THE TOURIST RAILWAYS
OF FRANCE

RICHARD HAWORTH

SECOND EDITION

RAPID TRANSIT PUBLICATIONS

ISBN 0 948619 05 8
Second edition 1996

Previous editions
First edition 1995

Maps by Richard Haworth

Typeset in Gill Sans 8.5 and 9 point
by Rapid Transit Publications, London.

Printed by
Hobbs The Printers Limited
Totton, Hampshire

RAPID TRANSIT PUBLICATIONS
37 Wellesley Road, Ilford, London, England

CONTENTS

ACKNOWLEDGEMENTS

First Edition

This guide has been compiled from personal visits and research. Any errors, therefore, are mine. However, much help has been freely given by many people, without whose encouragement this guide would not have been completed. I am especially grateful to: L. Baussant, N. Blondin, M. Brun, J. Carel, Y. Crue, J. Daffis, J. David, A. Duchesne, B. Duchesne, H Gauge, A. Guenet, I. Haworth, Mrs J. Haworth, R. A. Haworth, M. Hull, D. Jones, A Lecomte, G. Le Gat, A. Marti, P. Merlet, J. Met, J. Milet, P. Nicholson, G. Nickson, M. Normand, R. Orsini, G. Perruqeti, A. Pierreschi, J. Piernet, C. Randall, E. Relton, C. Remery, A. Scaccaglia, M. Sidorski, Col. N. Williams, B. Zieguner; the staff of French Railways Ltd (SNCF), and innumerable enthusiastic operators of the various railways.

The use of information sourced from IGN maps is gratefully acknowledged.

Richard Haworth
August 1994

Second Edition

In addition to the help in preparation of the First Edition, the updating in the Second Edition has only been possible with the assistance of the following to whom I am most grateful: J. Banaudo, Y. Baussant, G. Bernard, M. Breuze, J. Carel, B. Caunesil, J. Dannhauser, J. David, N. Denmare, B. Duchesne, M. Gala, P. Gilot, C. Guilman, I. & J. Haworth, J. Hughes, J. Hull, G. Jagneneau, S. Kottmann, A. Lacher, A. Lecomte, C. MacPherson, J. Maginot, N. Mailliary, M. & Mme. Messener, P. Mills, S. Oliver, P. Pacey, C. Randell, K. Sprimont, R. Taymans, M. Waish, G. Wizeman and F. Zielinger. Especial thanks are due to Mr. S. Oliver for contributions on the delights of various SNCF lines.

The contents of this guide were prepared in December 1995. In order that any future editions may be made as accurate as possible, I would welcome any information which readers think may help in this regard.

Richard Haworth

Crowcombe Cottage
1 Berkley Drive
Chester   CH4 7EL
Great Britain

December 1995

Front Cover: The Train à Vapeur des Cévennes **(98)** crosses the River Mailet on the Mescladou Viaduct. The 0-6-0T locomotive number 030T8158 was built in 1953. The front four carriages are open sided, and are very popular with school parties in summer. **Photo: TVC**

Back Cover: On the Chemin de Fer Touristique de la Brévenne **(60),** the 2-6-0T number 880 157 is a former Italian Railways (FS) loco now owned by CFTB. It is in a dull matt green livery, a contrast with the bright red four-wheel coaches. **Photo: CFTB**

INTRODUCTION

Welcome to this guide to the tourist and leisure railways of France. It has been prepared with the aim of introducing visitors to the pleasures of its amazing variety of railways.

Although the number of railway preservation sites in France does not approach that in Great Britain, the variety of types of preserved and tourist railways in France is far wider. This is a result of the geography of France and the history of railways in the country. Amongst the lines described here will be found steam, diesel, electric (overhead and surface), petrol and battery powered railways. The railways are of innumerable gauges ranging from standard gauge with enormous steam engines and double deck railcars, to miniature railways, rack railways and some of the steepest funicular and adhesion railways in Europe. There are canal railways, underground railways, military and pleasure park railways, and even a standard gauge railway you drive yourself. A train can be found which is powered by engines built for luxury cars, a passenger train consisting only of track repair vehicles and trains which spiral inside and outside mountains, in the style of the renowned railways of Switzerland. There is a train running along a valley side at an altitude of 6500 feet, and others running amongst sand dunes, across bogs or along Mediterranean beaches.

There are industrial railways, military lines, pleasure park lines and roadside steam tramways. Trains pass through forests, gorges, caverns, quarries and mines. Others cross a ranch, a zoo, and international boundaries. Dual gauge lines can be identified, and even a station with three different gauges. Possibly, the more unusual features (at least to British eyes) are a 15-inch gauge passenger railway which crosses public roads without signals or barriers, and a passenger train operated by SNCF on the national railway network using carriages without a roof!

What the Guide offers

The guide gives details of each tourist railway. It describes the main features of the railway and its geographical, historical or industrial setting as appropriate. A full descriptive entry in the guide is made for the majority of railways. A shorter description is given for the minor lines. In every case a table of essential data is presented which summarizes the key features of the railway, the rolling stock and the opening times.

Because this guide is intended for visitors to a foreign country, much effort has been put into showing the location and the access details for reaching each site. This information is presented in the form of maps, identification of the most appropriate SNCF station and method of access from there, the route by road from the largest town in the area and finally the identification of the site by a grid reference on a summary map and on the French Ordnance Survey (IGN) maps, which are widely available in Britain and in France. Sources of further information are also included.

What is a Tourist Railway?

For the purpose of this guide, tourist railways have been defined as those which you may use for enjoyment and the pleasure of the journey, not primarily as a means of transport. These pleasures may be to view the scenery, including that not otherwise approachable, or to experience the atmosphere of railway travel of an earlier epoch; to experience aspects of industrial archaeology, to examine preserved railway equipment or marvel at feats of engineering. A selection of SNCF lines are described where travel is recommended to experience their scenic and other attractions. Also, modern tramways and funicular railways have been included where they are likely to be of interest to visitors. Many of these have been opened recently in France and more are being developed or extended today, illustrating central government support for rail-based transport.

The Origins of Today's Tourist Railways

Local narrow gauge railways

Following the effective completion of the French national network of standard gauge railways built by private companies (but in many cases with government aid), the desire to supply railway services to rural areas remained in the last decades of the 19th century. The distances and sparse rural communities were unable to justify the expense of standard gauge railways, but as in other countries, a narrow gauge was found practicable. The French system was to delegate the judgement of need to the local *département* (i.e. provincial) authorities. The arrangement varied from one *département* to another, with some building and operating lines themselves, some directly subsidizing lines, but most initially guaranteeing a rate of return to a *concessionaire* (licence holder) over a fixed term.

A number of these lines were considered to have national importance and were classified as of *Intérêt Général,* with central government contribution to funding. The majority were of *Intérêt Local* or *Tramways* with local funding only. *Tramways* in this context were light railways, with the majority of their length along public roads. A preserved example of this arrangement can be seen at Pithiviers. By the beginning of WW1 the length of local lines had reached almost 25 000 km.

Initially restricted by law to 750mm or metre gauge, the metre gauge generally became the norm for local railways. The standardization of features of these railways led to the same station designs, for example, to be found throughout the country. A number of 600mm gauge lines were also constructed often using the light railway equipment marketed by the Decauville company: a change in the law was necessary. The success of this system, particularly as a WW1 military resource, can be seen today in the large number of Decauville locomotives preserved on the various tourist lines of 600mm gauge. Other gauges were also laid for practical, economic or strategic reasons. The results of this proliferation of gauges can be seen today at various preservation sites: a prime example is the transport museum at La Barque.

The surviving lines retain the atmosphere of the old *départemental* railways. Perhaps the best examples of this are to be seen today on the metre gauge railways of Corsica and Provence. However, what has been lost is an indication of the once enormous extent of such lines in France.

Others built originally for industrial purposes have become tourist attractions and now carry passengers as their primary function. The line to La Mure is in this category, having been built to carry anthracite but now exclusively carrying tourists on a remarkable route through the gorge of the River Drac.

Funicular and rack railways

Early purpose-built tourist rail lines were built in the Alps and Pyrénées in particular: funicular or rack railways giving access to spas, viewpoints and, more recently, for skiing. A number of the earlier lines survive very successfully today and have been joined by a number of modern funicular lines. The most historic survival is the Capucin funicular at Le Mont-Dore, but there are many others, and proposals remain to revive some of the closed funiculars. The popularity of winter sports has given rise to a spate of very modern funicular railways in France in recent years.

Narrow Gauge Pleasure Railways

Many lines have been built specifically to encourage tourists and day visitors. The *Parc d'Attractions* around France are set out for day visitors with a range of simple entertainments and activities. A narrow-gauge railway is a common feature. Perhaps the best known and certainly the longest established is in the Bois de Boulogne in the centre of Paris. Perhaps more unusual are the narrow gauge lines which are dressed up in the style of fairground rides but which operate on lines some miles long. Two on the west coast are at Cap Ferret and St. Trojan.

Standard gauge tourist lines

Standard gauge preservation has a rather different basis and one probably unique to France. The country has retained a very large number of branch lines which are used only for occasional freight trains. Many of these lightly used lines are in picturesque rural settings and are ideal for use as tourist railways. After some resistance by SNCF, the Transport Ministry directed that access to the tracks should be made available to groups wishing to operate tourist trains on days when freight services are not operated. This opened up lengths of railway which had not seen passenger trains for many years and attracted an encouraging patronage. With the maintenance of the track largely paid for by the State, the operation of one or two trains on Summer weekends was a viable operation, especially if uncomplicated diesel railcars were employed. However, many of these operations offer steam locomotive hauled passenger trains; for example the lines to Richelieu and Les Herbiers.

During the 1980s, SNCF were finding that the light railcars, built in the 1950s to maintain rural branch line rail services, were redundant. Many were obtained by local preservation societies. The most numerous and distinctive of these preserved railcars are of the type known as "Picasso", due to their unconventional design. The driving compartment of these railcars is placed on the roof. This is possible because of the high loading gauge of French railways. The driver sits sideways in this cabin and is able to see the track ahead in whichever direction the vehicle is travelling. In fact the cabin is strategically placed to enable a single unpowered trailer car to be attached without impairing the driver's visibility. These railcars have become synonymous with French preservation operations on standard gauge branch lines.

Some preservation operations, of a type more familiar to British visitors, have also grown up. In these cases the operating group has a closer stake in the ownership of the track and/or trackbed. Therefore these lines are generally operated on more days, due to the need to raise sufficient revenue to maintain the infrastructure. Almost all lines, however, have a great deal of support from local authorities, who consider the tourist trains to be an asset in encouraging visitors to areas where the development of tourism is important. By this process it has been possible for tourist trains to blossom, to the benefit of locals and visitors alike. Recently, financial pressures on SNCF has led to the withdrawal of much freight from lightly used branch lines. This has resulted in the total cost of track maintenance falling upon the tourist operations; a burden they are completely unequipped to withstand. A number of the earlier tourist lines have regrettably closed. Those which have survived this upheaval have generally been those operated by the most determined groups, supported by local and regional councils. There are many examples of this type of arrangement; the line between Evian-les-Bains and St. Gingolf is one such.

Some of the standard gauge tourist trains operate on railways owned not by SNCF, but by other State authorities or commercial undertakings. In these cases it is possible for a preservation group to operate trains on just a few days per year as its outgoings are limited to rent of the track and maintenance of the stock. Examples of trains operating under these arrangements are to be found alongside the River Rhine at Port Rhénan and alongside the Atlantic Ocean at Soulac.

Main line steam trains

As in Britain, following removal of steam locomotives from the national rail network, there was an effective ban on all use of steam trains on the French network. However, in 1981, SNCF relaxed this policy and arranged for certain steam locomotives to run "specials". This was followed in 1983 by permission for selected privately owned locomotives to operate on the national network. These arrangements permit the operation of some very large locomotives which are unsuitable for use on the generally short and more lightly maintained track of tourist lines. A number of societies arrange steam trips on SNCF lines using a limited range of large locomotives. SNCF also permit specifically certified private diesel railcars to operate on its rail network. This arrangement has enabled some of the societies operating weekend tourist trains on freight branch lines to extend their activities and offer rail trips in preserved rolling stock. These are often along rail routes which are no longer served by passenger trains. This guide indicates some of the societies offering these trips.

Use of the Guide

The guide is split into four regions and presented in the following order: North, East, South and then West. The major railways of each region are followed by the minor lines of that region. For each railway, the key data is presented in the form of a standard summary table highlighted with identification symbols. Each table is laid out in the following order:-

※   the main stations on the line,

✣   a reference number unique to the line and the map grid references,

✷ ♨ ✷ the propulsion method employed, the gauge of the track, and its length,

☞   the access route by public transport

☛   the access route by road

✓   the opening times and dates

✉ ✆   the correspondence address and telephone number for further information.

◉   cycle hire available at SNCF station.

Stations. ※

The main stations on the line (or the location for single sites) are indicated in the table and also appear in the index.

Reference number. ✣

The reference number appearing before the title of each railway at the head of each page is also given on the summary map on page 14. The railways are numbered sequentially through the book, and in a general clockwise order round the country, beginning in Normandy.

Grid references. ✣

Two grid references are given for each line: the first for the summary map (Map A) in order that the general area of the location can be simply identified, and the second for the local French ordnance survey Institut Géographique National (IGN) 1cm = 2.5km map in order to reveal the accurate location of the railway's site.

In the case of the summary map, the location of the railway is within the square on the map indicated by two letters: a capital letter for the east/west position and a lower case letter for the north/south position. For example the Baie de Somme railway will be found at grid reference "Ga". That is, "G", half-way across the map from west to east and, "a", right in the north of France.

The grid reference on the IGN 1:250,000 maps system is indicated in the tabulated data by the map number followed by a letter-and-number combination. For example, in the case of the Baie de Somme railway as follows: IGN 101 B2 indicates that the main stations on the line (Noyelles and St. Valery-sur-Somme) are shown in segment B2 of IGN map number 101. The IGN maps are recommended as they clearly indicate the contours of the land and railways and are freely available in Great Britain. The Green Series maps at 1:100,000 scale are the primary recommendation but the Red Series at 1:250.000 give excellent information and cover the whole of the country in only sixteen sheets.

Motive power, gauge and track length. ✿ ⚘ ✿

The gauge and track length are given in metric measurements. For unusual gauges, the equivalent imperial measurement is also quoted.

Access by public transport. ☞

The table for each railway indicates the location of the nearest SNCF station which has services on the days on which the tourist line is operational. (Many tourist trains only operate on Sundays when some minor SNCF stations are not open). Also given, except in the case of major terminii, is the Table No. in the SNCF railway timetables. (The timetable comprises well over 2000 pages in four volumes. The line number simplifies identification of train service details). Not all of the tourist trains are within walking distance of the SNCF station. In some instances buses available between the station and the site are indicated. On occasions car or cycle hire may be a sensible option. Where cycle hire is available at the nearest SNCF station this is indicated, in the table for the particular railway, by the ☉ symbol. Cycles can be hired at 47 SNCF stations. Standard "traditional", touring "randonneur", and mountain "tout terrain" cycles are available. Hiring is possible for any period from a half-day. Transport of accompanied cycles by passenger train is available (free) on most trains throughout France, including those in Paris (except rush hours). Cycles must be placed in the baggage car (often limited to three cycles per train). Cycles can also be sent in advance of travel as luggage. Car hire is available at 196 SNCF stations. Cycles and cars can be booked in advance.

Access by road. ☛

The road route is given from the nearest large town. This can be easily followed on a road map and is a further way to find the location of the site. The route described has been chosen for simplicity of identification. It is not necessarily the recommended access route, which is left to the traveller to determine.

Opening times. ✓

A number of the railways described in this guide are genuine public transport services and hence operate daily all year round. Some others are commercial tourist attractions and generally operate on most days throughout the holiday season. The majority, however, are barely-commercial operations and function only on Sundays and national public holidays and only in the summer months of the year. Most of the operating societies will consider running trains for groups on additional days if booked in advance.

Obtaining further information. ✉ ✆

The lines are generally operated by unpaid volunteers. It is most appropriate to write in French and expect a response in French and include a (French) stamped addressed envelope or international reply coupon. When telephoning it should be borne in mind that many of the lines are operated by unpaid volunteers. Care is required in selecting an appropriate time to telephone which will not be unreasonable to the recipient of the call. Throughout most of the year French local time is one hour ahead of that in Britain. Very few of the lines will have respondents who will have the facility to converse in English.

The telephone details given in the tables are in the form of an eight-digit number. In France there is split in the use of telephone system between (**A**) the region of Paris/Ile de France (*départements* 75, 78, 91, 92, 93, 94 and 95) and (**B**) the rest of the country. The département number is given in the details of each railway as the first two digits in the post code given in the last line of the correspondence address. To telephone within France from **A** to **A** or from **B** to **B** the use of the eight-digit telephone number given in the data table is all that is required. When telephoning from **A** to **B**, it is necessary to first dial **16**, pause, then dial the eight-digit number. When telephoning from **B** to **A** first dial **161**, pause then dial the eight digit number.

When telephoning from England to area **B**, dial **00 33**, pause, then dial the eight-digit number. For telephoning to area **A**, the number is **00 33 1** followed by the eight-digit number.

A further source of information is the system is known as Minitel, a computer monitor style system available to France Telecom subscribers. It is used by a number of the lines to distribute information. Access to the Minitel system is straightforward. Firstly it is necessary to dial **36 15** on the telephone and at the sound signal touch the "Connection" key on the Minitel terminal. Then type "RAIL" and touch the "Envoi" key. There is a help-line, **49.70.12.17**, in case of difficulty.

GLOSSARY

autorail:	diesel powered railcar
baladeuse:	open sided carriage used on narrow gauge pleasure park railways
berline:	type of small (usually tipping) rail wagon used in mines
chemin de fer:	railway
crémaillère:	mountain rack railway
département:	administrative area similar to English county
draisine:	four-wheeled vehicle designed for transport and support for track work
fourgon (à bagages)	(luggage) van
locotracteur:	diesel shunting locomotive often used for haulage on minor lines
Picasso:	Nickname of French railcars with driving cab situated off-centre on roof with the driver sitting sideways.
standard gauge:	railway track of 1435mm (4 ft 8½ in) between rail centres
tramways:	tramcar or tramway: a light railway running alongside a roadway
transverser:	system to move rolling stock at right angles to normal motion
vapeur:	steam (locomotive)
voie ferrées:	railway or railway track

INTERPRETATION OF SYMBOLS

✳ Name of site or station(s)

✛ Grid reference on Map A/ Grid reference on IGN "red series" map

✴ Principal motive power used on the line

⚒ Gauge of railway track

✳ Length of railway line

☞ Public tranport accesss to site including name of nearest SNCF passenger station

☞ Road route to the site from the largest town in the area.

✓ Time and date of operation

✉ Correspondence address for information

℡ Telephone number for information

◉ Cycle hire available at SNCF station

MAP A

KEY TO GRID REFERENCES

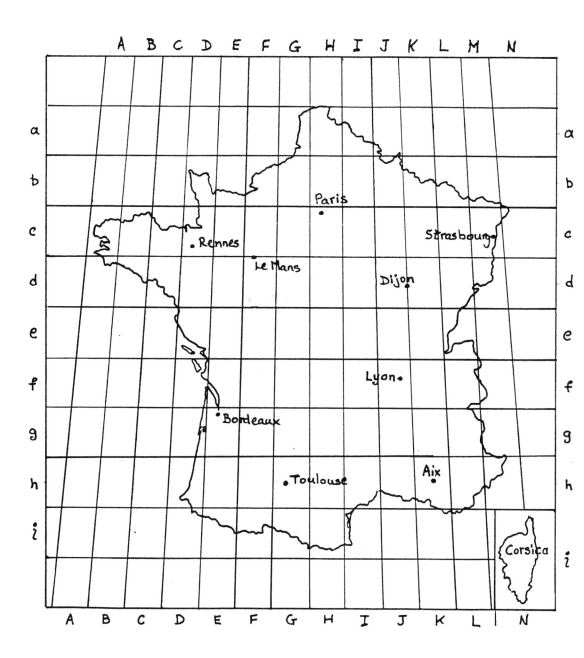

ABBREVIATIONS

AJECTA:	Association des Jeunes pour l'Exploitation et la Conservation des Trains d'Autrefois
am:	morning
AMTP:	Association du Musée des Transports de Pithiviers
Apr:	April
Aug:	August
Ave:	avenue
begin:	around the beginning (of the month)
BH:	(French) public holiday
Blvd:	boulevard
CF:	*chemin de fer*: railway
CFD:	Compagnie des Chemins de Fer Départementaux
CFF/SBB:	Swiss national railway/ access station for tourist train
CFT:	*chemin de fer touristique*: tourist railway
CH:	Switzerland
CITEV:	Compagnie Internationale des Trains Express et Vapeur
Dec:	December
degF:	degrees Farenheit
DFB:	German WW1 military railway equipment
DM:	diesel mechanical locomotive transmission
DR:	National railway system of post-1945 Germany or the former East Germany
E:	east
Etat:	Chemin de Fer de l'Etat (French State Railway)
FACS:	Fédération des Amis des Chemin de Fer Secondaires
Fri:	Fridays
FS:	Italian national railway system
hp:	horse power
Hz:	hertz (cycles per second)
ic:	internal combustion
IGN:	Institute Géographic National (French ordnance survey) map No. and grid reference.
Jun:	June
junc.:	junction
km:	distance (1km = 0.62 mile)
m:	distance or altitude in metres (1 m = 39.4 inches)
Mar:	March
Mem. Sec.:	membership secretary
mid:	around the middle (of the month)
Midi:	Chemin de Fer Midi (railway company)
mm:	track gauge in millimetres (one inch = 25.4 mm)
N:	north
No:	number
NW:	north west
Oct:	October
o/h:	overhead wiring
O&K:	Orenstein and Koppel
Nov:	November
PLM:	Paris-Lyon-Mediterranée (railway company)
pm:	afternoon
PN:	*passage á niveau* : level crossing
PO:	Chemin de Fer de Paris à Orléans (railway company)
RD:	*route départemental*: minor road number
RN:	*route national*: main road number
S:	south
sae:	Stamped addressed envelope (or International Reply Coupon)
SACM:	Société Alsacienne de Construction Mécaniques
Sat:	Saturdays

SE:	south-east
Sept:	September
SNCB:	Belgian national railway system/ access station for tourist train
SNCF:	French national railway system/ main passenger station for access to site
SSE:	south-south-east
Stn:	station
Sun:	Sundays
TGV:	*Train à Grande Vitesse* : French high speed train
TT:	*train touristique*: tourist train
Tues:	Tuesday
UK:	United Kingdom
V:	volts
W:	west
Wed:	Wednesdays
WT:	well tank locomotive
WW1:	First World War
WW2:	Second World War

LOCOMOTIVE BUILDERS

Alco/ Alco-Cooke:	American Locomotive Co. (USA)
Arn Jung:	Arn Jung Lokomotivfabriik GmbH, Jungenthal (D)
Bagnall:	W G Bagnall Ltd, Stafford (UK)
Baldwin:	Baldwin Locomotive Works, Philadelphia (USA)
Batignolles:	Société de Construction des Batignolles, Paris (F)
Berliet:	Établissements Berliet, Lyon (F)
Berry:	Berry, Lille (F)
Billard:	Établissements Billard & Compagnie, Tours (F)
Blanc-Misseron:	Les Ateliers de Constructions du Nord de la France, Blanc-Misseron(F)
Bondy:	Les Ateliers de Bondy, Paris (F)
Borsig:	A Borsig GmbH, Berlin (D)
Brissonneau & Lotz:	Société Anonyme des Établissements Brissonneau & Lotz (F)
Brown-Boveri:	Brown-Boveri & Compagnie (CH)
Buffaud & Robatel:	Buffaud & Robatel, Lyon (F)
Cail:	Établissements Cail, Denain (F)
Campagne:	Établissements Campagne & Compagnie, Paris (F)
CFD:	Compagnie des Chemin de Fer Départementaux (F)
Cockerill:	Société Anonyme John Cockerill, Seraing (B)
Comessa:	Établissements Comessa, Strasbourg (F)
Conferna:	Société de Constuctions Ferroviaires & N de l'Ouest, Les Sables d'Olonne (F)
Corpet:	L Corpet, Paris (F)
Corpet-Louvet:	Corpet-Louvet & Compagnie, La Courneuve (F)
Couillet:	Société Anonyme des Usines Métallurgiques du Hainaut, Couillet (B)
Crochat:	Établissements H Crochat, Paris (F)
Davenport:	Davenport Locomotive Works, Davenport (USA)
Decauville:	Société nouvelle des Etablissements Decauvlle-Ainé, Corbeil (F)
Deutz:	Klöckner-Homboldt-Deutz Aktiengesllschaft, Köln (D)
de Dion/Dion-Bouton:	Automobiles de Dion-Bouton, Paris (F)
Fives-Lille:	Compagnie de Fives-Lille, Fives-Lille (F)
Franco-Belge:	Société Anonyme Franco-Belge de Matériel de Chemin de Fer (F) (B)
General Electric:	General Electric Co, Pennsylvania (USA)
Gmeinder:	Gmeinder & Co GmbH, Mosbach (D)

Haine-St.Pierre:	Société Anonyme des Forges, Usines & Founderies, Haine-St.Pierre (B)
Hartmann:	Sächsische Maschinenfabrik AG, Chemnitz (D)
Heinz:	Heinz, Strasbourg (F)
Henschel:	Henschel & Sohn GmbH, Kassel (D)
Hohenzollern:	Hohenzollern AG, Dusseldorf (D)
Hugh Phillips:	Hugh Phillips Engineering, Tredegar (UK)
Jung:	Arn Jung Lokomotivfabriik GmbH, Jungenthal (D)
Krauss:	Lokomotivfabrik Krauss & Co AG, München (D)
Krauss-Maffei:	Krauss-Maffei AG, München (D)
Krupp:	Friedrich Krupp, Essen (D)
La Meuse:	Société Anonyme des Ateliers de Construction de la Meuse, Liège (B)
LLD:	Société Anonyme des Locomotives & Locotracteurs Diesel (F)
Moyse:	Établissements Gaston Moyse, La Courneuve (F)
North British:	North British Locomotive Co Ltd, Glasgow (UK)
Orenstein & Koppel:	Orenstein & Koppel AG, Berlin (D)
Pétolat:	Usines A. Pétolat, Dijon (F)
Pinguely:	Société Pinguely, Lyon (F)
Plymouth:	Plymouth Iron Works Corporation, Plymouth (USA)
Renault:	Régie Nationale des usines Renault, Billancourt (F)
Ruston:	Ruston & Hornsby, Lincoln (UK)
SACM:	Société Alsacienne de Constuctions Mécaniques, Belfort (F)
Schneider:	Schneider & Compagnie, Le Creusot (F)
Severn-Lamb:	Severn-Lamb Ltd, Stratford-upon-Avon (UK)
SLM:	Schweizerische Lokomotivfabrik & Maschinenfabrik, Winterthur (CH)
Socofer:	Société Socofer, Tours (F)
Soulé:	Soulé Fer & Froide, Bagnères de Bigorre (F)
Vulcan:	Vulcan Ironworks, Pennsylvania (USA)
Whitcomb:	Whitcomb Locomotive Co. Rochelle (USA)

MAP B

LOCATION OF RAILWAYS

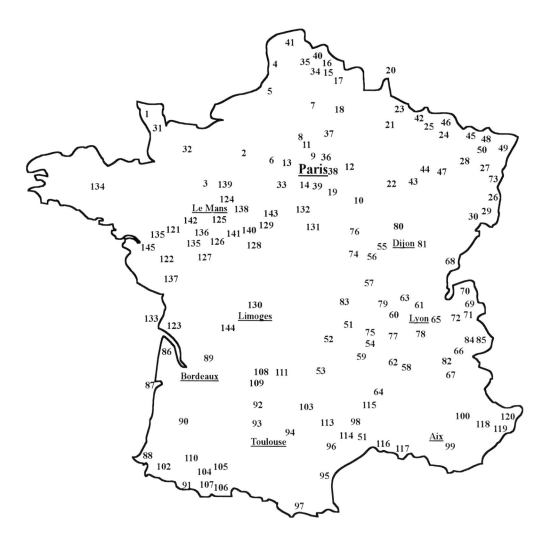

NORTH

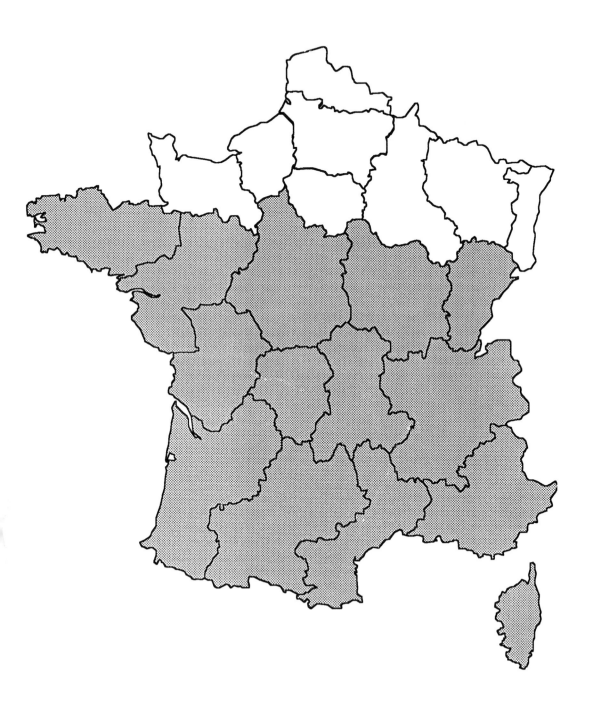

1: TRAIN TOURISTIQUE DU COTENTIN

✳ **Carteret** to **Portbail**
✣ Db/IGN102 B2, ✱ Diesel, ⛾ 1435mm, ❊ 10km
☞ Table 320: SNCF Cherbourg then bus (35km)
☛ Carteret is 35km from Cherbourg via RD904. TTC station is to right on entering the town
✓ am & pm. Tues, Thurs, Sun & BH: begin-July to begin-Sept. Also occasionally in Winter
✉ TT du Cotentin, Clos St.Jean, 50270 St.Jean de la Rivière, ✆ 34.62.80.20 (evening)

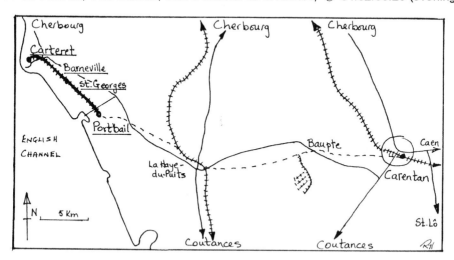

Until relatively recently, the Cotentin (Cherbourg) peninsular was well served by railways. A line ran from the south-west, up the centre of the peninsular to reach Cherbourg on the north coast. The upgraded main line from Paris runs from the south-east at Carentan to reach Cherbourg. In addition a branch line cut diagonally across the peninsular from Carentan in the south east to reach Carteret, a small harbour on the west coast mid-way along the peninsular overlooking the Channel Islands. This line was opened in 1894, and crossed the western line at La Haye-du-Puits; it lost its passenger services in 1966. The western end was closed to all traffic in 1979. Fortuitously, the track was retained and as result survived into the era of seasonal passenger services supported by local authorities to encourage tourists into this rural area.

An initial tourist train ran on the eastern end of the line between Carentan and Baupte from 1986. A second section was re-opened for tourist passenger trains in 1990. This latter operation, known as the "Train de la Côte des Îles", runs from Carteret to Portbail calling at stations at Barnville-sur-Mer and St.Georges-de-la-Rivière. This section of the line runs parallel to the west coast. Both Carteret and Portbail are small harbour towns. Carteret is a growing yachting centre with numerous chandlers, cafés and souvenir shops. Portbail is also a tourist centre but is set further back on an estuary. It has a fortified church and a ancient stone bridge and causeway across the saltmarsh. The train has developed a market combining pre-organized groups (predominantly schoolchildren or retired people), individual holiday visitors, and local people using the train once again as a public transport service. Passenger loadings are particularly heavy on Portbail market days.

The western end is somewhat more hilly than the rest of the line. The train, in a distance of only 9km, passes a variety of scenery from town settings, small woods, cuttings and the salt marsh. Beyond Portbail the line swings decisively inland towards La Haye. The starting point of the Train de la Côte des Îles is situated in the old goods yard at Carteret: the track has been cut back from the old passenger station, which is now used for SNCF summer camps. The station at Portbail is situated just beyond the level crossing over the RD264. It is well maintained and very welcoming.

The rolling stock used consists of railcars, trailer car, also various diesel locotracteurs and two ex SNCF "Bruhat" bogie coaches.

The present restricted length of track gives a most pleasant journey between two delightful towns of completely different character. The extension of services towards a connection with the earlier Carentan operation now looks a forlorn hope due to a lack of official support. The Carentan to Baupte tourist trains have not operated since 1994.

Around Baupte is a large area of bog where an extensive network of 600mm gauge railways bring peat to the factory at Baupte. Passenger tours over part of the network are operated in association with the leisure complex here **(31)**.

1. Pinguely 0-6-0T No. 101 with a train for Noyelles awaits departure from Le Crotoy on the Chemin de Fer de la Baie de la Somme [5]. *(Photo: G. Nickson)*

2. A young enthusiast admires the Neumeyer 0-4-0T No. 2 in the museum on the Chemin de Fer Froissy-Cappy-Dompierre [7]. This locomotive operated the early services on this successful 600mm gauge railway. *(Photo: R. Haworth)*

3. CdF Froissy-Cappy-Dompierre locomotive No. 1 prepares to depart from the halt at Cappy-Port beside the Somme canal [7]. *(Photo: APPEVA)*

4. Metre gauge Billard locotracteur and a Pinguely 0-6-0T of the Musée des Transports de la Vallée de Sausseron at Valmondois [8]. *(Photo: B .Duchesne)*

5. 40hp Baldwin petrol locotracteur and "Margarete", an Arn Jung 0-4-0T of 1937 at the Moncourt station of the Tacot des Lacs [10]. *(Photo: B. Duchesne)*

6. One of the Renault locotracteurs takes fuel at the park station at the Jardin d'Acclimatation, prior to the return journey through the Bois de Boulogne to Porte Maillot in Paris [13]. *(Photo: R. Haworth)*

7. ↑ On the 600mm gauge line at Evry, the ex-German military locomotive "Bondoufle", an 0-8-0T Henschel of 1917, takes a train of baladeuses through the Bois de Saint-Eutrope [14].   *(Photo: B. Duchesne)*

8. ↓ A 1927 vintage ex-Lille "Mongy" tramway, No. 304, stands on the operational line at the Marquette depot of the Tramway Touristique de la Vallée de la Deûle [16].   *(Photo: Breuze)*

2: CHEMIN DE FER DE LA FORÊT DE LA LONDE

✷ From **Elbeuf-Ville** to **Moulineaux-La Bouille** and **Petit Couronne**
✛ Fb/IGN102 B9, ✱ Diesel, 𝄞 1435mm, ✱ 16km
☞ Table 302: SNCF Elbeuf-St.Aubin
☛ Elbeuf is 24km S of Rouen via RN138 and RD 132
✓ am & pm. Sun & BH: Mid-Apr to end-Sept
✉ Club Ferroviaires d'Elbeuf, gare d'Elbeuf-Ville, 76500 Elbeuf ✆ 35.78.26.40

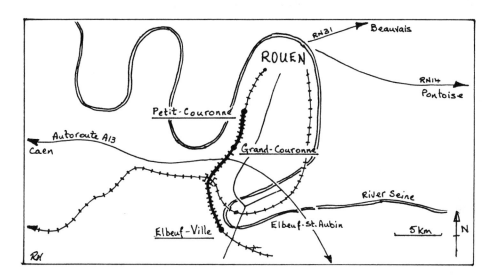

Around Rouen the River Seine meanders tightly in a fairly steep-sided and constricted valley. The banks are typified by industrial developments for some distance either side of the city. These have led to the retention of a network of railways along the valley and also across the intervening hills, which rise to 150m and are covered in deciduous woods. Two railways pass through the conurbation of Elbeuf to the south of the city. One, at this point on the right bank of the Seine, retains SNCF freight and passenger services. The other is operated as a freight branch, having lost its passenger services in 1965 and being truncated just beyond Elbeuf. It was, however, originally opened in 1883 as part of a through route from Rouen to Orléans. It is on this route that tourist trains are operated on days when freight trains do not run.

The base of operations is at Elbeuf-Ville, south of the town centre and hard against the valley side a few kilometres up-stream of Rouen. The line crosses the town on a 16 arch viaduct and runs along the side of the valley before passing through two tunnels under the Forêt de la Londe. The views along this stretch are particularly fine; firstly over the roofs of the town and then across the valley at a particularly tight hairpin bend of the river.

The next section of the route runs through the woods for about 4km. There is a further tunnel immediately before reaching Moulineaux-La Bouille station where the line is once again on the left bank of the river, but this time down-stream from Rouen because the river has yet again doubled back on itself. Moulineaux was initially the end of the tourist train journey, but since 1992, the run has been extended along the edge of the wood to terminate at the town of Grand-Couronne.

The enormous station at Elbeuf-Ville has survived its years of disuse reasonably intact and has now been well restored. The stock collected together at the old freight depot here consists of "Picasso" railcars (X3801, X3823 and X3971), trailer cars, two diesel locotracteurs of 1936 and 1960 vintage, and also various carriages and freight wagons. These items are in various stages of preservation. The railcars used for the tourist trains are well turned out.

This fairly new operation offers a variety of scenery both urban and rural, with some significant civil engineering structures, and is situated close to some of the ferry ports from southern England: Dieppe, Le Havre and Caen (Ouistreham) in particular. The two-hourly five-train service enables the locality to be explored from any of the intermediate stations. Hêtre à l'image station appropriately gives immediate access to the forest. The château de Robert le Diable is just a mile west of Moulineaux station.

3: CHEMIN DE FER TOURISTIQUE DU MONT DES AVALOIRS

✳ From **Alençon** to **Pré-en-Pail**
✤ Fc/IGN102 D6, ✻ Diesel, ⚑ 1435mm, ✱ 27km
☞ Table 335: SNCF Alençon (CFTMA station is 0.5km to N of SNCF station, on W side of Caen road)
☛ Alençon is 48km N of Le Mans via RN138 (E402)
✓ am & pm. Sat, Sun & BH: begin-July to mid-Sept. Also occasional Sun in May & June
✉ Syndicat d'initiative, Place du Marché, 53140 Pré-en-Pail, ✆ 43.03.89.38

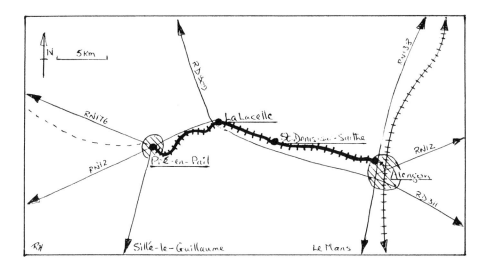

From a junction just north of Alençon station on the SNCF line from Caen to Tours, an SNCF branch runs westward for 27km to Pré-en-Pail. This section was opened in 1888: its passenger service ceased in 1938. The line used to form part of a cross country route from Alençon to Pontaubault. This line has been severed and each section progressively cut back over the years. This eastern section has retreated from Domfront to Juvigny, then Couterne, and now as far as Pré-en-Pail.

The freight traffic remaining today is solely block trains of fertilizer from the company Société Masdac situated at Pré. With the co-operation of this company and SNCF, it has been possible for the enthusiast group, CFTO, to run a tourist train service. They have operated diesel railcar services since 1991, on days when freight trains do not run.

The group previously operated the Chemin de Fer du Mont St.Michael tourist trains on the line from Pontabault, which was the western section of this same line. The Pontaubault CFMStM tourist trains were operated using both a diesel railcar and a steam locomotive. By contrast, the stock used for the Mont des Avaloirs service is exclusively 1950's railcars: X2423 and "Picasso" X3867 and trailer cars.

Starting from an immaculate halt, established on the west side of RN138 just to the north of the centre of Alençon, the train calls at each station along the line: Damigni, Lonrai, St.Denis-sur-Sarthon, Forêt de Multonne, Lalacelle and Pré-en-Pail. It passes through the heart of the Normandie-Maine regional nature park, a large area of varied scenery situated between the chalk of the Paris basin and the plateau of Brittany. Each station has possibilities for walks to explore this rural countryside. Two long distance footpaths cross the line: these *Grandes Randonnés* can be approached from St.Denis and Pré-en-Pail stations. There are picnic sites at each of these locations: refreshments are available at Alençon and Pré-en-Pail. At an altitude of 303m, Lalacelle is claimed to be the highest station in western France. Mont des Avaloirs is a 417m high hill close to Lalacelle station. It is possible to walk the summit or to the Chappel of Sainte-Anne between trains by alighting at Lalacelle.

The well presented railcars are fitted out so that commentaries can be made during the journey. From the train there is a wide panorama over the Forest of Multonne and the wooded hills of Butte Chaumont to the north of the line and Mont des Avaloirs to the south.

This line is situated between the Channel ports and the Valley of the Loire; a convenient and worthwhile point to pause for British visitors to France travelling further south.

4: BAGATELLE PLEASURE PARK

✴ At **Bagatelle** Parc d'Attractions
✣ Ga/IGN101 B2 ✳ Diesel and steam ⚒ 600mm ✳ 1.5km
☞ Tables 200 & 205: SNCF Étaples ⊙, or Rang-de-Fliers then bus to park entrance
☛ Between Le Touquet and Berck on RD940
✓ am and pm. Daily: Beginning April to end-Sept.
✉ Bagetelle Parc d'Attractions, 62155 Merlimont, ℂ 21.89.09.99

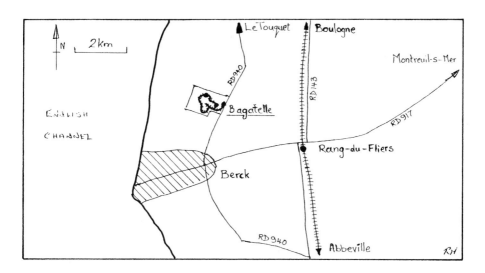

South of Boulogne and Calais lie a string of resorts along the Channel coast. Each has wide beaches and fine silver sand. They are popular holiday locations for the inhabitants of the northern towns and offer such diverse attractions as sand yachting and ice rinks. Among these is situated one of the uniquely French pleasure parks. These have a wide range of simple entertainments including a range of adult-sized children's playground style amusements - swing boats, revolving drums, eccentric bicycles, etc.- enthusiastically utilized by adults and children alike. In the case of Bagatelle, these attractions are complemented by a monorail, fairground, boating lake, and zoo and an extensive narrow gauge railway.

The railway is of 600mm gauge, running in a contorted loop of about 1.5km length around the park. There are a number of branches. The normal operation is a clockwise service around the circuit. The total length of track including the public service circuit extends to about 2km. Three stations are situated roughly equidistant around the route. A very frequent service is offered. This enables visitors to use the train as a convenient means of transport between the various attractions of the site. The train, like other features of the park, is free to use once the entrance fee has been paid. The service is maintained by a collection of 0-4-0 ex-industrial diesel locos. They haul trains of up to nine gaily-coloured "baladeuses" (covered but open-sided, bogie or four wheeled carriages). These give a comfortable ride on the well-maintained track.

The journey takes one through the woods, which are a feature of the site, through two short tunnels and over the boating lake on a low viaduct. At three places, the railway is crossed by a modern electric monorail. The two modes of transport make an interesting contrast. The monorail enables aerial views of the railway to be obtained and affords useful photographic possibilities. Interchange between monorail and railway is made at 'Gare Saint-Hubert'.

Previously a delightful 1912-built O&K 0-6-0T steam locomotive was displayed by the park entrance, on one of the branch lines, and made a pleasing welcome. This locomotive operated services occasionally. Since 1994, a superbly presented 0-6-0T Soquet pulls trains at peak times in the holiday season: this loco carries the name "Bagatelle". In keeping with the aims of the park, this engine and its train of baladeuses entertains visitors of all ages.

5: CHEMIN DE FER DE LA BAIE DE SOMME

✳ **St.Valéry** to **Le Crotoy** via **Noyelles**. Also **St.Valéry** to **Cayeaux**
✤ Ga/IGN101 B2, ✱ Steam & diesel, ⚒ 1000mm and dual l000 + 1435mm, ✳ 27km
☞ Table 200: SNCF Noyelles-sur-Mer ☉, or SNCF Rue ☉ then bus to Le Crotoy
☛ From Calais/Boulogne via RN1 to Nouvion then D111 to Noyelles.
✓ pm only. Sun & BH: mid-Apr to end-Sept. Daily (except Mon) in Jul and Aug
✉ CFBS, Gare de St.Valéry, BP31, 80230 St.Valéry-sur-Somme. ℂ 22.26.96.96

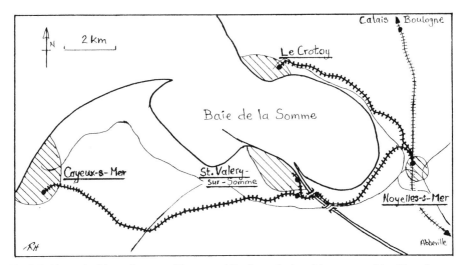

On the English Channel mid-way between Dieppe and Boulogne is the wide estuary of the River Somme. Along both the north and south shores of this bay are the metre gauge lines of the CFBS which meet at the SNCF station of Noyelles-sur-Mer. These lines are not only the most accessible French preserved lines for English visitors but also the most typical example of the once extensive network of local narrow gauge railways in France.

These lines carried produce from this important agricultural area and also supplied local passenger services. During the summer season they carried tourists from Paris and the towns of northern France to the resorts of Cayeux, St Valéry and Le Crotoy. A peculiarity of this network is the provision of four rails between Noyelles and St.Valéry which enabled metre gauge locomotives to propel standard gauge wagons. This unusual feature is still in place.

The preserved railway operation is based principally at St.Valéry. The depot is situated at St.Valéry-Canal, immediately before the line crosses the swivel bridge, which carries the road and railway across the Abbeville Canal. At this point and within St.Valéry, the railway runs along the centre of the road as a tramway. A short branch leads the train alongside the pretty quayside at St.Valéry. This port is today a centre of yachting. It has historic connections with Joan of Arc and was the point of departure of William of Normandy en-route to his invasion of England.

The section of line from St.Valéry-Ville to Cayeaux is the least used and has changed little since pre-preservation days. Unlike the other lines of the network, this section is used only on Sundays and holidays in July and August.

The lines to Le Crotoy and St.Valéry run parallel on their departure from the junction at Noyelles. The opportunity of a race as the two trains depart together is rarely foregone. After leaving Noyelles both lines cross flat fenland scenery with drainage channels crossed by small bridges. The St.Valéry line runs along the sea defence embankment.

Three of the diesel locotracteurs are originals from the Somme operation. A more recent arrival is that obtained when the Blanc-Argent line ceased freight operations in 1989. The steam locomotives include a 2-6-0T Corpet-Louvet of 1906, an 0-6-0T Pinguely built in 1904, three 0-4-0T Corpet-Louvet of 1921, 1925 and 1927 vintage, an 0-6-2T loco built by Buffaud and Robatel in 1909, and a 2-6-0T built by Haine-St Pierre in 1920. A 2-6-0T steam locomotive built for the construction of the Panama Canal was brought from the USA in 1994. This locomotive was built in France by Cail in 1889, and had been preserved in the USA for many years before removal to St. Valery. The carriage stock is distinctive. Bogie carriages with end balconies, used previously for the heavy summer resort traffic, are still in regular service today. In addition a magnificent saloon carriage has been refurbished for use on charter trains.

The CFBS is in the premier league of tourist railways in France. The charm of the Somme estuary, the collection of preserved stock and its position close to the channel ports, make this a highly recommended destination.

6: CHEMIN DE FER DE LA VALLÉE DE L'EURE

✳ **Pacy-sur-Eure** to **Bueil** (and to **La Croix St.Leufroy**)
✢ Gc/IGN102 C10, ✱ Diesel, ✇ 1435mm, ✱ 11km (26km)
☞ Table 320: SNCF Évreux (14km) . ◉ at SNCF Vernon.
☛ Pacy is 55km S of Rouen via RN15 to Louviers then RN154 to Aquigny and RD 836 to Pacy
✓ Dates of operation to be announced
✉ ALVE, BP6, 27730 Bueil ℭ 32.36.04.63

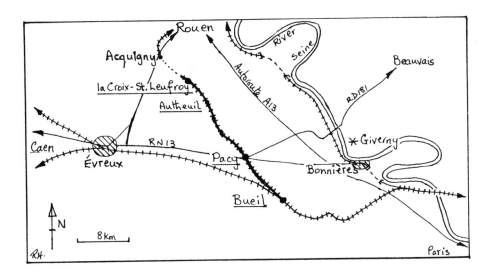

Remnants of the old Rouen to Orleans line remain. Sections have been lifted between Aquigny and La Croix-St.Leufroy (9km) and between Bueil and Croth-Sorel (14km). The 26km long section from Bueil to Pacy-sur-Eure and La Croix-St.Leufroy last saw passenger trains at the beginning of the 1950s and freight trains at the end of the 1980s. For strategic reasons this section was not immediately lifted, which has made possible the use of the line for tourist trains.

The ALVE group (Amis des Locomotives de la Vallée de l'Eure) have since 1991 been working towards establishment of a tourist train operation: Exhibitions have been held at Pacy station to gain the awareness the local population, rolling stock has been acquired and the assistance of local and national authorities obtained. The stock based at Pacy has been refurbished and track cleared of weeds in anticipation of services beginning in 1996, when it is planned that initial operations will be on the Pacy to Bueil section.

The stock being prepared for this operation are diesel railcars and locotracteurs. The railcars are Renault units X3601, built in 1949, and X5506, of 1950, and trailer cars.

The state of the track and railway infrastructure is remarkable considering the length of time that the line has been disused. Level-crossing gates, signs and station/freight buildings remain in place and in good order. The atmosphere of a railway from an earlier age pervades the line, and should form an excellent basis for a preserved railway. Through the whole of its length, the line closely follows the River Eure.

The line is close to the garden of the impressionist painter Claude Monet (Giverney is only 10km from Pacy). Points of railway interest in the area include the Elbeuf based Chemin de Fer de la Forêt de la Londe [2] and, close to the station at Bonnières-sur-Seine (10km from Pacy), an excellently preserved vertical boilered Cockerill 0-4-0T locomotive (built in 1924) may be seen from the SNCF train. The locomotive is in the private ground of the St.Éloi metal works. Its mention in this book does not imply that access is pemitted.

7: CHEMIN DE FER FROISSY-CAPPY-DOMPIERRE

✳ **Froissy** to **Dompierre** via **Cappy**
✤ Hb/IGN101 C4, ✱ Steam and diesel ⚒ 600mm ✻ 7km
☞ Table 221: SNCF Albert. Then (weekday) bus.
☛ From Amiens or St.Quentin: RN29 then N towards Bray-sur-Somme
✓ pm. Sun & BH: Begin-May to end-Sept. Also Wed & Sat: mid-Jul to begin-Sept. Thurs in Aug.
✉ APPEVA, BP106, 80001 Amiens Cedex, ✆ 22.44.55.40

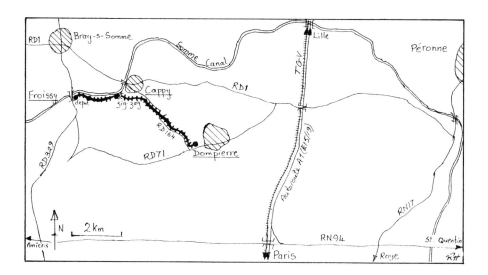

The River Somme has cut a deep groove in the chalk plateau covering the region north of Paris. This has been formed into a broad canal to the east of Amiens. This area was the scene of front line battles during WW1. One of the innumerable narrow gauge railways, which played such a significant role supporting troops in these battles, has survived into preservation and runs between Froissy and Dompierre. Both the German and Allied troops employed 600mm gauge railways. The German army built a line to bring ammunition up from the Somme Canal to defensive positions on the plateau. For many years after the armistice, the line was used to bring coal from the canal to a sugar refinery at Dompierre and to distribute its produce. During this period the track was renewed and a tunnel built to reduce the severe gradient.

The present track runs from the edge of Dompierre (about 500 m from the refinery) then alongside the D164 before following the zig-zag to drop down from the plateau and behind Cappy village, to reach the canal-side via a short curved tunnel. The line then follows the canal tow-path from Cappy lock to the RN329 road bridge at Froissy terminus. The track rises towards the end of the line to enter the simple station at road level. Parking is on the far side of the bridge over the canal. There is an extensive depot, workshop and museum beside the line close to Froissy with access by train.

Train services usually involve a steam locomotive on the canal-side stretch from Froissy to Port de Cappy where an exchange of locomotives takes place. A diesel locomotive is used for the more difficult section through the tunnel and up the zig-zag. The return journey includes a stop at the depot to enable passengers to visit the exhibited stock. It is also possible for non-passengers to visit the displays on payment of a modest fee.

The CFCD is one of the major 600mm gauge preservation operations in France. An important collection of historic stock is maintained and displayed at the Froissy depot. This includes the reassembled WW1 train with typical bogie wagons dating back to 1880, and a 1917 Alco 2-6-2T locomotive. In addition there are about a dozen steam locomotives (including two Henschel's, an 0-8-0T of 1917 and an 0-4-0T of 1937, two Decauville 0-6-0Ts of 1916-17, a Franco-Belge 0-6-0T, Borsig 0-4-0T, 0-8-0 Vulcan of 1928, and Krauss Feldbahn 0-8-0T of 1918. Amongst the numerous diesel locomotives are three which worked at the sugar refinery operation on the line from 1942 until closure in 1972: two Conferna 100hp 0-6-0 and a 75hp Plymouth 0-4-0.

8: MUSÉE DES TRANSPORTS DE LA VALLÉE DU SAUSSERON

✳ Museum situated at **Valmondois**, Butry. Line runs to **Le Bois Thibaud**
✣ Hb/IGN103 B5, ✱ Steam and diesel ✌ 1000mm ✱ 1km
☞ Tables 26 & 28: SNCF Valmondois. Museum is behind SNCF freight depot
☛ About 35km NW of Paris. From RN1 via L'Isle Adam and RD64/RD4. At SNCF station
✓ pm. Sat, Sun & BH: Mar to Nov. Museum: pm. Sat, Sun & BH: Mar to Dec.
✉ MTVS, mairie de Butry, 95430 Butry-sur-Oise, ✆ 34.70.04.40

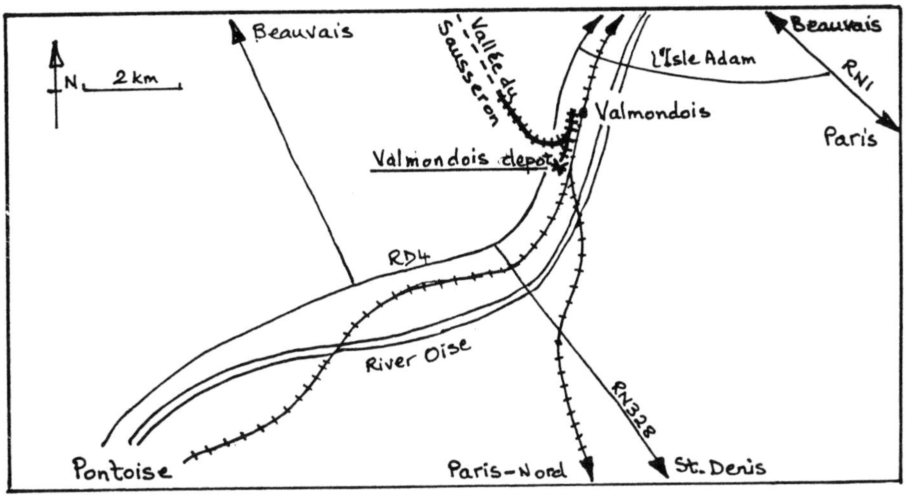

The River Sausseron is a tributary of the Oise which it joins near Valmondois, about 35km north of Paris. The existing SNCF line serving the town follows the valley of the Oise. From 1891 to 1946 a metre gauge line followed the Sausseron valley to reach Marines from the junction station at Valmondois.

Since 1976 a museum has been established at the old depot of the Marines line at Valmondois. A major collection of metre gauge equipment has been preserved and is exhibited here, and a short section of line has been re-laid on the trackbed of the old line. This extends to 1km along the track of the old rural railway. The terminus has been established at Le Bois Thibaud pending authority to extend further.

Historic stock from some of the once extensive network of French rural narrow gauge railways has been assembled at Valmondois. The stock is maintained in immaculate condition, as might be expected at a museum operated by a group of enthusiastic volunteers. Some of the locomotives are classified by the French government as of historic importance and as a result receive significant contributions to their restoration and maintenance. The group also has had strong support from the local authorities.

The rolling stock includes two double ended 0-6-0T steam tram engines built by Blanc-Misseron in 1897 and 1898 for use on the Tramways de la Sarthe. These are undoubtedly the star exhibits. A collection of contemporary four-wheel coaches, with balconies at either end, has been painted in matching livery. When teamed with one of the tram engines they make a magnificent sight. The operational locomotive is "No. 60 Le Ferte Bernard", built in 1898. The second loco, ("No. 16 St. Denis d'Orgues") is restored cosmetically only.

Other metre gauge stock are two Corpet & Louvet 0-6-0T locomotives of 1909 and 1925, an 0-6-0T Pinguely of 1897, an ex-Portuguese 2-6-0T built by Decauville in 1913, and another 2-6-0T built by SACM in 1924.

The diesel stock includes an 0-4-0 DM locotracteur built by Billard in 1947 and two 0-6-0 DM locotracteurs constructed in 1948 at the Montmirail depot of the CF Départmental railway network and used on the Corsican and Baie de Somme systems.

A range of metre gauge freight wagons is preserved here including a number from the Blanc to Argent line which still carried significant freight traffic until the end of the 1980's. The extensive yard includes complex 1000mm, 600mm, and dual gauge track. The operating line crosses two roads. Its extension is at present restrained by some local residents.

9: MUSÉE DES TRANSPORTS URBAINS , ST.MANDÉ

✳ At St.Mandé, 12th arrondissement, **Paris**
✤ Hc/IGN103 C6, ✲ Electric & steam, ⚐ 600, 1000 & 1435mm and others, ✲ 0km
☞ Porte Dorée station, Metro line 8 (direction: Créteil-Préfecture) or RATP bus 46, 86 or 325
☛ From Place de la Bastille take ave.Daumesnil to Porte Dorée then ave. Ste.Marie is on left
✓ pm. Sat & Sun: Begin-Apr to end-Nov.
✉ MTU, 60 avenue Ste.Marie, 93160 St.Mandé, Paris ✆ 43.28.37.12

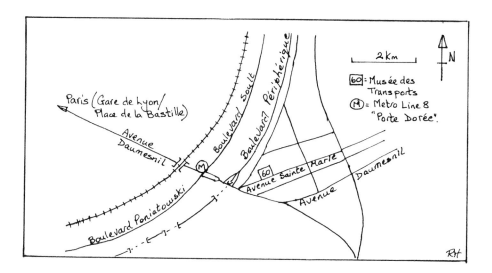

This long established museum of urban transport remains open after a period of uncertainty. An amazing collection of horse, steam and electric tramcars, together with a magnificent set of early Parisian buses are well displayed within the old tram sheds on avenue Sainte Marie in the twelfth arrondissement. There is a short demonstration tram line.

The collection was begun in 1957, and has been continuously added to since then under the protection of AMITUR, the Association pour le Musée des Transports Urbains, Interurbains et Rural. The collection was moved to the Avenue Sainte Marie depot in 1973. It includes various secondary items of railway stock, tramcars, metro cars, buses and trolleybuses: well over 100 items in all. There are six horsedrawn vehicles: buses of various dates from 1863 and a Swiss (Neuchâtel) tramcar of 1894. Amongst the numerous tramway exhibits is a Glasgow tram car (No.488 built in 1900): another British exhibit is a London trolleybus. The bus collection is superb, with examples from around France in addition to a comprehensive collection of Parisian buses of all periods, including horse drawn, petrol and diesel vehicles. Steam locomotives of 600 and 1000mm gauges are on display and include a vertical boilered example. The 1908-built vertical-boilered 0-4-0T Cockerill locomotive is a standard gauge design converted to metre gauge operation. Other steam engines are of Koppel, Decauville, Cail, Piguet and Blanc Misseron manufacture. A rack railway item, the motor carriage built for the Laon line in 1899, is exhibited on a sloping track, as is a funicular carriage from the Fourvière funicular at Lyon. One of the funicular cars replaced during the rebuilding of the Paris Montmartre line in 1990 is preserved at St.Mandé. The tramcar collection contains items from Swiss and many French tramways. The collection of Paris metro stock includes a motor carriage dating from 1904. A prototype rubber tyred metro carriage is available for inspection.

A visit to this museum cannot be recommended too highly. The collection has very many items of historic importance. In addition to a unique collection of passenger vehicles, various items of auxiliary equipment, models and photographs are displayed. Access by bus or metro is easy. The museum is laid out as a series of separate halls, each dedicated to a different aspect of urban and inter-urban transport, and has a bookshop containing a wide range of associated literature.

10: TACOT DES LACS

✳ At Grez-sur-Loing. From **Port au Sable** to **La Plaine**
✤ Hc/IGN103 D6, ✽ Steam & diesel, 🚋 600mm, ✻ 2.5km
☞ Table 540: SNCF Bourton-Marlotte-Grez then bus (4km) to Montcourt canal bridge
☛ Montcourt bridge is 5km N of Nemours. Depot station access via track 0.5 km N of bridge
✓ pm. Sun & BH: mid-April to mid-Nov and (diesel) Saturdays: mid-May to begin-Oct
✉ Association du Tacot des Sabliers de Bourron, 77880 Grez-sur-Loing ✆ 64.28.67.67

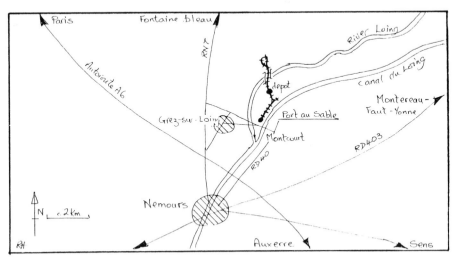

Tacot is a word used by the French to affectionately describe a ramshackle railway. To be fair, the Tacot du Lac is operated in as professional a manner as the resources of a dozen or so enthusiastic volunteers will permit. Visitors are made very welcome and the "affection" is justified.

The line has been rebuilt since about 1985 on the site of an old rail system used to transport sand from workings in the valley of the River Loing to the SNCF line at Bourron-Marlotte just south of Fontainebleau. Complete rebuilding was necessary when the present operation began, as the original track had been removed ten years earlier. The line runs through what is in effect a public access area through the woods and around the lakes which have been left by the old sand extraction. Plenty of photographic opportunities therefore exist. This free access does not apply to the centre part of the line which is fenced off to protect the stock storage area situated in a clearing in the woods. Access is by train.

A couple of standard gauge wagons beside the bridge over the Loing canal at Montcourt mark the station car park from where the line begins. Interestingly these wagons are of US origin with diamond bogies. The little station here offers no more than a rudimentary platform and shelter. The track, and the run round loop for locomotives, which is situated here, are very lightly laid on shingle. Along most of the line they are buried in the sand. On leaving the station the train briefly runs alongside the canal before it swings away along one side of a large triangle of track. At this point the line runs through woods and across numerous watercourses, passes through the gated storage area with lines of stock awaiting restoration. The train finally emerges into a wide sand covered area with lakes on both sides. The main depot and station are situated here. The operational locomotives are stored within the workshop building. In the siding area beyond is a large collection of stock awaiting attention. The line then runs slightly uphill to cross the River Loing on a 35 m long steel girder bridge before reaching the terminal station at the site of the old sand workings.

A large collection of stock is present on this line, and will be displayed in the new building. The operational steam locomotives are "Margarete" an 0-4-0T Arn Jung (built in 1937 and originally operated on the sand line here), "Caroline" 0-8-0T an immaculate Henschel DFB of 1917. Also on the line are an 0-4-0T Decauville, an 0-4-0T O&K, and a Baldwin 4-6-0T which was converted by its industrial operator to become a diesel-mechanical locomotive. Other items are Billard and Whitcomb locotracteurs, two more DFB 0-8-0Ts and an ex-Réseau Breton draisine.

Unlike so many French tourist lines, the Tacot des Lacs operates for most of the year (weather permitting). British visitors seem to be not infrequent. All are made welcome at this line which is operated by and for enthusiasts. A great deal of interesting stock and reasonable access make this a practical choice, even out of season. Montcourt is only 70 km from Paris.

11: CHEMIN DE FER DES CHANTERAINES

⁜ **Pont d'Epinay** to **Pompidou, Verdure** and **Gennevilliers**
✣ Hc/IGN103 B5, ❃ Steam and diesel, ✌ 600mm, ❃ 5km
☞ RER line C Gennevilliers station or RATP bus 137 to Porte de Claincourt
☛ Autoroute A86 then RN186 to Villeneuve-la-Garenne. Entrance on Boulvd Chas.de Gaulle
✓ pm. Wed, Sat, Sun & BH: March to November. Winter services depend on the weather
✉ CF des Chanteraines, A.Dubout, 46 ave George Pompidou, 92390 Villeneuve-la-Garenne,
✆ (1)40.85.86.20

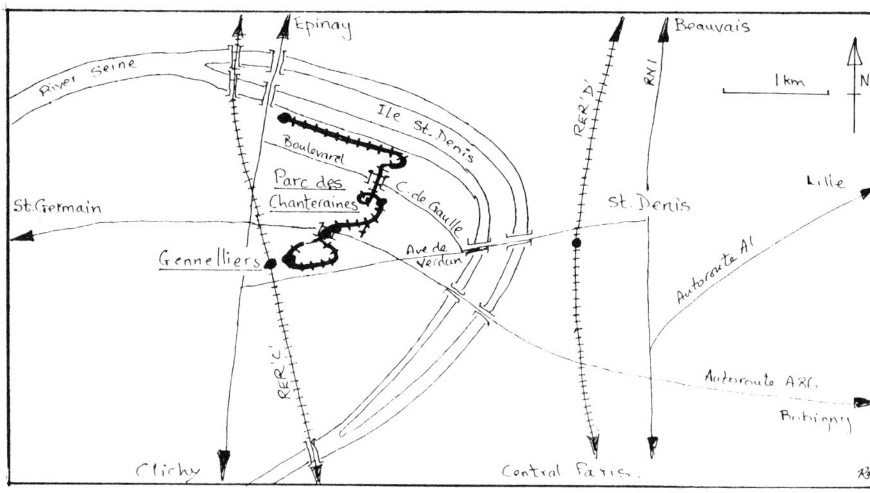

The leisure park of Chanteraines was created by the *département* of Hauts de Seine during the 1970s. This covers an area of about 70 hectares on either side of autoroute A86. A narrow gauge railway was gradually extended through this park during the 1980's. This has been professionally constructed using heavy grade rail on reused SNCF sleepers. A large, modern depot has been built and a significant collection of stock has been assembled.

The track starts from a terminal station close to the Pont d'Epinay which crosses the river Seine in two stages via the Ile St.Denis. This island extends along the middle of the river for about 4km. The track runs along the left (south) bank of the river for 1.3 km before curving sharply south on entering the park. It then follows a sinuous course, firstly to the station at Avenue George Pompidou then, by a reverse curve, it rises up to cross boulevard Charles de Gaulle on a long metal bridge close to the park entrance. The line then falls down to the station at the children's farm via a spiral loop. Beyond this the railway runs close to the lake, across lawns and amongst trees to rise once again to cross the autoroute on a wide concrete bridge. Just as this climb begins, the track splits with a branch running down to the depot.

The next station, Passage de Verdure, is situated on the bridge over the motorway. After this the line splits again at a triangle of track and runs right round the edge of the western section of the park to reach Gennevilliers RER station. The setting offers a range of photographic opportunities.

The stock used for services on the line is of equal standard to the infrastucture. It includes two modern (1981) Socofer locotracteurs, two Decauville steam locomotives, (an 0-6-0T built in 1920, and an 0-4-0T of 1911); closed and open bogie carriages and some "freight" wagons. Outside operating periods, the stock is securely locked in the sturdy depot building. This has four tracks, a service pit and workshop facilities. Additional tracks run beside the building for the storage of the carriage stock. The modern locomotives are Socofer four wheel diesel hydraulic machines. There are also Plymouth, Decauville and Campagne diesel locomotives preserved here.

Up to three trains operate simultaneously on peak days. Each train has three carriages, each capable of carrying 20 passengers. Over 30,000 passengers are carried each year. Visiting locomotives are often operated on special "enthusiast" days. Restaurant and entertainment facilities etc are available in the park, for which entrance is free.

12: EURO DISNEY RAILROAD

⁂ At **EuroDisney** resort park at Marne-la-Vallée
✣ Hc/IGN103 C7, ❃ Steam, ✌ 914mm (3 feet), ❃ 2.2km
☞ RER line A and SNCF (TGV): Marne-la-Vallée-Chessy. Direct Eurostar service from UK
☛ At Marne-la-Vallée, 32km E of Paris. Signposted from autoroute A4(E50)
✓ am & pm. Daily: all year
✉ Resort EuroDisney, Marne-la-Vallée, ✆ 49.41.49.10

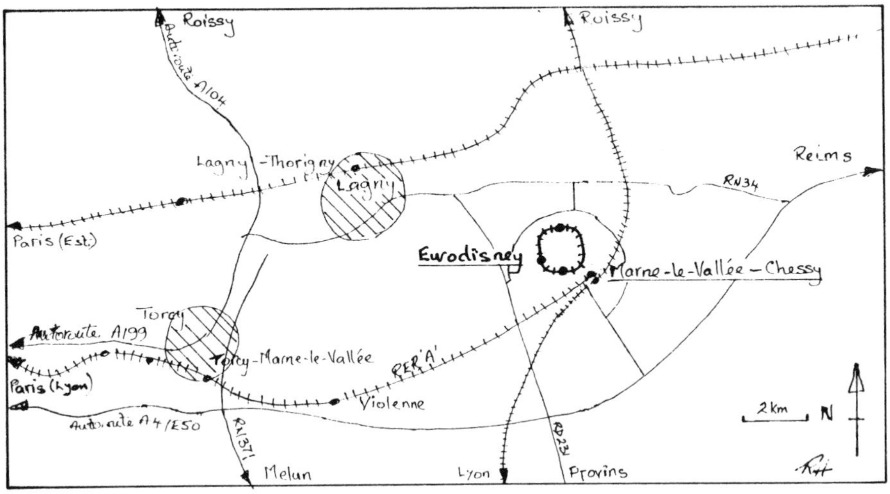

Unlike every other tourist railway in France, the EuroDisney railroad takes no benefit from the countryside. The whole location has been designed and built independently of the original geography. In fact this railway could, literally, be situated in any part of the world. The infrastructure and railway are, in all major respects, identical to those in the other Disney theme parks. Each railway operates 4-4-0 tender locomotives of "wild west" style with large wooden cab, conical chimney and enormous head lamp based on the design of locomotives once owned by a certain Walter Disney.

The four locomotives at EuroDisney, each with a train of 5 bogie carriages, have all been built in Britain in the last few years by Hugh Phillips and Severn Lamb. The gauge is a very non-metric three feet (914mm). The locomotives, stations and attire of the railway staff give a fair representation of a US railway of civil war vintage. The carriages by contrast are reminiscent of early twentieth century wooden bodied stock. The locomotives, numbered 1 to 4, are named "W F Cody", "C K Holliday", "G Washington", and "Eureka" respectively. Each carriage is named after a locality in the USA.

The line runs clockwise around the perimeter of the essentially circular pleasure park and links each of the individually themed "lands". From the two storey, Victorian style Main Street Station at the park entrance to the south of the site, the train travels clockwise passing Grand Canyon, Frontierland Depot Station, Fantasyland Station, Small World and Cinemagique, giving a brief view of each..

The whole railway and its setting is immaculately manicured, undermining the illusion of a real railway. This is in reality a large fairground ride. However, it is of the highest quality and is 100% steam operated, except for a diesel draisine (also built in South Wales by Hugh Philips Engineering) used for maintenance work. The trains give the passenger an excellent view of the features of the park. A diorama is presented in the tunnel which is entered immediately after Main Street Station. A circuit of the line takes twenty minutes, giving up to twelve trains per hour. Despite this, waiting for a place on the train can be very lengthy experience, although less so at either end of the day. This is particularly the case at Main Street Station, and boarding at Frontierland or Fantasyland is an advisable alternative.

A frustrating feature of this line is the difficulty of access and lack of photographic opportunities. Access to the platforms is strictly controlled and access to the round house depot appears impossible. By contrast, the other rail based transport system, the horse tramway along Main Street, is freely accessible. Another item of railway interest is the Thunder Mountain Railway, giving a rather different ride!

13: PETIT TRAIN DU JARDIN D'ACCLIMATATION

※ **Porte Maillot** to the **Jardin d'Acclimatation** in the Bois de Boulogne in central Paris
✧ Hc/IGN103 C5, ✳ Petrol, ⚖ 500mm, ✱ 1.8km
☞ Metro line 1 (direction: Pont de Neuilly) or bus line 73 to Porte Maillot Station
☛ Parking at Porte Maillot: junc. of Ave .Charles de Gaulle(RN13)/Boulevd Périphérique (A1)
✓ pm. Wed, Sat, Sun & BH. Also daily during school vacations
✉ Jardin d'Acclimatation, Bois de Boulogne, 75116 Paris, ✆ 46.24.10.80

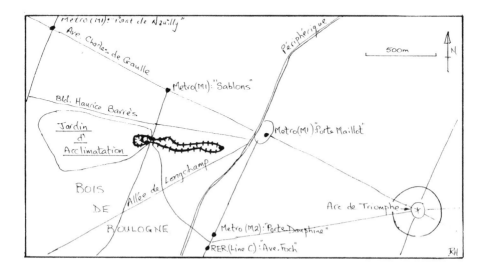

In 1860 a pleasure garden was opened in Paris in the Bois de Boulogne public park. This institution thrived and continues to offer entertainment to young and old. Today many of the facilities are more biased towards the young than previously. However, the restaurants and 45 acres of gardens ensure that the whole family is catered for and that a very large number of visitors are attracted each year.

In 1880 an extensive line was built right around the gardens and then out across the Bois de Boulogne to Porte Maillot, the entry to the "Bois" nearest to the centre of the city. This 5km long line was operated by horses until about 1910. The horse trams were replaced by trains of open carriages hauled by petrol engines of various designs. About twenty years later the line was reduced in length by removal of the circuit within the gardens and also by being cut back to accommodate a subway at the Porte Maillot road junction. The line was thus reduced to a little under 2km in length. The present Renault locotracteurs were delivered to the line in 1960. The passenger stock had roofs added in the 1950's but otherwise remain as built in 1910. The seven Renault locomotives have steam outline bodies. They are brightly painted to match their individual trains of five carriages. The locomotives are petrol driven, the supply being taken from a vintage pump situated at the end of the departure platform within the gardens.

The railway is laid out as an elongated loop to carry visitors over the 800m distance between Porte Maillot and the entrance to the gardens. The platforms at Porte Maillot are served by a rustic ticket office building. The lines out and back briefly run side-by-side. As trains are operated in a clockwise direction they travel to the left along this stretch as in standard gauge main-line practice. For the remainder of the journey they run independently through the open woods. The whole length is enclosed by impressive 2m high rustic railings. Just before entering the garden the lines again converge to cross a public road at an open crossing.

Trains return via a loop immediately inside the garden entrance where the platforms are situated. The line however extends further in the form of a large loop which encircles the park office building and the railway depot. Here there are five covered tracks to accommodate the complete trains and also maintenance facilities. The trains neatly lined up here are a fine sight in matching livery. They are clearly lovingly maintained.

This is a line is well suited for British visitors to the French capital. It has great ambience, is conveniently located, and operates for much of the year.

14: CHEMIN DE FER DE SAINT-EUTROPE

✳ At Bois de **Saint-Eutrope** near Évry
✦ Hc/IGN103 C6, ✽ Steam & diesel, ᪥ 600mm and others ✸ 2.5km
☞ Tables 82 & 84: SNCF Evry-Coucouronnes then bus No 403 (3km)
☛ Beside the racetrack on N side of RN446 between Évry and Montlhéry
✓ pm. Sat (diesel), Sun & BH: Easter to mid-Nov. Also some Weds in season.
✉ Société Études et Équipment, 5 Square Montsouris, 75014 Paris, ✆ (1) 45.89.76.49

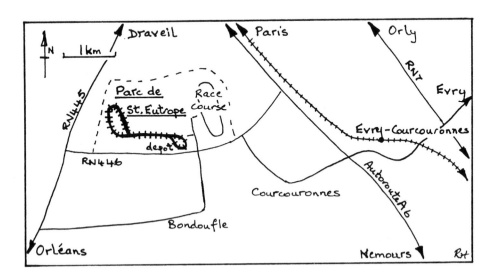

Évry is a new town on the southern outskirts of Paris. The desire of the local authorities to develop leisure activities around the town coincided with the plans of railway enthusiasts to find a site to operate the collection of industrial narrow gauge locomotives owned mostly by an individual collector. As a result, the land required was provided close to the Hippodrome des Arcades race track. The necessary facilities were created and the extensive collection of rolling stock was moved to the site prior to the opening of the railway in 1978.

The railway is laid out in a country park of woods and open areas. A large depot has been created which also acts as an exhibition area close to the entry car parking. The station and depot are positioned on the outside of a large loop of track which leads to the beginning of the single-line route through the woods and fields. The train offers a transport service within the park, which excludes motor cars. Its primary purpose however is to enable the collection of railway equipment to be demonstrated in operation.

The stock is immaculately maintained. This is in essence a private museum collection. Up to eight steam locomotives are on display together with about ten diesel locotracteurs The steam stock includes two 0-8-0T Henschel, three 0-6-0T Decauville of 1916 to 1920 vintage, an 0-4-0WT built by Jung in 1918, a 1910 constructed Couillet 0-6-0T and an 0-8-0T built by Krauss in 1918. The diesel collection includes examples of Deutz, Gmeinder and Billard industrial engines. There is also an extensive collection of passenger, freight and tramway stock.

Trains operate from 14.30 with steam operation on Sundays and public holidays. It is possible to walk the length of the track, giving ample opportunity for photography. Despite being a recent creation the atmosphere created is one of a real railway. This is assisted both by the wooded setting and by the design of the wooden railway buildings.

In addition to the 600mm gauge railway, lines of 184mm (7¼inch) and 400mm have been laid. These are operated on Sundays. The 184mm line is used for a battery operated miniature tramway for children.

Évry was the birthplace of the Decauville company which established 600 mm railways as a French standard. Many of the tourist railways described in this book have examples of Decauville locomotives. A museum dedicated to Decauville equipment is being established at Évry. At the time of writing it appears likely that this will be at the CF de Saint-Eutrope site.

15: TRAIN TOURISTIQUE DE LA VALLÉE DE LA SCARPE

❄ At **L'Anguille** to **St.Amand-les-Eaux**. (Also **St.Amand** to **Maulde-Mortage**)
✢ Ia/IGN101 B6, ❋ Diesel, ⸗ 600mm, ❋: 1.5km (and ⸗ 1435, ❋ 8km)
☞ Table 271: SNCF St.Amand-les-Eaux
☛ St.Amand is 40km SE of Lille via Autoroute C27 and RN17
✓ Narrow gauge operation on Sunday mornings all year. (Standard gauge: when advertised)
✉ AAMCS, Office du Tourisme, 91 Grand Place, 59230 St.Amand-les-Eaux
✆ 27.48.13.13

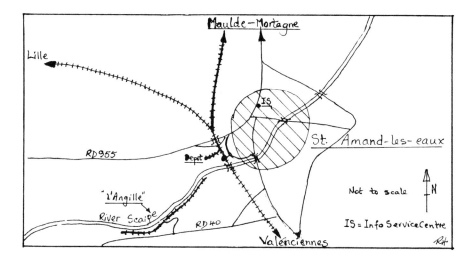

St.Amand is situated on the canalised River Scarpe in northern France close to the Belgian border. It is the junction on the SNCF line from Valenciennes to Lille where the freight branches to Millonfosse and to Maulde-Mortagne diverge. Maulde-Mortagne was the border station on the old line to Tournai (Belgium).

An active railway enthusiast group (AAMCS) is based here. It has three inter-related operations based at separate sites in the town. The first is situated at Espace Caron at the Info Centre, rue de Rivoli (immediately north of the town centre). Here the members of the group have created an extensive (12m x 5m) 1/87 scale model railway. This is open to public viewing each Saturday afternoon all year.

A narrow gauge operation is based at the depot built on the western edge of the town at a location known as L'Anguille (beside the D4 road to the SW of St. Amand). The depot is beside the River Scarpe. A 600mm gauge track is being built along the towpath on the south bank of the river. Trains are regularly operated each Sunday morning all year round. The rolling stock collected here is quite extensive and includes about a dozen ex-industrial diesel locotracteurs. These have been collected largely from brickworks and sand quarries and include items built by Baldwin, Jung, Plymouth, CACL and Deutz. In addition, a steam locomotive is undergoing restoration at L'Anguille. This is an 0-8-0T WW1 Feldbahn locomotive. The line has a collection of 600mm freight wagons and four carriages used for the passenger operation which is known as the Train Touristique de la Vallée de la Scarpe (TTVS).

The same name is used for the proposed operation along the remaining 8km section of the standard gauge line, from St.Amand to Tournai in Belgium, which now terminates at Maulde-Mortagne at the Belgian border. This single track branch retains some freight connections. Standard gauge stock has been obtained by the group. A diesel railcar (X2448) built by Decauville in 1954, a diesel locotracteur built by Berliet in 1924 and freight wagons have been collected since 1989: all are in operational state. The railcars are approved for operation on SNCF and SNCB tracks, and using the railcars, AAMCS operate advertised day trips to various locations in France and Belgium. These trips are often to open days on other preserved railways: details are advertised locally and are also available from the Office de Tourism. In addition, a number of other operations using the AAMCS railcars on SNCF/SNCB lines are organised by other groups.

16: TRAMWAY TOURISTIQUE DE LA VALLÉE DE LA DEÛLE

✳ Marquette-lez-Lille to **Wambrechies**
✣ Ia/IGN101 A5, ✳ Electric tramway, ⚿ 1000mm, ✳ 2km
☞ SNCF Lille Flandres then bus (Lines 3, 9 or 18), or Table 227: SNCF La Madeleine (2km)
☛ Marquette-lez-Lille is 5km N of Lille via RN17 (rue du General de Gaulle) and RD108
✓ pm. (Museum am & pm) Sun & BH: Begin-April to October
✉ AMITRAM, 1521 rue de Bourbourg, 59670 Bavinchove, ✆ 20.42.44.58

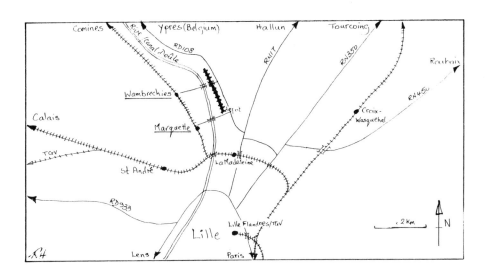

Historic trams from the Mongy **(40)**, the Lille interurban tramway, form the nucleus of an extensive collection of urban transport equipment at the Centre cultural d'historiques, scientifiques et techniques des transports. This museum is based at rue Lavoisier, Marquette-lez-Lille on the northern outskirts of Lille. The collection has been assembled since 1968. It contains buses and tramcars from various parts of France and Europe. A couple of dozen trams and buses are preserved here as well as some lorries and service vehicles. The Lille trams include examples of most of the classes previously employed on the Mongy system. Vehicles from Swiss tramways are also well represented (eg Genève, Berne, Neuchâtel and Fribourg). The range of trams includes a car originally horse drawn, and a prototype version of the *VAL* rapid transit system, which has now become the French standard for these sytems. Various traditional electric trams from the museum are used to operate occasional vintage excursions on the interurban network.

Since 1989 the AMITRAM preservation group, which manages the museum, has been building a metre gauge line with overhead electrical supply line, to demonstrate, and offer rides on, a selection of trams from its collection. This tourist tramway has been built alongside the canalised River Deûle. It starts from the Pont Mabille bridge at Marquette-lez-Lille, just south of the tram depot with its passing loop, siding and tram shed. The route then runs parallel to the river with another passing loop about mid way. It reaches the final loop and terminus by passing under the RN349 which crosses the tramway and river on the Pont de Wambrechies.

The line initially runs through an industrial area but it gradually leaves the town to cross a less urban area and reach the pleasant village of Wambrechies.

Being a new installation, this tramway does not have the historic relevance of the various preserved tramways or those still operational - for example the Mongy itself. However, the ride has the atmosphere of pre-war interurban tramways and the leisurely ride one associates with trams of the era. The opportunity to travel in examples of the preserved stock adds an active dimension to a visit to this superb collection of urban transport.

17: TRAIN TOURISTIQUE DU HAINAUT/ TRAIN TOURISTIQUE DES HOUILLÈRE

❄ **Denain-Mines** to **Arenberg** mine
✢ Ia/IGN101 B6, ✹ Diesel, ⚒ 1435mm (also 570 and 600mm) ✻ 8km
☞ Table 255: SNCF Denain (1km)
☛ Denain is 10km SW of Valenciennes. RN30 for 8km then RN45 W for 5km.
✓ pm Sun in July, Aug and Sept
✉ CEF-Nord, c/o M G Grépier, 6 chemin du Moulin, 59144 Jenlain, ✆ 27.49.78.52 (evenings)

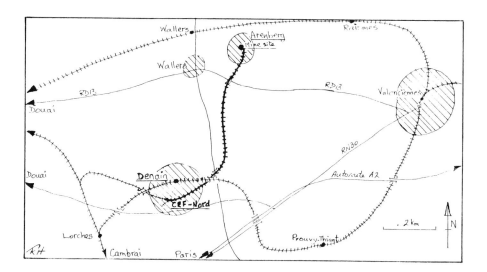

The coalfields and industrial areas of northern France along the border with Belgium have had a close association with railways for over 100 years. In recognition of this, the CEF-Nord group of enthusiasts has, since 1980, amassed a collection of railway rolling stock and created a regional railway museum. This is situated at Denain, an old mining town close to Valenciennes. The location is the site of the old coal mine to the west of the town. The large collection of narrow gauge vehicles includes stock of 600mm gauge used in mines in the Pas de Calais *département*, and 570mm gauge which was standard in the Nord *département*. About eighty of these items have been obtained. In addition to a large number of *berline* wagons, the narrow gauge collection includes locotracteurs built by Baldwin, Deutz, Gmeinder and Jung, and wagons adapted for particular purposes (including personnel transport). The collection includes some WW1 military items.

Despite the quantity of the narrow gauge equipment, the more important items are among the standard gauge stock. These include the largest collection of preserved standard gauge wagons in France: some are truly historic items, dating from 1873 for example. Other items include a collection of rail mounted cranes built by Bondy, Bucyrus and the Industrial Works of Michigan, USA (in 1913). The locomotive stock includes a number of small steam locomotives with three vertical boilered locomotives (one built by Cail in 1913 and two by Cockerill in 1920 and 1928). There are also diesel and petrol locomotives, a Night Ferry sleeping car and a locally-built Picasso railcar (X4046 by ANF, Blanc-Misseron in 1963). Stock for the museum collection is primarily items associated with the area, either by having been built locally or having worked in the area before becoming redundant.

Since 1989 the preservation society has operated an occasional passenger service on the now disused mineral line from its depot at the old Denain mine to the mine location at Arenberg, some 8km to the north. Part of this route is along one of the earliest railway lines in France: the Denain to St Waast (Valenciennes) line was built in 1838. The route followed by the passenger service passes right across the town before following a surprisingly rural route to Arenberg, to reach the remaining pit shaft winding gear. Much of the route is through the recently-extended regional nature park. The Picasso railcar and a Decauville-built trailer car are used for these passenger services. The train operates on selected dates each summer: usually on Sundays. Due to the irregular nature of the passenger service, a telephone call in advance is recommended. Occasional trips are also operated to other sites in the area, for example to St.Waast where the some of the original 1842 station buildings remain.

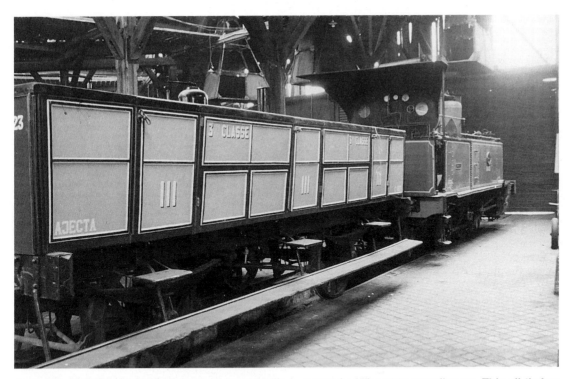

9. ↑ The AJECTA preservation site at Longueville is centred on the 1911 roundhouse. This all-timber structure contains the "St. Germain" train which comprises the 1867 loco "Rimaucourt" and examples of contemporary 1st, 2nd, and 3rd class carriages. [19]. *(Photo: R. Haworth*

10. ↓ The Givet line operated by the Belgian group connects with the SNCB network at Dinant. Preserved diesel railcar 4611 is seen here connecting with a single Class 45 SNCB diesel railcar on the service to Namur. [20]. *(Photo: R. Haworth*

11. The Dinant to Givet line runs alongside the River Meuse. At Annseremme the railway passes through a rock tunnel. The CFV3V railcar is No. 4611, travelling towards Givet. [20].　*(Photo: R. Haworth)*

12. Picasso railcar X3877 is standing at Vigy station ready to form the Sunday afternoon train to Hombourg-Bundange. [24].　*(Photo: R. Haworth)*

13. Loco 141TB4 with a train of 4-wheel end-balcony coaches on the CdF Touristique du Rhin in Alsace [26]. This loco is classified as a *Monument Historique*. *(Photo: C. Gerrer*

14.This 400mm gauge train transports visitors from the car park through the park grounds to the entrance of the model railway museum at Clecy in Calvados [32]. *(Photo: R. Haworth)*

15. At the Historic Mine Centre at Lewarde, the 600mm gauge railway uses mine man-rider wagons to transport visitors around the various buildings. [34]. *(Photo: Centre Historique du Minier de Lewarde*

16. One of the well-disguised Billard diesel locomotives waits to depart from "Babagattaux" station at the Mer de Sable pleasure park, Ermenonville, to the north of Paris. [36]. *(Photo: La Mer de Sable)*

18: CHEMIN DE FER TOURISTIQUE DU VERMANDOIS

⁂ **Saint Quentin** to **Origny-Sainte-Benoîte** via **Ribemont**
✣ Ib/IGN101 C6, ❃ Steam & diesel, ❀ 1435mm, ❃ 22.5km
☞ Tables 253: SNCF St.Quentin (Platform 5)
☛ St.Quentin is 45km NW of Laon. Access via RN44 (rue General Leclerc)
✓ am & pm. Sun & BH: Begin-June to end-Sept (Diesel: am, steam & diesel: pm)
✉ CFTV, BP152, 02104 St.Quentin Cedex, ✆ 23.07.88.02

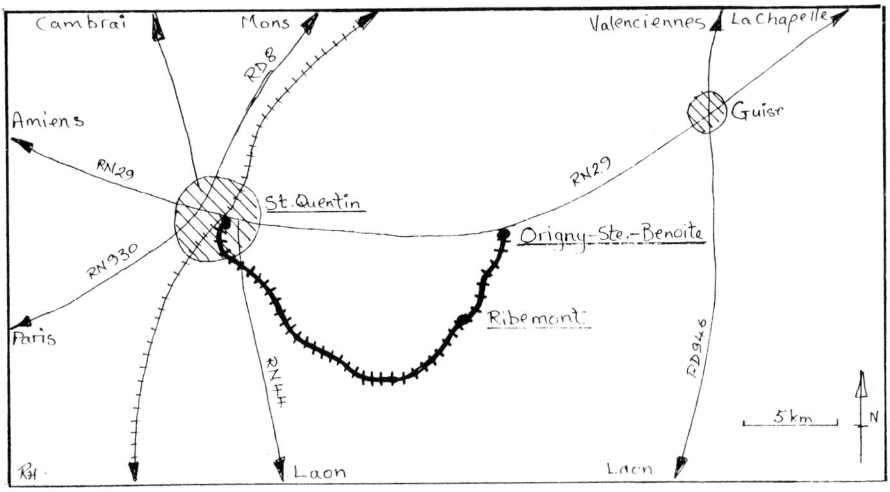

The Vermandois is a lowland plateau to the west of River Oise and about 150km north of Paris. It is crossed by the main Paris to Brussels rail routes. During the second half of the nineteenth century, a network of branch lines were built to serve this area of highly productive agriculture. These railways were built by local companies. The Compagnie du Chemin de Fer de St.Quentin à Guise opened a route in 1874 from a junction with the main line at St.Quentin; initially as far as the small town of Origny-Sainte-Benoîte and then, the following year, to Guise. For fifty years this railway formed part of a network of lines not only providing an indispensable passenger service but also transporting the large quantities of sugar beet, cereals, milk and the production from the various agricultural industries of the area.

This stable situation was abruptly halted by military action during WW1. For strategic reasons, the German army destroyed the railway including the track and infrastructure. Ribemont, midway along the line, was the only station building to survive. This is now maintained as an "historic monument". Following WW1 reconstruction took place but road competition commenced. Passenger services were operated by Billard and Renault railcars from 1927 in an attempt to reduce costs but closures were to occur between the wars. The final passenger services, between St.Quentin and Origny, ceased in 1968, but cement and agricultural products continue to be carried on this remaining section.

The CFTV preservation group was founded in 1977 and using railcar X5830 (built in 1954) began weekend passenger trips. Negotiations with SNCF were successful despite this early tourist operation pre-dating the change in SNCF attitude to use of its tracks by amateur groups. The tourist service has continued and a "living museum" has been created based at St.Quentin.

The rolling stock maintained by CFTV includes an 0-6-0T steam locomotive built by Fives-Lille in 1933; three diesel railcars: X5830; X3623, a Renault ABJ4 of 1950; and "Picasso" X3866; and numerous ex-SNCF carriages including stock from the Night Ferry service. In addition, the society has responsibility for the magnificent SNCF 2-8-0 locomotive No 140C314. This is owned by the FACS association, and is used for main line excursions.

The CFTV trains run on days when freight services do not operate. The train initially runs through the south west part of St. Quentin, but soon emerges into the rural area through which it climbs at a steady 1 in 60 past Itancourt to reach the watershed between the rivers Somme and Oise. The line then falls at the same gradient through Mézières-sur-Oise which was the junction for the old La Fère branch. Having crossed the Oise and its canal, the line follows the valley on a level course for the remaining 12km to Origny. Ribemont is on this section. It was the junction station for the old line to Le Ferté-Chevresis. The early afternoon train is usually a Picasso railcar. This runs as far as Ribemont only. There are two CFTV depots in St. Quentin.

19: LONGUEVILLE RAILWAY MUSEUM

✳ At **Longueville**
✢ Ic/IGN103 C8, ✿ Steam, ⚒ 1435mm
☞ Table 170: SNCF from Paris (Est) to Longueville (5 minute walk)
☞ From Paris via RN19 (or RN4 & D231) to Provins then D412 to Longueville
✓ am & pm. Sat, Sun & (some) BH all year. Annual open day usually at beginning of October.
✉ AJECTA, BP1, 77650 Longueville, ✆ 64.08.60.62 or (1)43.86.94.49

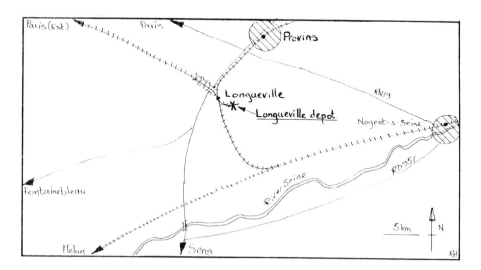

Longueville is situated at the extremity of the Paris suburban railway network. The locomotive depot here was established by the Est railway as base for its operations in the Brie region to the south east of Paris.

The AJECTA preservation group was formed in 1968 and took the lease of the redundant depot from SNCF in 1971. From that date the collection of stock here has steadily expanded to include approaching 100 pieces of rolling stock.

The facilities of the depot include the semi-circular locomotive roundhouse, with turntable, a large storage area with numerous long sidings and a comprehensive workshop. The roundhouse is built exclusively of timber, a possibly unique feature: it is classified as an ancient monument, as is a large part of the rolling stock. It was built in 1911: it is photogenic and provides an excellent setting for the museum and locomotive storage/workshop. Close to Longueville is the small town of Provins. This is a preserved medieval town with more developed tourist facilities than Longueville. Hotels and restaurants are available here.

Despite the attraction of the depot and region, the primary reason for visiting the Longueville site must be the collection of rolling stock which in France is second in size only to the national railway museum collection at Mulhouse. The stock at Longueville varies from time to time due to stock loans etc. However, the following steam locomotives are in the Longueville collection: 2-6-0 Schneider built in 1862, 0-8-0 by Cail in 1866, 2-6-0 built by the Epernay works of the Est railway in 1883, "Rimaucourt" an 0-6-0T built by Batignolles in 1887, "Suzanne", an 0-4-0T vertical boilered tram style locomotive built by Cockerill in 1896, 2-8-2T from Blanc Misseron in 1913, 0-4-0T Corpet of 1918, 0-6-0T Schneider of 1920 and 0-6-0T built by Davenport Locomotive Works in 1942 for the US Army Transportation Corps. An interesting item for British visitors is 2-8-0 tender locomotive No 140C231 built by North British Locomotive Company in 1916.

There is a particularly large collection of carriages here also. This includes items from the Golden Arrow train. Of especial note are the 1st, 2nd and 3rd class carriages which form the "de St.Germain" train with "Rimaucourt". This immaculately prepared train is typical of travel of the 1860's and vividly illustrates the contrast between the open 3rd class wagon and the luxury of the 1st class carriage. A visit to Longueville is worthwhile for experiencing this train alone.

The AJECTA society offer items of stock for use on tourist railways and for use in film, TV and advertising photography. Specific mainline items of stock make frequent runs on the SNCF network. These often involve a start from one of the main Paris termini. These tourist trains are well advertised in the railway literature and give the opportunity to travel over selected lines in the Paris area in 1930's carriages hauled by steam. Loco 2-8-0 No. 140C231 is often used.

20: CHEMIN DE FER VAPEUR DES TROIS VALLÉES

✳ **Givet** from Dinant (Belgium)
✛ Ja/IGN101 C10, ✳ Steam &diesel, ⚑ 1435mm, ✳23km
☞ Table 132: SNCF Givet
☛ Givet is 55km N of Charleville-Mézières via RD988 to Fumay then RN51.
✓ pm. Sat & SunBegin May to end Sept. Also occasional other days. Steam 10 days per year.
✉ CFV3V, Chausée de Givet 49, B5560 Mariembourg, Belgium ℗ (+32) 31.24.40

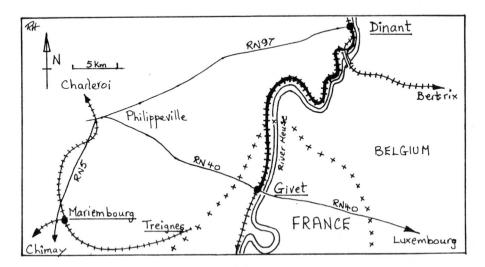

The operations of the Belgian association Chemin de Fer Vapeur des Trois Vallées are included here because two of the lines run into France. The association has a very large collection of rolling stock including two dozen steam locomotives, a dozen powered railcars and a dozen diesel locomotives. The main depot is at Mariembourg with a large roundhouse and water tower and full servicing facilities.

Tourist trains are operated on three lines by the CFV3V: Mariembourg to Treignes (SNCB line132), Mariembourg to Anor (SNCB line 156) and Dinant to Givet (SNCB line 154). Anor and Givet are both in northern France close to the Belgian border.

The operation on the Mariembourg to Anor line has been recently cut back to terminate at Momignies on the Belgian side of the border, and the service frequency reduced due to the poor state of the track. The operations on the route to Givet, however, are in fine fettle with regular diesel railcar and occasional steam train operations since 1990.

The Dinant-Givet trains leave from Platform 3 of the SNCB station at Dinant and then runs along the Bertrix line (SNCB line 166) for 3km. The Bertrix line then swings away right and then left to cross the River Meuse on a long steel lattice bridge. The Givet line runs close beside the river, passing through a striking rock formation in this tight valley. The line follows the left bank of the river for the whole of the journey, passing through the woods and grounds of the Château du Freyr. The train reaches the French border at Heer-Agimont before the final 3km to reach the expansive SNCF station at Givet.

Although there are usually two return journeys, only one completes the full journey to Givet. This reaches Givet at tea time and gives an hour here before the return working to Dinant and back to the depot at Heer-Agimont. There are exceptions to these arrangements. These usually occur on French public holidays and in mid November on the day of the Onion Festival "Fête aux Oignons" at Givet.

Points of interest on the route are the citadel, grotto and museums at Dinant, the château and gardens at Freyr, and the fort and town at Givet. Throughout the journey the valley of the Meuse is of constantly changing interest. The rocks of the valley sides south of Dinant are striking. The grounds of the château are quickly followed by extensive woods.

Fifteen kilometres to the south-west of Givet is the large CFV3V railway museum at Treignes (rue Bassidaine 13, 5670 Treignes. ℗ (+32) 31.24.40. Open daily except Monday).

21: CHEMIN DE FER TOURISTIQUE AMAGNE-LUCQUY CHALLERANGE

✳ From **Attigny** to **Amagne-Lucquy** and to **Challerange**
✤ Jb/IGN101 D9, ✳ Diesel, ▓ 1435mm, ✱ 40.3km
☞ Table 130: SNCF Amagne-Lucquy (0.5km) or SNCF Rethel (20km from Attigny)
☛ Attigny station is N of town, 57km NE of Reims: RD980 (towards Vouziers) and RD987
✓ am & pm to Challerange. pm to Amagne-Lucquy. Sun & BH: Mid-Jun to mid-Sept
✉ CFTSA, cour de la gare, 08130 Attigny, ℰ 24.71.47.60 or 24.26.63.84

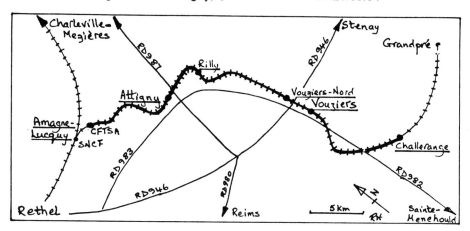

The line between Amagne-Lucquy and Challerange runs through some of the charming scenery of the south west hills of the Ardennes. It was built in two stages, opening from Ameragne to Vouzièrs in 1873, and to Challerange in 1878: The whole route came under the control of the Chemin de Fer de l'Est company in 1881. Passenger services were withdrawn in 1969, but significant freight traffic remains to Attigny, Vouziers and Challerange.

The *département* and local authorities, wishing to stimulate the under-developed tourist and leisure activity in the area, joined with a local group to organise tourist trains on a line in the area. The enthusiast group, les Amis de la Traction Vapeur en Ardennes (ATVA) took up the challenge. Having obtained two Picasso diesel railcars (X3850 and X3897) and trailer car, it operated advertised trips between Rethal and Grandpré in 1987. The present regular service between Amagne and Challerange has operated since 1988, and since 1991, a second ATVA train has been based at Mouzon operating services between Pont-Maugis and Stenay **(23)**. Confusingly both lines operate under the title of Chemin de Fer Touristique du Sud des Ardennes (CFTSA).

The railcars used for both these services are part of the ATVA stock which consists of three Picasso railcars (X3838, X3850, X3897), railcar X2468 and two trailer cars. Picasso X3838 has recently been allocated to the Mouzon based operation. The remainder are based at Attigny, which is situated about a quarter of the way along the line from Amagne. The association has the use of the old freight depot which has been refurbished. A collection of historic railway items is gradually being assembled.

Amagne-Lucquy is a junction station on the main SNCF line between Reims and Charleville-Mézières. The CFTSA station at Amagne-Lucquy is situated on the branch just beyond the junction and about 0.5km from the SNCF station. Between Amagne-Lucquy and Vouziers the train follows the valley of the River Aisne, initially on the right bank as far as Rilly. It then runs along the left bank beside the Canal des Ardennes hugging the valley side: this is the most scenic part of the journey. After Vouziers, the nature of the line changes as the train swings up to the plain above and crosses wide areas of agricultural scenery.

This rural area of rounded hills makes a pleasant setting for a leisurely journey. Organized trips to explore the local scenery and places of interest are available on arrival at Challerange; alternatively it is possible to alight from the train at one of the stations along the Aisne valley and take a boat ride. There are boarding points close the stations at Attigny, Rilly and Condé. The numerous stations along the line enable rambles to be made between the various picturesque villages along the valley. The connection with SNCF trains at Amagne-Lucquy is an additional advantage of this tourist line. The SNCF stopping trains between Reims and Charleville-Mézièrs are, however, infrequent and the timetable should be checked with care. Road services replace the trains in many cases.

An annual railway festival is held at Attigny in August. A variety of operating and preserved locomotives visit the line on these occasions.

22: WASSY STATION
CF DE BLAISE-ET-DER (ST. DIZIER TO DOULEVANT)

✳ At **Wassy** also **St.Dizier** to **Wassy** and **Doulevant-le-Château**
✛ Jc/IGN104 C3, ✳ Diesel (also diesel & steam), ⚘ 1435(&600)mm, ✳ 40(& 2)km
🕮 Table 126: SNCF St.Dizier or SNCF Chevillon (13km from Wassy)
☛ 75km from Reims(via RN44 to Vitry-le-François, RN4 to St.Dizier and RD2 to Wassy)
✓ pm
✉ Assn des Amis de la Gare de Wassy, 52130 Wassy ℂ 83.27.84.85
✉ Office de tourisme, Tour du Dome, 52130 Wassy ℂ 25.55.72.25

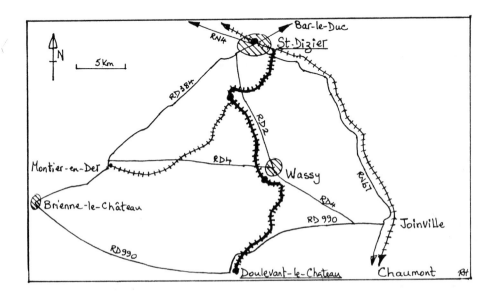

St.Dizier is an industrial town on the River Marne and the Marne-Saône Canal. From St.Dizier a branch line swings SW to Eclaron-Branncourt. when the route splits in two: to Montier-en-Der, and southwards to follow the valley of the River Blaise to Doulevant-le-Château. The railway closely follows this tributary of the Marne. The gently sloping valley is pastoral with woods and makes a picturesque setting for the line. The only significant station along the line is at the hamlet of Wassy. The line was opened in 1868. It lost its passenger trains in 1952 and its freight services in 1989. The track remains in place, however, and the 130 year old station is well preserved.

For some years a militaria and railway preservation society has been based at Wassy station. A 600mm railway has been laid for two kilometres along part of the trackbed of an ancient tramway. Stock includes three diesel locotracteurs and an 0-8-0T Feldbahn steam locomotive.

Both the station and line have recently been purchased by local interests. The station is used by the museum society and a tourist train has been operated since 1994 along the whole line between St.Dizier and Doulevant under the title of the Chemin de Fer de Blaise-et-Der. Railcar X5830 is used and a diesel locotracteur operates reinstated freight services. The standard gauge tourist train services and the narrow gauge operations are both based at Wassy.

23: CHEMIN DE FER TOURISTIQUE MOUZON-STENAY

✳ **Mouzon** to **Stenay** (also to Pont-Maugis)
✤ Kb/IGN101 D11, ✷ Diesel, ⚒ 1435mm, ✷ 22km (+13)
☞ Table 131: SNCF Sedan or SNCF Carignan
☛ Mouzon is 60km N of Verdun via RD964: the station is E of the village on RD19
✓ am & pm. Sun & BH: End-May to begin-Sept
✉ CFTSA Cour de la gare, 08130 Attigny, ✆ 24.71.47.60 or 24.26.63.84

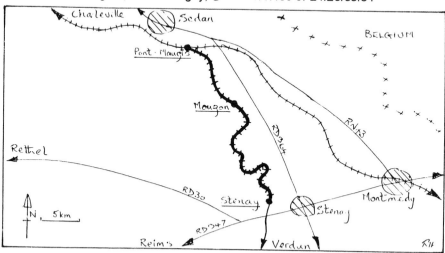

Following the success of its first tourist train, the CFT des Sud Ardennes, on the Armagne-Lucquy to Attigny line **(21)**, the operating society ATVA has run a second line since 1991. This is on part of the Pont-Maugis to Verdun route. Once again it is a summer season service using preserved diesel railcars. Confusingly both lines operate under the title of Chemin de Fer Touristique du Sud des Ardennes (CFTSA)

Along the whole of its length, the line between Pont-Maugis and Verdun runs close to the French/Belgan border. It was seen as militarily strategic and hence a double track line was laid. The potential military importance has also resulted today in the unused southern section of the line, between Stenay and Verdun, being maintained by the army. The northern section retains regular freight traffic to Mouzon and to the paper mill at Stenay. The line, which was built in 1876, lost its passenger service in 1958. The recent opportunity to travel the route once again has proved popular.

This is an area of well-wooded hills and narrow valleys and is a picturesque setting for tourism. The whole length of the line closely follows the meandering course of the River Meuse, always remaining on the west bank. The valley becomes particularly narrow between Muzon and Stenay and to the north of Verdun.

The tourist train operation starts from Mouzon where a Picasso railcar and trailer car are based during the season. The intermediate stations of Létanne-Beaumont, Pouilly, Inor and Luzy-St.Martin are served. Additional journeys are possible for pre-booked groups including northwards from Mouzon to Pont-Maugis, the junction station with the SNCF electrified route between Charleville-Mézièrs and Longuyon.

The railcars used for these services are part of the ATVA stock (3 Picasso railcars X3838, X3850, X3897, railcar X2468 and two trailer cars). Picasso X3838 has recently been allocated to the Mouzon based operation. If the passenger loadings justify it, the use of diesel locomotives and carriage stock is envisaged for future operations. Another future development is the possibility of operations along part of the retained line south of Stenay. This is likely to be along the 13km length of track from Stenay to Dun-sur-Meuse.

The station at Mouzon is situated on the western edge of the town, just over the river. Most of the other stations are well away from the locality from which they take their name. The string of villages are situated on RD964 which follows the far bank of the river. A result of this is that the train follows a completely rural route. The present terminus at Stenay is beside the paper mill, almost 2km from the town: visiting the town before catching the return train requires a significant walk. However, the timetable gives the opportunity of three, four or seven hours to visit the town with its brewery museum. The timetable also makes possible leaving or rejoining the train at intermediate stations and walking along this delightful valley. A further possibility is afforded by the fact that the river is navigable, and a river cruise service is available offering connections with the train at Mouzon and at Pouilly. Combined trips by train and boat are therefore possible.

24: CHEMIN DE FER DE LA VALLÉE DE LA CANNER

❋ Situated in Lorraine, the line runs from **Vigy** to **Hombourg-Budange** via **Bettelainville**.
✤ Lb/IGN104 A6, ❋ Steam & diesel, ǂ 1435mm, ❋ 12km
☞ Tables 160 & 154: SNCF Thionville then SNCF bus to Budange (1km from Hombourg-Budange station)
☛ Vigy is 15km NE of Metz via RD1/RD2 to Antilly then RD52. Station on town approach
✓ pm. Sun & BH, end-Apr to begin-Oct
✉ ALEMF, gare de Vigy, 57640 Vigy, ✆ 87.77.97.50

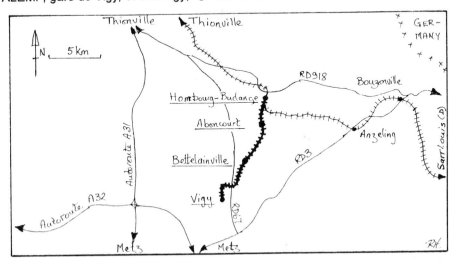

The region of Alsace-Lorraine has been under both French and German administration at various times during the past 150 years as a result of the fortunes of war. The strategic importance of the area affected railway development over this period. The preserved line between Vigy and Hombourg-Budange was no exception to this situation, which affected the development and nature of the line. The section Vigy to Bettelainville was laid as part of the German Elsass-Lothringe, double track, line from Metz to Anzeling which opened in 1908. The following year work began on the building of the single track link from Bettelainville to Merzig via Budange. These lines had strategic importance during WW1 and WW2. They were badly damaged between 1940 and 1944 whilst once again under German (DR) administration. Various sections were not rebuilt. However, the line between Hombourg and Vigy fared better and retained an SNCF freight service until 1976. Local authority action and the efforts of the ALEMF group of railway enthusiasts saved the line for preservation.

The geography of the location required the two strategic lines, of which the tourist line forms part, to negotiate a succession of valleys and low hills. The earlier, southern, line avoided excessive gradients by use of some notable engineering structures. The northern line however was built more cheaply and as a result the 5km section from Aboncourt to Hombourg has an average gradient of 1 in 100. This presents a reasonable challenge to the steam locomotives which operate the tourist trains.

The ALEMF society developed from railway modelling to the restoration of standard gauge steam locomotives in the 1970s. Using "Vesta" an 0-4-0T locomotive (built by Fives-Lille in 1927) the group operated a tourist service on the Etival to Senones line. Transfer to the Vigy line occurred in 1977. The locomotive stock now includes "Barbara", an 0-4-0T Hohenzollern locomotive of 1900, "Canner" an 0-6-0T Krupp built in 1925 and an 0-8-0T built about 1920. Also preserved at Vigy are "Picasso" railcars X3837 and X3877 built in the early 1950s, an 0-6-0T built by Fives-Lille in 1949, and a train of ex-Alsace-Lorraine balcony ended carriages. An Alsace-Lorraine baggage van has been converted to a buffet car. The steam locomotives are classified as historic monuments with central government support for preservation, as well asa superb third-class non-corridor carriage which has been immaculately restored.

The line has recently been sold to the preservation group for a nominal sum: they are purchasing the station at Hombourg-Budange from SNCF. The line runs through the gentle hills of the Lorraine plateau. For the whole of its length, the railway follows the wooded valley of the River Canner. This presents a pleasant and varied photographic setting for the trains. Access is relatively easy since the local road RD118 follows and crosses the line at a number of points. Access to the preserved stock is possible, on occasion, at Vigy depot. An additional attraction is a series of pre-booked locomotive driver training sessions held on certain weekends.

25: MUSÉES DES MINES DE FER, NEUFCHEF & AUMETZ

❊ At **Neufchef** 14km SW of Thionville and at **Aumetz** 20km NW of Thionville
❖ Lb/IGN104 A6, ❊ Steam & diesel, ⚒ 600, 700 & 1000mm
☞ Table 153: SNCF Hayange (4km)
☛ From Metz via RN52.To Hayange (28km) then RD13 to Neufchef or RN52 to Aumetz.
✓ pm. Daily except Mon: All year (Neufchef) and May to Sept (Aumetz).
✉ Both sites: Musée des Mines de Fer de Lorraine, Ste.Neige, 57700 Neufchef, ℂ 82.85.76.55

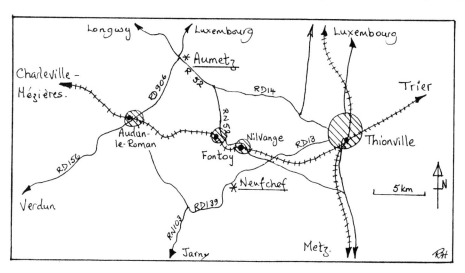

The iron ore basin of Lorraine extends over an area of France from the Belgian and Luxembourg borders to Metz and Nancy: over 3000 km² in all. Of the 56 mines which were operating in 1960 only two remain active. Mining in the area included open cast, drift mines and mines with vertical shafts.

Mine museums at Neufchef and Aumetz were established in 1984 with the express intention of preserving the memory of the mining industry of the region. This is one museum on two sites. They are located close to the Luxembourg border. The old Hamevillers mine at Neufchef is a drift mine with access from the Ste.Neige valley situated to the SW of Thionville. Aumetz is a shaft mine situated NW of Thionville. The Lorraine basin extends across the border. Less than 10km from Aumetz is the National Luxembourg Mine Museum at Rumelange.

The museums display aspects of iron ore mining from the earliest mining in the area in the middle ages to the present day. Much of the exhibited material is railway related because of the vital relationship of rail transport in the mines during the last two centuries.

At the Neufchef site, visitors are taken on guided tours of the underground galleries which extend to about two kilometres. The tour lasts over an hour and is conducted by ex-miners. Be sure to wear warm clothes for the visit underground.

The various galleries show successive stages of work of the mine. Static railway displays underground include a section of 700mm gauge track with battery electric locomotives and mine wagons.

Railway exhibits on the surface include examples of the specialised locomotives which were developed to haul heavier and heavier loads within the confines of restricted tunnel diameters. An especially impressive example is a three-section articulated locomotive with two pantographs.

The route to the Aumtez site is well sign posted. It is also identifiable by the pit head gear which lowered the cages into the shaft. In the car park area at the entrance to the site an overhead cableway has been erected to demonstrate the method by which spoil or waste material was transported in tipping buckets to a disposal site.

There are a number of railway exhibits at the Aumetz site. These include items of 600, 700, 1000mm and other gauges. An immaculately preserved Thomson-Houston 80hp mine locomotive with tipping wagons and a metre gauge Alsthom bogie electric locomotive of 1930 are of particular note amongst the large collection.

26: CHEMIN DE FER TOURISTIQUE DU RHIN

❊ **Volgelsheim** to **Sans Soucis** (and **Marckolsheim**) via **Port Rhénan**
✛ Mc/IGN 104 D10, ❊ Steam and diesel ⚒ 1435mm ✳ 8 km (16km)
☞ Table 190/1/2: SNCF Colmar ⊙ then bus (12km)
☛ From Mulhouse 40km NE via RD39 and RD52. From Strasbourg 70km S via RD468
✓ pm. Sat, Sun and BH: mid-May to mid-Sept
✉ CFTR, 26 rue des Cordiers, 68280 Andolsheim ✆ 89.71.51.42 (eve), 89.72.55.97 (w/ends)
✉ Office du Tourisme, 4 rue des Unterlinden, 68000 Colmar ✆ 89.20.68.92

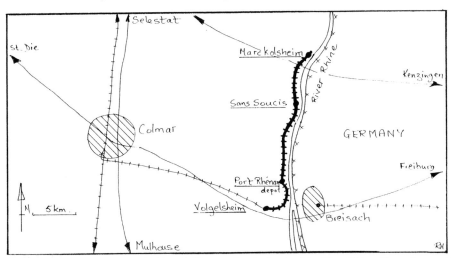

A network of lines remains around the French /German border lands of the River Rhine. These have retained significant freight traffic. Until the bridge was destroyed in 1945, international services were operated along the east/west line from Colmar (France) to Freiburg (Germany). The freight traffic was stimulated by the construction of a branch northwards from Vogelsheim to Marckolsheim. The track is now owned by the local community. An agreement exists for weekend tourist trains to use the line when freight services are not running. An effective locomotive depot and museum has been created at Port Rhénan.

In recent years, the local community has purchased Neuf Brisach station from SNCF. This station (renamed Vogelsheim) has been refurbished and put at the disposal of the group of enthusiasts who operate the museum and the tourist trains. The main base however remains Port Rhénan. Most of the stock preserved here is operational.

Locomotives based at Port Rhénan often operate steam trains on the SNCF system. The collection of rolling stock here includes items from the French national collection and SNCF locomotives as well as items owed by groups and individuals. As a result some interesting, even unique, stock may be found here but the stock list is subject to change. Stable items include a 2-8-2T No 141TB424 built by the Est railway, a travelling post office vehicle, two Belgian-built 0-6-0T ex-Alsace-Lorraine railway locomotives built in 1900, Nos 030TB130 and 030TB134, a modified 0-4-0T vertical boilered Cockerill engine built in Belgium in 1913, two locotracteurs: a large ex-SNCF diesel electric No A1A-A1A62029 built in 1946 and a smaller diesel mechanical engine built in 1962, No Y2402. The majority of these items are preserved in operational condition. Further items in the collection here are: an industrial ex-quarry Henschel engine built in 1901, 0-4-0T Fives-Lille and 0-4-0 fireless locomotives, some four-wheel diesel locotracteurs (a Gaston-Moyse, a Decauville and a Batignolles) and various diesel railcars, freight wagons and carriages.

The passenger stock includes four-wheel coaches with end balconies. These ex-Alsace-Lorraine railway coaches built in the 1920's enable passengers to travel outside and make the most of the steam railway atmosphere and also gain access to the buffet car which forms part of the tourist train. They complement the Alsace locomotives admirably. Also preserved at the Port Rhénan site are some narrow gauge items: a four-wheel Alsthom canal haulage locomotive of 600mm gauge from the Alsace Canal and a metre gauge electric tramcar from the Swiss tramway of Neuchâtel.

Port Rhénan is situated immediately beside one of the large locks which are typical of this stretch of the Rhine. At this point is one of the landing stages of the river boat trips. There are others close to Sans Soucis and Marckolsheim stations of the CFTR, enabling a combined boat/train circuit to be taken. Services to Marckolsheim at the northern end of the line are operated on an occasional basis.

27: CHEMIN DE FER DE OTTROTT/ ROSHEIM

✳ Depot at **Ottrott.** Possible operation once again between **Ottrott** and **Rosheim**
✛ Mc/IGN104 C9, ✳ Steam, 🐇 1435mm, ✳ 8km
☞ Table 124: SNCF Rosheim or SNCF Obernai (4km to Ottrott)
🛥 25km from Strasbourg (RN422/RD426 to Obernai then RD422/RD35 (or RD109 to Ottrott)
✓ To be announced
✉ Societe des Carrieres 67, St.Nabor 67530 Ottrott
✉ Syndicat d'initiative, Le Mairie, 67530 Ottrott ✆ 88.95.80.24

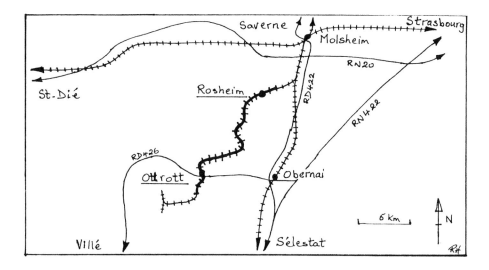

This was one of the earliest of the modern wave of French standard gauge tourist railways. It operated from 1969 to 1988. The 12km long branch line from Rosheim, on the Strasbourg - Molsheim - Sélestat route, to St.Nabour was opened in 1902. The primary use of the line was to move ballast material from the quarry at St.Nabour; for use on the network of railways in Alsace-Lorraine. The line also had passenger services from the start. There were both passenger and freight connections at Rosenheim and also with the Strasbourg metre-gauge tramway at Ottrott. Passenger services ceased in the 1950s since when the line has been under the control of the St.Nabour quarry operator.

In addition to diesel locotracteurs used for the haulage of the mineral wagons, one of the three steam locomotives previously used commercially on the line has survived and remains at Ottrott. This is an 0-6-0T built by Borsig in 1906. The successful tourist train operation was managed by the quarry company which also owned the stock. It used the Borsig locomotive and three four-wheeled ex-SNCF carriages.

The "Train Folklorique Ottrott-Rosheim" ceased operation in 1988. The stock remains at the Ottrott depot. Recent reports suggest that re-establishment of some steam operation on the line may be possible. The quarry continues to despatch freight trains daily on the line carrying ballast for SNCF use. Two steam locomotives are now in the Ottrott depot. The local authorities have now become involved, and re-establishment of the tourist operation seems once again to be a possibility. The line runs along the edge of the Vosges and is truly beautiful. It could quickly become once again a primary tourist attraction.

28: CHEMIN DE FER D'ABRESCHVILLER

✳ From **Abreschviller** to **Grand-Soldat** via **Romelstein**
✣ Mc/IGN104 B8, ✳ Steam and diesel, ⚒ 700mm, ✺ 6km
☞ Tables 103 & 108/9: SNCF Sarrebourg then SNCF bus (18km)
☛ From Metz via RD955 to Herring then D41 and D44 to Abreschviller
✓ am & pm. Sat, Sun & BH: Begin-May to begin-Oct. Also daily: mid-Jul to end-Aug
✉ M Baillet, Hôtel des Cigognes, 57560 Abreschviller, ☏ 87.03.79.12

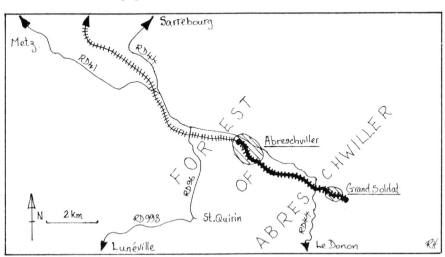

A vast area of forest stretches across the Vosges hills of the Alsace and Lorraine border region of NE France. It has been an important area for timber production for at least 150 years. The hills rising to over 1000m are covered in fir and deciduous woods. The exploitation of the forests was hampered by inadequate transport links in the 1880's and the forest authorities began to lay logging railways. At this time the area was under German administration. As a consequence the German military railway gauge of 700mm was chosen. This is the only system of this gauge in France.

Abreschviller became the hub of the network of forest railways which extended to well over 70km in total. Two violent storms of 1892 and 1902, which brought down vast areas of timber, were the main spur to this development. Abreschviller is situated at an altitude of 290m. The lines radiated up into the hills to a height of 635m. The bulk of the timber was brought out of the forest via the railway. However, by 1966 the railway had become life expired and it was decided to switch the traffic to road transport.

Occasional passenger trains had been operated for parties for some years prior to closure. These had latterly become fairly regular, demonstrating the potential for a tourist railway operation. With support from the forestry service and local authorities, retention of the 6km section from Abreschviller to Grand-Soldat for tourist trains was successful.

The railway starts from the old depot and sawmill of the forest service which is situated close to the SNCF station at Abreschviller. A small station with booking office, shop and waiting room has been established here. The train initially runs below the town, crossing roads on the level. Along much of the route, the train runs close to the River Sarre Rouge which is glimpsed occasionally through the trees. The line twists and turns, crossing pastures and clearings in the woods following an old forestry track. After crossing the river and a local road, the train runs as a tramway alongside the road at Grand Soldat. The terminus of the line is shortly beyond the edge of the hamlet. The small station and museum have been built beside the road in the bottom of the valley. A picnic and play area have been created here. The journey is usually broken by a stop at the intermediate station of Romelstein where the steam locomotive is exchanged for a diesel locotracteur for the onward journey to Grand Soldat.

Most of the locos are preserved originals from the railway when it was a viable commercial enterprise: No 1 is an 0-4-4-0T Mallet built by Maschinenfabrik-Heilbronn in 1906 for use on the Abreschviller lines. No 2 is an 0-6-0T Decauville built in 1928. No 3 is an 0-6-0 diesel hydraulic locotracteur constructed by Conferna in 1953. Also original from the Abreschviller network are two draisines: a Renault car converted by the railway workshops in 1925 to run on the line and a twelve seat unit constructed locally. Items of rolling stock which have subsequently been acquired by the preservation group include No 4 which is an 0-6-0 tender locomotive built by Jung in 1944 for the German military and an 0-4-0 Deutz diesel locotracteur.

29: NATIONAL RAILWAY MUSEUM, MULHOUSE

❋ At Dornach, **Mulhouse**
✧ Md/IGN104 D9, ❋ Steam, diesel, electric and petrol, 🜚 1435mm, ✳ 1.5km
☞ Tables 190 & 195: SNCF Mulhouse-Dornach. The museum is 0.5km E. at the end of ave.Alfred de Glehn
☛ Mulhouse is 30km N Basle via RN66/A35. The museum is to E of town at Dornach
✓ am & pm. Daily all year, except Christmas and new year
✉ Museum Français du CF, 2 rue Alfred de Glehn, 68200 Mulhouse, ✆ 89.42.25.67

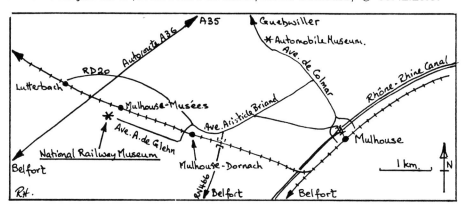

Mulhouse is rightly renowned for the motor museum located in an old spinning mill on Avenue de Colmar. This contains an immense collection of prestigious cars, including 123 Bugattis, which were collected privately by Hans and Fritz Schlumf. The town has a large number of other museums including the French national railway museum. This is situated in a purpose-built building located at Dornach, beside the SNCF line from Mulhouse to Strasbourg. The museum contains the railway collection assembled by SNCF and the Wagons-Lits company. The items exhibited are of the highest quality and are displayed in immaculate condition. The museum building has been designed to display the items in an ideal environment. It is spacious and well lit. In places viewing from a balcony gives a different perspective.

A full list of the this unique collection is impossible here. Personal inclination will lead the visitor to specific items. The British foundation of the French railways system is well represented by three 2-2-2 locomotives of the 1840s: "No33" by Buddicom in 1844, "L'Aigle" by Stephenson of Newcastle in 1846 and "Sezanne" of similar design built by Hallette in France in 1847. Other steam locomotives included in the collection on display are a dozen large passenger engines and a similar number of freight engines. Included are a 2-4-2 built for the PO system in 1882, a 4-8-2 built for the Est railway in 1925, a 2-8-2T in PLM livery and the magnificent "Chapelon", a 4-6-2 built for the Nord railway in 1936. Unfortunately the Nord "Baltic" No 3-1102 has been cut open to reveal the boiler tubes, details of the motion and steam passages etc.

The collection contains a number of electric locomotives and power cars as is to be expected in view of their important place in the history of French railways. Less prestigious items are a tramcar of 1935 manufacture from the Lille tramway system and a metre gauge powercar from the St.Gervais line. Diesel items displayed include the remarkable, 1936 built Michelin type 22 railcar which has eight-wheel bogies and rubber tyred wheels. Most magnificent of all is the Bugatti "Presidential" railcar of 1936 powered by four Bugatti Royale 12.5 litre car engines. This item, also with eight-wheel bogies, is worthy of a visit to Mulhouse in its own right and is likely to prompt an associated visit to the magnificent Bugatti collection on Avenue de Colmar.

Other items of rolling stock include the lovingly restored luxury carriages of the Wagons-Lits company, and very early railway passenger stock. For example a Nord first class carriage clearly showing the lines of its horse drawn predecessors and WW1 vans for soldier or horse transport although similar items to these may been seen at Longueville and Connerré respectively. The double deck suburban carriages of 1850s design are particularly striking as are the various state, imperial and presidential coaches.

Altogether this is a most interesting and superbly presented collection of railway equipment. However, there are some disappointing gaps in the items displayed: a lack of modern equipment, industrial railway items, and aspects of the narrow gauge railways which covered France not so many years ago. This in no way detracts from the spectacular quality of the standard gauge items so wonderfully displayed at Mulhouse.

30: CHEMIN DE FER TOURISTIQUE DE LA VALLÉE DE LA DOLLER

✳ **Cernay** to **Sentheim** via **Burnhaupt**
✤ Md/IGN104 D9, ✽ Steam & diesel, ⚙ 1435mm ✳ 15km
☞ Table 195: SNCF Cernay (Bus service Sun & BH)
☛ Cernay terminus in SNCF yard; south of town centre. Depot at Burnhaupt. Both via RN83.
✓ am & pm. Steam: Sun & BH June to Sept.. Also diesel: (pm only) Wed to Sat in July & August
✉ CFTVD, 10 rue de la Gare, BP5, 68780 Sentheim, ℰ 89.82.88.48

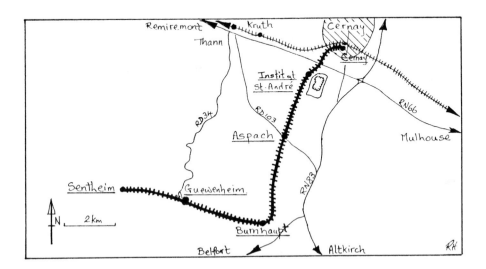

The branch line, in Alsace, from Cernay to Sewen was opened in stages between 1869 (to Sentheim) and 1901. Regular passenger traffic ceased in 1967 and freight traffic in 1972. However, special trains, for walkers to access the hills from the Sewen end of the line, were operated and led to a preservation attempt for that section of the line. Due to local pressure, the preservation operation transferred to the St André/ Sentheim section. With local authority assistance, trains operated from 1975. With the opening back to Cernay in 1978, freight movement onto SNCF tracks was again re-established.

The tourist train is run by a preservation group who maintain a noteworthy collection of stock at Burnhaupt, which is situated half way along the route. Additional stock is stored at Sentheim. The first and last trains of the day collect passengers from Cernay by historic railcar. Passengers transfer to the steam train at Burnhaupt for the final section to Sentheim. Other trains operate steam throughout. The journey starts from the most southerly of the platforms at Cernay SNCF station. It then runs through the suburbs, across the busy RN66 by an open crossing and then alongside the extensive grounds of the St André hospital. The private 600mm line which runs around the grounds for the pleasure of patients can be seen at this point. The train then runs through flat agricultural land and woods before reaching the River Doller and lake which it crosses by an old military bridge, with very limited clearance, requiring special safety precautions. Immediately after the bridges is a minor level crossing and the station at Burnhaupt. The station buildings and depot are extensive and original. Time is available here to inspect the varied stock whilst the train takes water and preparations are made for the onward journey. The train then follows the River Doller through pleasant wooded scenery and some light industry towards the quiet town of Sentheim. Here food and souvenir stalls are set out at the station. The trackbed extends forward on the edge of the town as a footpath: the track has been removed.

The stock preserved on the line includes "Picasso" X5852, Billard and de Dion railcars of 1954, 1948 and 1938 respectively. The steam locomotives include a Meuse 0-6-0T of 1914, a Hainaut 0-6-0T of 1912, a 1911 Henschel 0-4-4-0T Mallet, a 1912 0-6-0T Couillet and an 0-8-0T Franco-Belge of 1945. The locotracteur stock includes an intriguing four-wheel Moyse: basically a chassis with a 30hp Ford engine.

This preservation site has one of the richest collections of stock typical of minor French standard gauge lines; all presented in a friendly and entertaining fashion.

31: LIGNE DE MARAIS DE GORGES

✻ Between **Le Prieure** and **Baupte-le-Lac**
✤ Db/IGN102 B3, ✱ Diesel, ⚒ 1000mm, ✱ 3km
☞ Table 320: SNCF Carentan (10km). Some connecting services available on the TT du Cotentin
☛ Baupte is 60km S from Cherbourg via RN13 to Carentan then W on RD903
✓ pm. Easter to September
✉ Office de Tourisme, boulevard Verdun, 50500 Carentan, ✆ 33.42.74.01

At the southern end of the Cotentin, or Cherbourg peninsular, is an extensive area of *marais,* peat bog and marsh. A level area of wide vistas; this is a regional nature park. Across these tracts immediately south of Baupte is a network of 27km of metre gauge railways used by a large chemical factory here. Peat is collected and brought to the works at Baupte between April and September. It is dried there for chemical processing or horticultural use. The company has established a leisure park at a lake in the *marais* and operates tourist trains along about 3km of its railway for visitors. The train consists of the LLD or Deutz locotracteurs normally used for peat transport, and an old tramcar from the Charleroi tramway in Belgium, which regularly transports workers to the peat-cutting areas.

32: MUSÉE DU CHEMIN DE FER MINIATURE

✻ Situated at **Clécy**
✤ Ec/IGN103 C5 , ✱ Diesel, ⚒ 400mm, ✱ 0.42km
☞ Table 330: SNCF Flers then bus (20km)
☛ Clécy is 35km S of Caen via RD562. Parking available at the site entrance to E of the town
✓ am & pm. Daily: Easter to end Sept. Also pm. Sun: Oct to mid-Dec & Mar to Easter
✉ Musée de Chemin de Fer Miniature, 14570 Clécy, ✆ 31.69.07.13

Close to the centre of Clécy is a small park built in an old quarry. This pretty area has a narrow gauge train running from the car park to the entrance of the renowned model railway display. This enormous layout is claimed to be the largest in Europe. It covers an area of 310 m² and has more than 600 items of rolling stock. The narrow gauge train consists of a four-wheel diesel mechanical locomotive and two open bogie carriages. From the small station with siding it runs across a short bridge and around the sides of the quarry to reach the entrance to the model display. The site and model are open daily but the narrow gauge railway has more restricted operating times.

33: RAMBOLITRAIN MUSEUM

✻ At **Rambouillet**
✤ Gc/IGN103 C4, ✱ electric, ⚒ 16.5 to 75 mm,
☞ Tables 350 & 054: SNCF Rambouillet (0.9 km via rue J. Gambette)
☛ Rambouillet is on RN10 and RN306 about 50 km SW of Paris
✓ am & pm. Weds to Sun, All year
✉ Musée Rambolitrain, 4 Place Jeanne d'Arc, 78120 Rambouillet ✆ 34.83.15.93

A grand town villa was given to Rambouillet town in 1965 by Jean Visbecq, together with a major collection of railway equipment and models which he had assembled. The collection is certain to enthral anyone with an interest in railways. The museum is arranged on two floors of the villa. Very many of the models are of the larger scales (gauges 1 to 3) and are quite magnificent. There is also a very extensive collection of commercially produced models mainly of smaller scales with particular emphasis on the HO scale (16.5 mm gauge). There are fine working layouts of HO and O scale. This collection shows how model railway practice has developed over the years. In the garden a train gives rides to children in summer.

34: LE CENTRE HISTORIQUE MINIER DE LEWARDE

✳ Just to the S of **Lewarde**
❖ Ha/IGN101 B6, ❋ Steam & diesel, ⅋ 1435 & 600mm, ✳ 0.5km
☞ Table 260: SNCF Douai (7km), SNCF Sin-le-Noble (4km), or Table 231: SNCF Montigny (4km)
☛ Lewarde is 30km W of Valenciennes via Autoroute A2 and RN45. Mine museum is 1km S
✓ am & pm. Sun & BH all year. Also Fri in July & Aug.
✉ Le Centre Historique Minier, Fosse Delloye, 59287 Lewarde, ✆ 27.98.03.89

Just south of the French/Belgian border, the old mines at Lewarde are in a surprisingly rural setting. They were finally closed in the 1970s but some shafts had not been used for many years. The old Delloye pit at Lewarde has been opened as a museum of the coal mining industry which illustrates the development of mining technology, and its social history. Many of the exhibits have railway interest. Original buildings and pit-head gear have been retained. Material displayed from the local coal industry includes standard gauge railway items: an 0-8-0T steam locomotive built by Fives-Lille in 1938, diesel and petrol locotracteurs, and rail-mounted crane. The majority of railway items are, however, 600mm gauge and include diesel-electric and battery-electric items designed for mine use. A site tour is operated using a 600mm gauge train. Included is a visit to a reconstructed mine tunnel, coal-handling facilities, stables, miners' infirmary, etc. A large glass hall has been added to exhibit mining equipment from other mines. Other railway exhibits are numerous berline wagons, and various specialised wagons and locomotives from the underground system. A buffet and well-stocked bookshop are open for visitors.

35: CENTRE DE LA MINE ET DU CHEMIN DE FER "DENIS PAPIN", OIGNIES

✳ On Rue de Libercourt at **Oignies**, Pas de Calais
❖ Ha/IGN101 B5, ❋ Steam, ⅋ 1435 also 127 and 184mm
☞ Tables 221/231: SNCF Libercourt (1.5km)
☛ Situated between Oignies and Libercourt 20km due S of Lille (Autoroute A1, RD954)
✓ pm. Saturdays
✉ CMCF, Service Relations, 9 Allée de la Sologne, 59650 Villeneuve d'Ascq ✆ 20.91.14.96

The recently organised museum at Centre Denis Papin is situated at the preserved coal mine site on Rue de Libercourt, Oignies. The museum is open weekly and describes the history of mining, the techniques used for extraction, and also aspects of the life of the mining community. In addition to underground mining equipment, aspects of the surface facilities are exhibited. The standard gauge railway stock includes two steam locomotives. These are a 1939-built SACM tank loco and an ex-SNCF Pacific No. 231C78. A 5 inch and 7¼ inch gauge miniature railway has been constructed and is operated on open days.

36: LA MER DE SABLE

✳ At **Ermenonville** pleasure park
❖ Hb/IGN103 B6, ❋ Diesel, ⅋ 600mm, ✳ 0.9km
☞ SNCF Senlis (12km)
☛ On RN330 2km N of Ermenonville and 12km S of Senlis
✓ am & pm. Weds, Sat Sun & BH: Begin-Apr to end-Oct. Also daily in June, Jul & Aug
✉ Centres Attractifs Jean Richard, 60950 Ermenonville. ✆ 44.54.00.96

In a sandy clearing in the Ermenonville Forest, a large leisure park and zoo was established in the 1960's. This, the Mer de Sable, remains a major attraction for French families. One of the attractions is the Desert Train which runs clockwise around a single track loop crossing a wide area of sand and through the woods. There are two stations on the line. "Babagattaux" is at the castellated entrance of the village area. "Le Sables" station is stated to be a copy of the SNCF station at Senlis. The locomotives are large, steam outline, Billard diesels. They are a fair representation of US wood burning locomotives of the American civil war. A particular feature of travel on this line is the attack by Indians in feather head-dress, as the train crosses the desert!

37: ARMISTICE MUSEUM

✳ At Clairière de l'Armistice in **Compiègne** Forest
✤ Hb/IGN103 A7, ⚒ 1435 mm, ✱ 0.2 km
☞ Tables 250/2/3/7: SNCF Compiègne (6 km)
☛ On RN 31 6 km East of Compiègne and 50 km NE of Paris via RN17 and RN 31
✓ am & pm. Daily except Tues: Beg-Apr to end-Oct
✉ Clairière de Compiègne, 60200 Compiègne ✆ 44.40.09.27

A clearing in a large forest to the east of Compiègne is a point of attraction: a French national pilgrimage site. This spot was the scene of the signing, in a Wagon Lits carriage, of the armistice in 1918 which concluded WW1. In 1940 the same carriage and exact location was insisted upon for the signing of the French surrender. Relaid rail track now crosses the memorial to Marshal Foch and enters a building in which are displayed relics from the original carriage. The prime exhibit is a sister carriage displayed in all the splendour of its 11 November 1918 condition. It is the subject of a continuous stream of visitors. This must be the most popular railway exhibit in France.

38: MUSÉE NATIONAL DES TECHNIQUES

✳ **Paris**
✤ /Hc/IGN103 C5,
☞ RATP Arts et Métiers (Metro 3 & 11), RATP Réaumur-Sébastapol (Metro 4 & 3)
☛ Bus 20, 38, 39 & 47. Museum located at junction of Rue St.Martin and Blvd de Sébastopol
✓ am & pm: Sun and pm: Tues to Sat: All year
✉ Consevatoire des Arts et Métiers, 270 rue St.Martin 75141 Paris Cedex 03 ✆ 42.71.24.14

This is a long-established technical museum in an old priory building in the centre of Paris. The museum is similar in concept to the Science Museum in London. A range of railway items are displayed, but some non-railway exhibits should not be overlooked, in particular a relic from the dawn of steam transport: a steam propelled munition carriage of 1776 (indeed claimed to be the first mechanical tractor in the world); and a steam passenger road carriage of 1873. The railway items include the cab of an electric locomotive, enabling the visitor to experience the driver's control position. Many fine models depict the evolution of locomotive technology and design (steam, diesel and electric). Dioramas are used to describe the effects of contours and landscape on railway civil engineering. Carriages and wagons are well represented.

39: LIGNE DU "TRANS GRIOTTIN"

✳ At the Port aux Cérises leisure park at **Draveil**. From **Juvisy** to **Vigneaux** at ends of park
✤ He/IGN103 C6, ✱ Steam & diesel, ⚒ 600mm, ✱ 3.3km
☞ SNCF (RER Line C) Juvisy
☛ Situated 15km S of Paris. To Draveil via RN6 then RN448
✓ pm. Wed, Sat, Sun & BH: All year. Also Daily: Begin-Apr to Sept.
✉ Base de Loisirs, Le Port aux Cérises, 91210 Draveil, ✆ 69.83.46.00

In the SE suburbs of Paris close to Orly airport, the "Port aux Cérises" pleasure park has been created by a consortium of local and regional authorities. A 600mm gauge railway was built here in 1985 and extended in 1995. Its patronage has grown steadily every year, so that now it is one of the main attractions of the park, and operates all year. Its success has been rewarded with extensions of the track towards the NE and SW corners of the park. The short train of baladeuses is hauled by a diesel on weekdays and by a steam engine on Sundays and public holidays (from the beginning of April to the end of October). The train is the only mechanised transport in this large public park. The stock is a Decauville 0-6-0T of 1915, and Billard, Deutz, O&K, and two Comessa diesel locotracteurs. Not all these items are in operable state. A Comessa is regularly used. The Decauville is classified as an historic monument. The open carriages are built on WW1 bogie munitions wagons.

17. ↑ The canal barge lift, the Ascenseur, at Fontinettes linked the River Aa and Canal de Neufosse. The two 600mm gauge tug locos from the Canal du Rhône au Rhin are displayed at the end of the 750mm barge-haulage track. [41].   *(Photo: R. Haworth*

18. ↓ A 600mm gauge tug loco is displayed at the small harbour at Bissert. [41].   *(Photo: R. Haworth*

← 19. At Coloy-Menillot, 0-6-0T Decauville "Simone" and 0-4-0T Bagnall "Charles" are viewed at the depot on the CdF du Val de Passey [43].
(Photo: CFVP)

20. ↓ The Museum of the Lorraine Coalfield runs a train for visitors to a nearby mine site. "Picasso" railcar X4042 stands in front of Shaft Nos. 1 and 2 at the Wendel mine.
(Photo: S. Kottmann)

21. ↑ A number of closed standard-gauge lines have been established as cycle railways, with four-seat draisines available for hire, by the hour or by the day. [47]. *(Photo: R Haworth)*

22. ↓ A Class X4300 railcar and driving trailer sit at Langogne before departure on the Nîmes service. The unrefurbished 1960s design is in keeping with the classic station. [51] *(Photo: A. Oliver)*

23. ← One of the Berry locotracteurs pulling a train up the twisting route of the CdF Touristique des Combes at Le Creusot [57]. The photo illustrates the nature of this recently-completed line, which has cuttings, embank-ments, a tunnel, and testing gradients. *(Photo: P. Pacey)*

24. ↓ The regular steam serv-ice on the metre gauge Chemin de Fer de Vivarais [58] gives four hours for lunch at Lamastre. Mallet 0-6-6-0T loco No. 413, built by SACM in 1932, is taking its siesta. *(Photo: B. Duchesne)*

40: LILLE, TRAMWAY "LE MONGY"

✳ Linking **Lille, Roubaix** and **Tourcoing**
✤ Ia/IGN101 B5, ✾ Electric (750V dc o/h), ⚱ 1000mm, ✱ 19km
☞ SNCF Lille Flandres (TGV), SNCF Roubaix and SNCF Tourcoing
☛ Parking is available close to the Mongy route in the centre of Roubaix and Tourcoing
✓ am & pm Daily all year
✉ Transpole, BP 1009, 59701 Marcq-en-Baroeul, ✆ 20.98.50.50

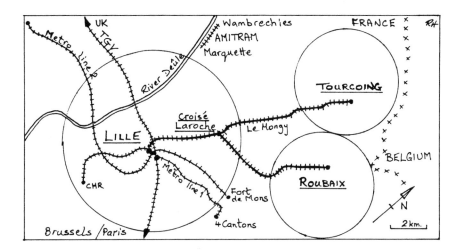

Lille has a thriving metre gauge tramway network linking it with the neighbouring towns of Roubaix and Tourcoing close to the Belgian border. In 1894 this became the third tramway in France to be electrified. The network is still referred to as "Le Mongy" after its original engineer, a local town planner. It is operated by overhead supply, originally at 600 V dc but recently increased to 750 V. It now complements the new *VAL* light metro system.

One hundred years after the opening, the tramways have been completely renovated and rebuilt, with ultra-modern tramcars. The original tramway was laid out with much reserved track, away from the road, along wide boulevards. The system was still carrying 8 million passengers in the late 1980s when the decision to renovate the system was taken despite the development of a network of light rapid transit *VAL* routes as part of an integrated urban transport system. The network is operated by Transpole. The tramway has had slight route changes to form an integrated system, and road crossing underpasses.

The tramway network is Y-shaped. Starting from SNCF Lille-Flandres station, the double track route emerges at the TGV station Lille-Europe, and then runs alongside the wide Avenue de la Republique. At Croise Laroche the routes divide towards Roubaix and Tourcoing. Both follow the wide avenues laid out by Mongy: Avenue de Flandre, and Avenue de la Marne respectively. This network is an interesting survival of the once extensive French urban tramway systems.

The new bogie tramcars are of Italian manufacture and are low floor design. Examples of the earlier tramcars survive both in the town collection and at the AMITRAM museum at Marquette-lez-Lille, 5km north of Lille **(16).** This is on Transpole bus routes 3, 9 and 18, which depart from outside Lille-Flandres station. Public transport service network and zone tickets are available from enquiry bureaux at Lille-Flandres, Place des Buisses at Lille, and at Roubaix and Tourcoing tramway terminii.

41: ASCENSEUR DES FONTINETTES

❋ At Les Fontinettes, in Arques
✢ Ha/IGN101 A3, ✿ Electric (750V ac), ⚒ 600 & 750mm, ✳ 0km
☞ Table 209: SNCF St Omer (5km)
☛ Arques is 3km from St Omer which is 30km SE of Calais via RN43. Signposted from Arques
✓ Sat, Sun & BH: March to October. Also daily in July & Aug and (externally) Daily: All year
✉ Office de Tourisme, boulevard P. Guillain, 62500 St Omer ✆ 21.98.70.00
✉ Association des Fontinettes, Mairie d'Arques, 62510 St Omer ✆ 21.98.43.01 or 21.98.59.35

The Canal de Neuffossé links the Rivers Aa and Lys. Where it joins the Aa at Les Fontinettes there is a water level difference of 13m which originally required a series of five locks for barges to negotiate. In 1888 these were replaced by the lift or ascenseur which can be visited in the backstreets of Arques. This device was itself replaced by a single enormous lift in 1967. The ascenseur operates on the same principles as the smaller one which can be seen at Anderton on the River Weaver in Cheshire. The mechanism is hydraulic with two enormous water filled tanks which carry a barge apiece. The section lowering a barge raises the barge which is being lifted. At Arques the structure is not only larger but also much prettier than that at Anderton. The massive mechanism is supported in a decorated brick built structure.

Beside the barge list at Arques, relics are displayed of the once extensive barge haulage railways. The track which remains in place alongside the canalized River Aa is of 750mm gauge. Two tug locomotives are of 600mm gauge and are displayed on a short length of track. each locomotive was originally operated by electric traction with collection via a trolley connecting with an overhead wire. Barges were hauled by a cable attached to an large hook fitted to the upper surface of the locomotive.

Other examples of these unusual locomotives can be seen beside various canals in northern France. There is one beside the canalised River Rhine at Port Rhenan [26], and others at Arziller on the Marne-Rhine Canal [50], at Bissert on the Canal des Houillères de la Sarre near Sarre-Union and also just east of Reims close to where Autoroute A4 crosses the Canal de l'Ansne à la Marne.

42: FORT DE FERMONT (MAGINOT LINE)

❋ At **Fermont**
✢ Kb/IGN104 A5, ✿ Electric (o/h), ⚒ 600mm, ✳ 1.2km (underground)
☞ Tables 131 & 161: SNCF Longuyon (6km)
☛ Fermont is 60km NW of Metz via RN43 to Beuveille then RD174. Well signposted locally
✓ pm. Daily Begin-Apr to end Sept
✉ AAOFLM, 9 rue Albert Lebrun, 54260 Longuyon, ✆ 82.39.35.34

This underground city housed 600 French soldiers in 1940. The complex was opened to the public in 1980. It consists of seven defensive turrets linked by a series of passages about 30m below ground level. Munitions etc were moved between the installations by an electric railway within the tunnels. This originally extended to about 3km. Now 1.2km of it is used for transporting visitors between the various blockhouses. The locotracteur used is a Vectra with overhead (single trolley) pick-up. A range of armaments is open to view together with the various support facilities. The whole gives a clear idea of the living conditions in the defensive works 50 years ago. Warm clothing is recommended. Other Maginot line fortifications with internal railways are open to visitors at Hackenberg **(46)**, Simserhof **(48)**, and Schoenenbourg **(49).**

43: CHEMIN DE FER DU VAL DE PASSEY

❋ At **Choloy-Ménillot** near Toul
✤ Kc/IGN104 B5, ❋ Steam & diesel, ⚙ 600mm, ❋ 0.8km
☞ Tables 101 & 116: SNCF Toul (8km)
☛ Choloy-Ménillot is 28km from Nancy, via B11 from Foug exit of Autoroute A33. Signed.
✓ A private line. Open to public on advertized days: usually Whitsun and two Sundays in Jun
✉ CFVP, c/o M J Maginot, 12 rue de Chazeau, 54220 Malzeviller

This private railway has been hidden away since the early 1970s in a wooded valley of a minor tributary of the River Meuse. The line runs from the depot, alongside a field and lane to the main halt, and then into the woods to the terminus. The passenger stock consists of wooden bodied carriages with end balconies. The locomotives are an 0-4-0 Gmeinder diesel and two pristine steam locomotives: an ex-sugar refinery 0-6-0T Decauville "Simone" and an 0-4-0T Bagnall "Charles" of 1919. The owner and operators of the line make the public very welcome on a few days each year, an event well worth watching out for. An enjoyable day is certain!

44: FORT DE VILLEY-LE-SEC

❋ At the west fort at **Villey-le-Sec**
✤ Kc/IGN104 B5, ❋ Diesel, ⚙ 600mm, ❋ 1km
☞ Tables 101 & 116: SNCF Toul (8km)
☛ Villey-le-Sec is 14km W of Nancy RN4 for 6km then a minor road SW through the Haye Forest
✓ pm. Sun & BH: Begin-May to mid-Nov
✉ M F Metzelard, 8 rue du Fort, 54840 Villey-le-Sec, ✆ 83.63.68.46

Around Toul is a ring of a dozen defensive forts which were located on hilltops to overlook strategic communication routes along the valleys of the River Moselle. The fortification at Villey-le-Sec is in three sections surrounding the village, which is situated on a steep-sided hill. The primary section is a square fort on the west side. This is open to the public as an historic monument. Over a period of four years, a narrow gauge railway has been laid around the immediate perimeter of the forest, with short branches into various parts of the building. The train consists of two open baladeuses and a diesel locotracteur: a Berry or a Billard.

45: MUSEUM OF THE LORRAINE COALFIELD

❋ Museum at **Wendel**. Trains between **Wendel** and **Forbach**.
✤ Lb/IGN104 A8, ❋ Steam & diesel, ⚙ 1435mm (and 700mm), ❋ 8km
☞ Table 151: SNCF Forbach (3km)
☛ Due E from Metz via Autoroute A32 for 50km to Forbach then 4km N.
✓ am & pm. Two Sundays each month begin-May to end-Sept. Museum open Daily except Wed.
✉ CCSTI, Musée du Basin Houilles de Lorrain, 57540 Petite-Rosselle ✆ 87.87.08.54

The Lorraine coalfield is located at the French/German border. The museum of mining created here has a particular emphasis on all aspects of the various railway systems which supported the mining operations. The museum stock includes a standard gauge Hanomag fireless locomotive built in 1923 which is exhibited in operating condition, various locotracteurs including Deutz and Moyse examples and a Baldwin of 1916 vintage in addition to a German ex-DB 2-8-2T and Picasso railcar X4042. These latter items are used to operate tourist trains over the mine company's track to an adjacent mine at Forbach. A 700mm gauge line using a DM locotracteur carries museum visitors around the exhibits. In the old mine workshops, diesel locomotives of many gauges are exhibited. At the end of 1995 an 0-4-0T O&K steam locomotive arrived at Wendel. This 1922-built loco is undergoing restoration to operational state.

Currently the standard gauge passenger trains are operated by the Picasso railcar and the Moyse locotracteur with three end-balcony four-wheel coaches. The route takes pasengers through a variety of settings: the industrial aspects and the coal mines (the mine shafts, slag heaps, and colliers' houses) and the deciduous woods which are typical of the area. Locally, narrow gauge mine locomotives are exhibited at Stiring-Wendel, Petite Rosselle, Belle-Roch, and Creutzberg, a suburb of Forbach, and a beautiful 0-4-0T steam locomotive can be seen at Neuver-Maison.

46: FORT DE HACKENBERG (MAGINOT LINE)

✻ The **Hackenberg** fortifications are within the hills between Lemsestroff and Budling
✤ Lb/IGN104 A6, ✿ Electric (o/h), ⚒ 600mm, ✱ 3.5km
☞ SNCF Metz
☛ Hackenberg fortifications are 15km E of Metz. Road distance 20km via RN153 and RD62
✓ pm. Sat & Sun: April to October
✉ Mairie, 57920 Veckring, ✆ 82.91.30.08

Hackenburg is one of the largest of the numerous fortifications built between 1930 and 1940 to defend France from the north and east. A significant portion of the 10km of underground chambers and tunnels here are open for inspection. Sections of the 600mm gauge overhead electric railway have been preserved. These were built to transport provisions and munitions within the fortifications, which were able to accomodate over 1000 soldiers. About 3.5km of the line is operational and used to transport visitors within the complex. Due to the cool atmosphere within the tunnels it is advisable to wear warm clothing. These fortifications were reportedly visited by Churchill and King George VI, travelling on the railway. Other Maginot line fortifications with internal railways are open to visitors at Fermont **(42)**, Simserhof **(48)**, and Schoenenbourg **(49)**.

47: MAGNIÈRES BICYCLE RAILWAY

✻ From base at **Magnières**. North 10km to **Gerbéviller** and south 4km to **Deinvillers**
✤ Lc/IGN104 C7, ✿ Pedal power, ⚒ 1435mm, ✱ 14km
☞ Tables 103 & 112: SNCF Lunéville then Table 113: SNCF bus to Magnières (23 km)
☛ Magnières station is to W of village, 23km S of Lunèville via RD914
✓ am & pm. Daily
✉ M. R Gagnieux, gare de Magnières, 54129 Magnières, ✆ 83.72.34.73

A standard gauge railway for cycling! The old SNCF line linking Lunéville and Rambervillers in the heart of the Vosges was originally opened immediately before WW1. Passenger services survived until 1980 and freight for a further ten years. The centre section between Gerbéviller and Deinvillers has been retained and offers the oportunity to ride at one's own pace along the pleasant valley of the River Mortagne. Being a level track, use of rail-adapted bicycles is practical. Book ahead to collect your *draisine* at Magnières. Each vehicle can take two pedalers, or two plus two passengers. Certainly an unusual experience: choose a sunny day and enjoy the fresh air!

48: FORT DE SIMSERHOF (MAGINOT LINE)

✳ **Simserhof**
✧ Mb/IGN104 B9, ✽ Electric (o/h), 𝆑 600mm, ✽ 5km
☞ Table 157: SNCF Bitche (5km)
☛ Simserhof is 70km NW of Strasbourg via RN63 and RN62 to Bitche then RD35
✓ Open one or two days a week; all year round. Prior booking is recommended.
✉ M. le Président AAS, rue du Général Stuhl, 57230 Bitche ✆ 87.96.14.55

The Maginot line fortifications at Simserhof were built between 1928 and 1934. The eight linked defensive turrets formed a huge underground military headquarters which extended over about ten kilometres. A total of 820 soldiers were accommodated within the complex. This remarkable fortress has been restored and is maintained by the army. Visitors are welcome but prior booking is advisable. Only one tour per day is available. This uses the 5km of restored underground railway to travel between the various facilities. Warm clothing is recommended. Other Maginot Line railways are also accessible: see **(42), (46)**, and **(49)**.

49: FORT DE SCHOENENBOURG (MAGINOT LINE)

✳ At **Schoenenbourg**
✧ Mc/IGN104 B11, ✽ Electric (o/h), 𝆑 600mm
☞ Table 106: SNCF Soultz-sous-Forêts (6km)
☛ Schoenenbourg fortifications are 50km of Strasbourg via RN63 to Haguenau then RD263
✓ First Sun of each month. Also some BH: Mar to Dec
✉ M.le Président AALMA, 32 rue du Chemin de Fer, Reichshoffen, 67110 Niederbronn

At the Maginot line forts at Schoenenbourg, six defensive turrets are open to the public. They are linked by a series of tunnels about 30m below ground. The whole network in effect formed a self- contained underground city for 630 soldiers in 1940. An extensive narrow gauge electric railway was used to transport munitions and material around the complex. Many of the wagons have been preserved. To these have been brought some old mine locomotives of identical design to those originally used in the fortifications. In addition a range of armament and munitions is exhibited, together with the various support facilities. Warm clothing is recommended. For other Maginot Line railways see **(42), (46)**, and **(48)**.

50: ST. LOUIS ARZVILLER INCLINED PLANE

✳ East of **Arzviller,** Moselle
✧ Mc/IGN104 B9, ✽ Electrically-driven funicular
☞ SNCF Saverne. Then SNCF bus, Table 103. The plane is situated between Lutzelbourg and St. Louis
☛ From Strasbourg follow RN4 to Saverne (40km) then RD38 for 10km and RD98 for 3km
✓ am & pm. Daily
✉ Association Touristique du Plan Incliné, Arzviller (57), ✆ 87.25.30.69

On the borders of Alsace and Lorraine the Marne-Rhine Canal crosses the Vosges mountains. The climb to the summit tunnel at Arzviller required an inordinate number of locks. A total of 17 of these were replaced in 1969 by an electrically operated inclined plane which lifts a section of the canal through a height of 44m. This operates in the form of a funicular railway. A section of canal which is raised is 45m in length and is counterbalanced by weights, also running on the inclined rails. The structure is available for viewing at all times. A guided tour of the control and machine rooms, and a ride by barge during a canal lift operation is available at certain times. A small museum has been created which describes the operation of this interesting feature and the canal. The original flight of locks and the replacement canal meet at the 2.5 km Arguiller tunnel, about 3 km to the west of the inclined plane. Here the old narrow-gauge tug-haulage railway is visible.

EAST

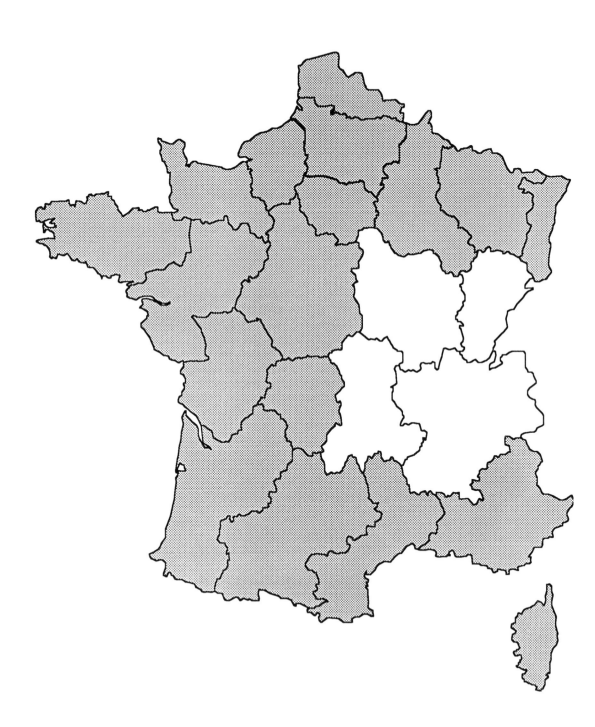

51: SNCF LINE: CLERMONT-FERRAND TO ALÈS AND NÎMES

✳ **Clermont Ferrand** to **Alès** and **Nîmes** (SNCF Table 543)
✢ Hh to Jh/IGN111 E3 to K4, ✳ Diesel, 𝄕 1435mm, ✱ 303km
☞ SNCF Clermont-Ferrand, Arvant, La Bastide, Alès, Nîmes. ☉ at SNCF Génolhac
☛ Alès and Nîmes are 70km N and 50km NE of Montpellier respectively
✓ am & pm. Daily: All year.
✉ Gare SNCF, ave de l'Union Sovietique, 63000 Clermont-Ferrand, ℂ 73.92.50.50
✉ Gare SNCF, 30100 Alès, ℂ 66.23.50.50
✉ Gare SNCF, boulevard Sergent Triaire, 30000 Nîmes, ℂ 66.23.50.50

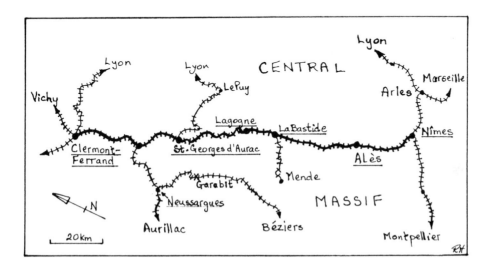

The is arguably the most scenic SNCF route in France. As a through route it is the French equivalent of the Settle-Carlisle line. It runs through the heart of the Central massif and Cévennes mountains. Try to travel on the through train, "Le Cevenol". This crosses the whole line in the afternoon with twin-locomotive hauled stock. The north and south trains generally pass at La Bastide-St.Laurent. This and the overnight trains are through services to/from Paris (a journey which takes 12 hours to Nîmes).

Starting your journey from Nîmes you will find the train reverses out of the station for a short distance to gain access to the Alès line. The departure from Nîmes is steep and gives a foretaste of the locomotive work to come. The running is brisk to Alès across the inhospitable Camp des Garrigues and then along the valley of the River Gard. Alès is a former mining town and the junction for Bessèges. Beyond Alès the line follows a pleasantly wooded valley once it has left the industrial remains. The train is running more slowly and after La Grande Combe the valley quickly narrows and the hard locomotive work begins. Tunnel follows tunnel as the line climbs through the Cévennes. Just north of Camborigaud the train crosses a high viaduct and then runs along the hillside overlooking the town.

The arrival of the two large trains causes La Bastide to briefly become a bustling junction with passengers jostling for the branch line train to Mende. This is the country made famous by R.L.Stevenson in "Travels With a Donkey in the Cévennes" and receives many British visitors exploring the area. The route onward towards Langogne continues through mountain meadows, full of flowers in the Spring. The line begins its long decent towards Langeac. The train snakes through numerous tunnels and remains close beside the tumbling River Allier which it crosses and recrosses in the tight, wooded valley. This is a truly delightful stretch of the journey.

Beyond Langeac the line parts company with the river Allier and crosses the now wide valley to reach the junction station of St.Georges-d'Aurac (5km from the hamlet of the same name) where trains from Le Puy make a connection **[59]**. The next significant stop is at Brioude, a pleasant little town which could make a suitable base for exploring the various lines of the SNCF network in this area. The line continues through Arvant, which is the junction for Aurillac **[53]**. The route from here to Clermont-Ferrand is more mundane. The mountain scenery is well behind you. But what a journey it has been. Can SNCF really bring themselves to close this line? One sincerely hopes not.

52: LE MONT-DORE TO LE CAPUCIN FUNICULAR

✳ **Le Mont-Dore** to **Le Capucin**
✤ Hf/IGN111 F2, ❋ Electric funicular, ⌁ 1000mm, ✳ 0.5km
☞ Table 550: SNCF Le-Mont-Dore (1km)
☛ The funicular is 0.5km S of Mont-Dore, 46km SW of Clermont-Ferrand via RN89/ RD983
✓ am & pm. Weekends in Jan, BHs, then daily mid-May to end-Sept and during Xmas season
✉ Office de tourisme, ave Libération, 63240 Le Mont-Dore, ✆ 73.65.20.21

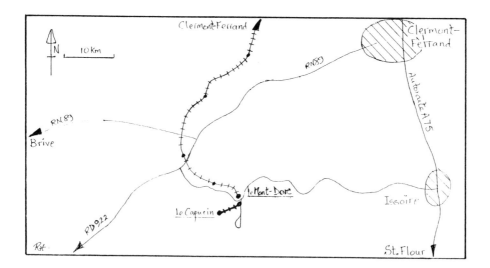

This is the oldest surviving funicular in France and was the first to be operated by electricity. It is virtually unchanged since its opening in 1897 and is now classified by the French government as an historic monument.

After many years of hand to mouth existence, the funicular has recently been subject to renewal schemes involving major trackwork, renewal of both carriages and the beechwood teeth of the giant cog wheels in the winch room. Despite this the resources available to the line are barely adequate to ensure survival.

The small town of Le Mont-Dore is situated right at the heart of the Mont-Dore mountains, which rise to over 1500m on all sides. The town is in the valley bottom, at the confluence of the various tributaries which join the River Dordogne here. Four valleys and numerous roads converge. It is also at the end of an SNCF branch line from Laqueuille on the Clermont-Ferrrand to Tulle line. The railway did not reach Le Mont-Dore until 11 years after the opening of the funicular. It was necessary to build a reservoir to provide the electricity for the operation. The promoters of the funicular must have had confidence in its success.

Given its location, Le Mont-Dore is a natural centre for winter sports and summer mountain recreation. Cable cars or chair lifts run up mountains on all sides of the town. Immediately to the SW is the Capucin mountain ridge which rises to 1465m. The funicular to the shoulder of this ridge was an early route to this wonderful vantage point. However, it is rather hidden at the rear of the town, set back from the main street. A slight climb from the town centre brings one to the lower station at an altitude of about 1000m. The upper station, which also houses the winch gear, is at an altitude of 1245m. With a track length of about 500m, the average slope is 1 in 2 and the maximum 1 in 1.8 (57%).

The carriages have recently been rebuilt on the original open-sided design with iron balconies at each end. These give a grand view, and a welcome breeze in summer.

The line is well worth a visit due to its historic interest: the stations, carriages, winch gear and track are exactly as built almost 100 years ago. However, the views are the main attraction. Those from the carriage, as it rises above through the trees, are magnificent. The scenery at the top is also excellent. Refreshments are available at the upper station before the return journey.

53: SNCF LINE: ARVANT TO AURILLAC

☀ Arvant to Aurillac (SNCF Table 542)
✛ Hg to If/IGN111 H2 to F3, ❋ Diesel, ⌇ 1435mm, ☀ 107km
☞ Table 556: SNCF Aurillac
☛ Aurillac is 174km SW of Clermont-Ferrand via RN89 for 43km then RD922.
  Arvant is on RN102 78km NW of Le Puy.
✓ am & pm. Daily: All year
✉ Gare SNCF Aurillac, rue F. Maynard, 15000 Aurillac ✆ 71.48.50.50
✉ Gare SNCF Arvant ✆ 71.02.50.50

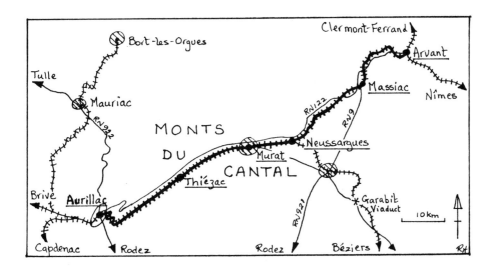

Arvant is only a village. It is a junction on the Clermont-Ferrand line [51] and the only remaining through east-west passenger line between Clermont and the Mediterranean. The line turns away to the north-west to reach the River Alagnon. Then it turns south-west into the gorge of the River Alagnon which it follows all the way to the junction at Neussargues. The narrowness of the valley forces the train to make some spectacular crossings of the river as far as Blesle. It then remains on the east bank as it climbs through Massiac (540m altitude) after which the valley widens as the train climbs to Neussargues (800m). The four-line junction here includes the electrified line south towards Béziers. This line is famous for the crossing of the River Truyère on the spectacular Garabit Viaduct which was designed by Eiffel. We are now in the heart of the Cantal, a magnificent area of volcanic formations

Five km after leaving Neussargues the line reaches Murat at 920m altitude and continues to climb along the hillside with a steep drop into the Alagnon valley below. The summit at Le Lioran is marked by a tunnel which takes the line through the mountain to the valley of the River Cère. The descent from St.Jaques-des-Blats (990m) to Vic-sur-Cère (680m) is very rapid. The countryside gradually opens out again as the line approaches Aurillac, which is a pleasant town about a ten minute walk from the station.

54: TRAIN TOURISTIQUE LIVRADOIS-FOREZ

✳ Between **Courpière** and **Sembadel**. (Different stretches on different days)
✢ If/IGN111 F4, ✳ Steam & Diesel, 🚂 1435mm, ✳ 60km (85km)
☞ Tables 558 & 565: SNCF Pont-de-Dore then SNCF bus Pont-de-Dore/Corpière/Ambert
☛ Ambert is E of Clermont-Ferrand. 88km via RN89 and RD906
✓ am & pm. Daily except Mon & Wed: mid-July to begin- Sept. Also advertised trips on routes in France & beyond
✉ Musée Agrivap, BP8, rue de l'industrile, 63600 Ambert, ✆ 73.82.43.88

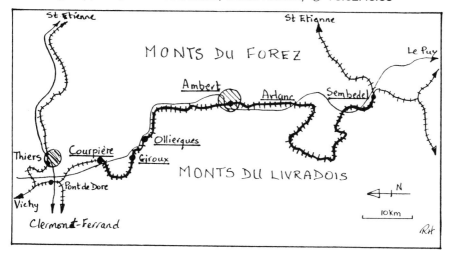

To the north of the Central Massif are the Forez and Livradois mountains which rise to about 1200m over a wide area. This beautiful region is designated as the Livradois-Forez Regional Nature Park. From a junction in the north at Pont-de-Dore, near Thiers, the PLM line was opened in stages between 1883 and 1902. The route chosen for the line closely followed the River Dore for the first seventy kilometres to Arlanc. The central portion of this northern section of the line passes right through the main range of the Livradois mountains via a narrow and sinuous gorge. Here the railway clings to the valley sides. It crosses and re-crosses the river and passes through numerous short tunnels. It then runs due south in a wide valley between the Livradois and Forez mountain ranges. Then, just beyond Arlanc, the line swings into the hills to climb rapidly to about 1000m to reach La Chaise-Dieu. On the climb the views are magnificent, and another superb vista opens up over the town as the train approaches La Chaise-Dieu. The climb towards La Chaise-Dieu is at 1 in 35. The line clings to the hillside as it follows the edge of the escarpment.

SNCF passenger services were finally withdrawn in 1980. Freight services were also being steadily reduced by the late 1980s. A group of preservation enthusiasts had established an agricultural machinery and steam equipment museum at Ambert in 1981 **(75)**. This group, known as Agrivap, began to offer rail trips on the line in 1987. For this purpose they have obtained Panoramic railcars, X4203, X4208. These have a double deck central section with a glass roof giving unrestricted views. These vehicles, built in 1959, were chosen not only for the comfort and views they provide, but also because they are well suited to the challenge of the gradients south of Arlanc. Other passenger stock includes Picasso X3934, a Billard railcar, various trailer cars, a couchette coach, and an open topped carriage. This last item is very popular in summer when the greenhouse-like qualities of X4203/8 are less desirable.

Since 1987, a syndicate, formed of local and regional authorities and Agrivap, have saved the line by purchasing from SNCF the whole length from Courpière to Giroux. Regular tourist trains, operated by a Picasso or Panoramic railcar, run on Sundays, Tuesdays, Wednesdays, and Thursdays in July & August, between. Ambert and La Chaise-Dieu. On Wednesdays & Sundays these run through from Courpière to La Chaise. On Saturdays steam trains operate from Ambert to Olliergues in July and August, using a 1948-built Corpet-Louvet 0-6-0T locomotive.

Perhaps the most remarkable feature of this tourist railway is that Agrivap are operating freight trains on the northern half. A locotracteur from the CF Est de Lyon and an 1800 hp ex-SNCF Co-Co diesel electric locomotive (CC65005) are owned by Agrivap in order to operate this service. Modern freight vans have also been purchased. Wood pulp, chemical products, and waste paper are the primary freight flows. This is a remarkable resurgence in the life of a line which appeared certain to close only a few years ago. The initiative taken by Agrivap and supported by the local authorities means that once again this scenic route can be explored by rail.

55: LE PETIT TRAIN DE LA CÔTE-D'OR

✳ From **Velars-la-Cude** to **Plombières (Le Lac Kir)**
✤ Jd/IGN109 A4, ✳ Steam and Diesel, ✇ 600 mm, ✳ 8 km
☞ SNCF Dijon-Ville then bus (11km)
☛ Velars is 11 km west of Dijon along the Ouche Valley on the RD10
✓ pm. Sat, Sun and BH: April to end-October. Daily in July and August
✉ APTCO, Gare de Plombières-Canal, 21370 Plombières-lès-Dijon, ✆ 80.45.88.51

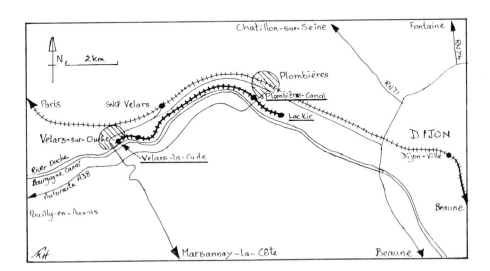

The Burgundy region is renowned for its wine: the *Côte d'Or,* or Golden Escarpment, is of especial note in this regard. The wines are claimed to be the best in the world: this is true if price is any indication. The range of hills forming this escarpment is cut through from the west to Dijon by the valley of the River Ouche. This forms a natural route through this barrier for road, railways and canal and more recently for autoroute A38 and the tourist line.

The 600 mm gauge tourist line runs along part of the trackbed of the old SNCF line from Dijon to Epinac-les-Mines. The original line was built in two main stages. A link between the coal mines at Epinac and the Canal de Bourgogne was opened in 1830. This was extended from Pont d'Ouche to Dijon at the very end of the last century. Part of the trackbed of the original section is used by the Vallée de l'Ouche tourist train from Bligny-sur-Ouche, the Côte-d'Or operation being on a part of the latter section **(56).**

The Côte d'Or line follows the Bourgogne Canal and the River Ouche along the whole of its 5km length. It starts from the old canal-side station at Velars-sur-Ouche which is situated adjacent to a lock on the canal. The line then runs to the recreational site of Kir Lake near Plombières. This is a level track running along the valley bottom through pastures and woods, all the the time close to the canal and River Ouche. The line is parallel to the main SNCF line from Dijon to Paris, which runs high along the north side of the valley. At Velars in particular the SNCF line runs on a high viaduct close to the narrow gauge line, giving interesting juxtaposition between the small diesel locomotives and TGV trains on the limestone viaduct of the line above. The Petit Train de la Côte-d'Or starts from a platform adjacent to the old SNCF station building at Velars, which survives intact and adds a certain authentic charm to this little line. The canal and railway setting at Velars is of industrial archeological interest. The rest of the line has the flavour of a leisure park railway giving pleasure to young and old.

The passenger carriages are open sided "baladeuse" type built on old wagon chassis. The motive power consists of a number of small four-wheel diesel locotracteurs previously used at slate mines. These have been neatly rebodied to resemble models of SNCF diesel shunters. An 0-4-0T Henschel steam locomotive built in 1928 is also on loan to the line.

Regular trains run during the afternoon on operational days. Additional trains operate, both morning and afternoon, when pre-booked for groups of passengers.

56: CHEMIN DE FER TOURISTIQUE DE LA VALLÉE DE L'OUCHE

❊ **Bligny-sur-Ouche** to **Les Cudilles** (extension to **Thorey** in progress)
✤ Jd/IGN109 B3, ❊ Steam and diesel ⚒ 600mm ❊ 5km (7km)
☞ Table 502: SNCF Beaune then bus (20km) or SNCF Dijon
☛ 20 km W of Beaune: On RD970 2km W of Bligny-sur-Ouche beside the leisure park.
✓ pm. (Steam) Sun & BH: Easter to mid-Sept. Also (diesel) Sat in July & Aug.
✉ ARVO, 4 rue Pasumot, 21360 Beaune,   ✆ 80.22.86.35

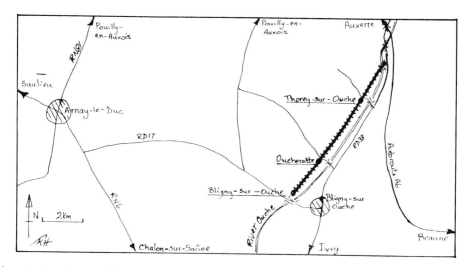

Before the development of the railway network, the Canal de Bourgogne was the main transport route for bulk goods from the valley of the River Ouche. Its route is dictated by the local geography, and reaches the Saône valley at Dijon by following the Ouche where it cuts thought the barrier formed by the hills of the Côte d'Or. As a result it did not effectively serve the area around Epinac to the south. When the transport of coal from the mines there became necessary in the 1820's, it was decided to build a railway between Epinac and Port d'Ouche, the nearest point on the canal. The route chosen passed close to Bligny. It was operated by horse power on the flat sections, and steam winch on the inclined sections. Being opened in 1830, it became one of the first railways in France. Subsequent development led to the extension to Dijon and also to the laying of a line from Beaune to Arnay, which crossed the Epinac line on the level at Bligny. Following closure of the mines the line was abandoned in 1970 and this (standard gauge) line was lifted. Fortuitously, these events coincided with the development of leisure activities by the local authorities, who purchased 7.2 km of trackbed with potential for a tourist railway running north from Bligny. About 5 km of track (600 mm gauge) has been laid. After some problems, laying of the northern extension is now proceeding. Thorey, at the limit of the available trackbed, will become the new terminus: the line will then be 7 km in length.

Since the original purpose of the line was to transport goods to the canal, its route was not chosen to serve the villages along the way. As a consequence, Bligny station is outside the village. It is situated to the west beside the leisure park on RD970. Fortunately the original PLM station buildings survived the removal of the SNCF track and now form a fine setting for the base of the tourist line. A substantial depot and station layout have been built here, including a wagon turntable - an unusual feature to install anew. The stock includes an 0-4-0T vertical boilered locomotive of 1925 and an 0-8-0 ex German WW1 military tender locomotive, plus an 0-4-0 Henshchel/Decauville built in 1947. In addition, the stock includes half a dozen diesel locotracteurs. Diesel traction is used for weekday train services.

Although a 600mm line laid on historic trackbed does not have the historic significance of a preserved railway, it is quite delightful, nevertheless. Any shortcoming in history is more than compensated by rural charm and locomotives. The operators have certainly achieved their aim of preserving the atmosphere of the era before the motor car.

A separate 600mm gauge tourist line uses a section of the old trackbed at the Dijon end. The Chemin de Fer de la Côte d'Or **(55)** runs between Velars and Plombières, some 25km to the north of Bligny-sur-Ouche. There is no chance of the two railways being joined because of the distance between them and the fact that the trackbed has been developed for other purposes.

57: CHEMIN DE FER DES COMBES

❋ At the **Gros Chaillot** leisure site at **Le Creusot**
✤ Je/IGN109 B3, ❋ Steam & Diesel, 𝄞 600mm, ❋ 5.3km
☞ Table 574: SNCF Le Creusot (4km), SNCF Montchanin (10km) or TGV Montchanin (12km)
☛ 100km SSW of Dijon via Autoroute A31 to Chalon, then RN80 to le Creusot. Site to north.
✓ pm. Sat, Sun & BH: begin-Apr to end-Oct. Wed in Jun and daily in Jul & Aug
✉ CF des Combes, rue des Pyrénnées, 71200 le Creusot, ✆ 85.55.26.23 or 85.55.02.46

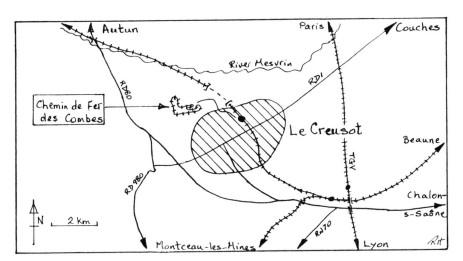

Above the town of Le Creusot is a wooded hill and vantage point known as Gros Chaillot. A leisure park has been established here offering various outdoor pursuits including go-carts, archery, clay pigeon shooting. A narrow gauge railway has recently been built. Begun in 1989, it was completed in 1993.

The railway has been developed by members of the town model railway club (ACMF) with the support of the local authority. The design of the circuit shows some allegiance to model railway practice which adds to its attraction to visitors. The route selected circles the summit of the hill and thus gives excellent views over the town and towards the neighbouring hills. The course forms a very convoluted loop with three stations or halts. A more spectacular section is the most recent which is very circuitous, following the landscape to gain height and complete the circuit back to the main station. The railway is notable for its gradients. As a consequence, the stock has been fitted with continuous air brakes (not a universal feature on French tourist railways). At the heart of the circuit is the main station building. This has been built to traditional French station design and adds significantly to the character of the station site. Close by is the large depot shed.

Along the west and south side of the loop, the line runs partially on the old trackbed of the standard gauge track of the Schneider ironworks which were situated here during the first half of the century. This short line carried waste material from the works for disposal. Aspects of the previous line can be discerned at certain points including the earthworks and metal bridges. The most noticeable of these features is the short single track tunnel, built in 1904.

The motive power used on this railway is a collection of ex-industrial Berry and Decauville four-wheel diesel locomotives and an 0-8-0T steam loco. Two locotracteurs originally built by Berry routinely operate services. The ex-German "Feldbahn" locomotive operates trains on Sundays.

The setting is excellent. The railway has settled naturally into the landscape - quite amazing for such a recent enterprise. The number of visitors is increasing each year. This is not surprising given the attractiveness of the site and the line which has two bridges, a long tunnel, a level crossing, cuttings, embankments, steep gradients and superb views.

A frequent and enjoyable ride is offered over an extended season and well worth a detour in its own right. Furthermore, a well established museum in Le Creusot illustrating the history of the activity of the area includes mining and steelworks. Two Schneider built standard gauge locomotives are preserved CF des Combes at Le Creusot. One of them, the enormous 1950-built 4-8-2 No. 241P17, is undergoing restoration. Visits are possible. A railway festival is organized at Le Creusot each year in mid-July. Close by is the Bligny to Thorey 600mm gauge tourist railway **(56)**.

58: CHEMIN DE FER DU VIVARAIS

✳ From **Tournon** to **Lamastre**

✤ IGN112 C2, ❀ Steam & diesel ⚒ 1000mm c 33km

☞ Table 503: SNCF Tain-Tournon (1km) or SNCF Valence then bus (18km)

☛ In Rhone valley 90km S of Lyon at SNCF Tournon freight station via RN 86, RN7 or A7.

✓ am & pm. Sat & Sun: End-March to mid-Nov.Also various days in Sept & Oct, and Daily begin-May to end-Aug (not Mondays until end-June)

✉ CFTM, 2 quai Jean Moulin, 69001 Lyon, ☎ 78.28.83.34

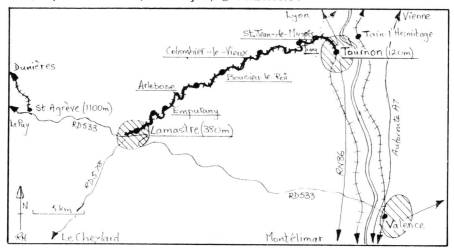

This well known line is one of the premier tourist railways of continental Europe. It has taken its name from the Réseau Vivarais which formed a network of metre gauge lines in the mountains of the Central Massif. The Vivarais is a region of central France occupying roughly the same area as the present day *département* of Ardèche. The lines serving this region were built between 1886 and 1891. The network had a total length of 200km formed of a basically north-south line from La Voulte-sur-Rhône to Dunières in the north, with branches to Lavoute-sur-Loire in the west, and from Le Cheylard to Tournon to the east. In each case the lines ran into the mountain range from the river valley on each side.

The last trains ran in 1968. Two sections were preserved following the closure of the system: from St.Agrève to Dunières in the north and from Lamastre to Tournon in the east. The northern section operated a tourist service between 1968 and 1986 and is now being progressively reopened. The eastern section forms the CF Vivarais. It has also operated since 1968 and has gone from strength to strength.

Tournon is a well preserved medieval town on the west bank of the River Rhône. Two SNCF lines follow the Rhône valley. The west bank line is a major north-south freight route. The narrow gauge tourist train shares the track for 2km as it leaves the town. This is achieved by the use of a third rail set between the standard gauge ones. The tourist line then swings away to the west and follows the valley of the River Doux for the remaining 31km to Lamastre. The valley has varied scenery with dammed reservoir, gorges, and wider heavily wooded stretches. It has exposed rocks for large parts of the route with vegetation clinging on to the rock outcrops. The train also seems to cling to the valley side as it steadily climbs along the valley. It crosses the River Doux on four occasions continually twisting and turning, opening up a new vista every few minutes.

Tourist train services are operated by the original Mallet locomotives and railcars which operated the old Vivarais network. There are a total of five 0-6-6-0T Mallets on the Vivarais: these retain the old Vivarais system of numbering, 401, 403 and 404, Swiss built by SLM in 1902/3; and 413 and 414, built by Société Alsacienne in 1932. Restoration of additional Mallet, 0-4-4-0T No 104, built by Blanc-Misseron in 1906, is expected to begin during 1996. Other locomotives include a twin cabin, tram style 0-6-0T Pinguely, and an 0-8-0T built by Corpet-Louvet. There are four Billard railcars and an articulated Brissonneau & Lots railcar built in 1935.

Train services operate out and back from Tournon. On most operating days, a steam hauled train departs mid-morning, returning from Lamastre mid-afternoon. This is followed by a railcar service on Sundays and holidays. Additional trains occasionally operate, including specials for photographers. Trains regularly stop at the quiet wayside halts, but also for an extended time at either Colombier-le-Vieux or Boucieu-le-Roi, for refreshments and water for the locomotive. A return journey on the Vivarais cannot be hurried - a long stop-over at Lamastre is a feature of the timetable. This allows the small town to be explored and its renowned restaurants to be visited. This magnificent line is well worth the time.

59: SNCF LINE: ST. ETIENNE TO LE PUY AND ST.GEORGES-D'AURAC

✳ **St.Etienne** to **Le Puy** and **St. Georges d'Aurac** (SNCF Tables 564 & 559)
✤ Jf/IGN111 F4 to H4, ✱ Diesel, ⚋ 1435mm, ✻ 110km
☞ SNCF St.Etienne-Chateaucreux
☛ St.Etienne is 60km SW of Lyon via RN42. Le Puy is 75km SW of St.Etienne via RN88.
✓ am & pm. Daily: All year.
✉ Gare SNCF St.Etienne-Chateaucreux, 42000 St.Etienne ✆ 77.37.50.50
✉ Gare SNCF, avenue C.Dupuy, 43000 Le Puy-en-Valay ✆ 71.02.50.50

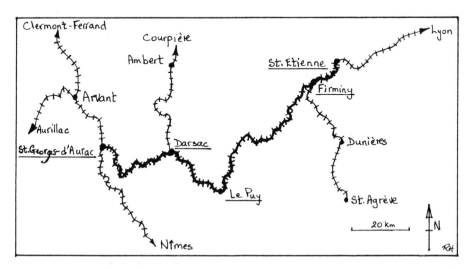

Le Puy-en-Velay is a most peculiar looking town dominated by the plugs of two extinct volcanoes. These are topped by a church and an enormous statue of Notre-Dame. Situated at an altitude of 600m, it is completely surrounded by level-topped mountains of 800 to 900m high. The three railways to the town, of necessity, follow the narrow twisting valleys of the River Loire and its tributary, the River Borne.

The line to Le Puy from St.Etienne passes through industrial suburbs as far as Firminy (15km) where the line to Dunières **[62]** branches to the south. After Firminy the line drops down to follow the right bank of the Loire. The valley is well wooded and quite picturesque for the next 10km before the valley opens out before the halt at Pont de Lignon (41km) where a plaque recalls an attack by the French resistance on a German troop train in 1944. Beyond here the line runs immediately beside the river in the bottom of the Loire Gorges and crosses the river five times. The class X2800 diesel railcar has plenty of speed restrictions to endure whilst meeting the tight schedule. The engine cuts in and out. The train brakes sharply. The final section of line approaches Le Puy through the Gorges de Peyredeyre. Here, close to Lavoute-sur-Loire, the train passes a chateau which looks more like a Scottish castle. Just before entering Le Puy, the freight line diverges southwards, heading across the Velay towards Langogne on the Clermont-Ferrand to Nîmes line.

A change of train and long wait is invariably required at Le Puy for onward travel to St.Georges-d'Aurac. However, Le Puy is a pleasant town with plenty of hotels and many tourist sites.

After departing from the station at Le Puy line skirts around the town giving good views before once again following a narrow valley to make an exit. The defile gradually reduces as the valley rises higher into the hills towards Darsac. Here the freight and tourist line from Pont-de-Dore, Ambert and Sembadel **[54]** swings off to the right about a kilometre beyond the station. The summit of the line is reached beneath Fix-St.Geneys (1000m altitude) in a 2km long tunnel. The line then descends, follows a sinuous route to avoid the numerous puys (remains of old volcanic cones) which are dotted about on all sides. This is a largely bare landscape with well defined pockets of woodland. About 12km beyond Fix-St.Geneys, the line swings through 300 degrees around the south side of Mont Briancon. At this point the line is only 3km from the Clermont-Ferrand to Nîmes line. However, that is on the far side of the Allier valley.

The remaining journey continues in the same manner across this wide area to reach St.Georges -d'Aurac. Unlike the trains at Le Puy, those at St.Georges are generally arranged to make practical connection with trains towards Nîmes and Clermont-Ferrand.

60: TRAINS À VAPEUR DES MONTS DU LYONNAIS /CHEMIN DE FER TOURISTIQUE DE LA BRÉVENNE

✳ From **L'Abresle** to **Ste.Foy-l'Argentière** via **Sain-Bel** and **Giraudière**
✤ Jf/IGN112 B2, ✸ Steam and diesel, ⚒ 1435mm, ✱ 20km
☞ Table 566: SNCF l'Abresle (connecting service)
☛ L'Abresle is 25 km NW of Lyon via RN7. The station is S of the town.
✓ am & pm. Sundays & BH: begin-June to mid-Sept
✉ CFT de la Brevenne, Place de la Gare, 69610 Ste.-Foy-l'Agentière, ✆ 74.70.90.64

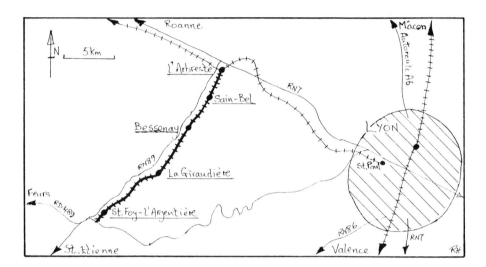

The Monts du Lyonnais is a range of hills immediately to the west of Lyon. The peaks of these hills reach a little under 1000m. They are heavily wooded in parts and deeply indented by numerous valleys. The range is completely divided in two by the valley of the river Brévenne, which follows an almost straight course from the SW above Ste.Foy-l'Argentière to the NE at L'Abresle.

The SNCF line from Lyon to the middle of France via Roanne passes to the north of these hills. At l'Abresle, about 25 km from Lyon, a branch line diverts to follow the Brévenne valley. Originally opened in stages between 1873 and 1876, it reached Montbrison. Passenger services ceased in 1955. The remaining freight services operate on weekdays only over the 12km to Giraudière. However, the track remains in place for 20km as far as Ste.Foy.

Tourist trains have operated along this line on Sundays in Summer since 1989. This followed the transfer of some rolling stock from the Chemin de Fer du Bréda which had been based at Pontcharra since 1980.

The operating stock includes a small Italian (FS) 2-6-0T steam locomotive No 880 157, and various diesel locotracteurs. The carriage stock includes three ex-DR "boîte à tonnerre" metal bodied four-wheel and the ex-SNCF bogie carriages. A smart red livery has been applied to the carriages to give a bright image to the tourist trains. The stock depot is at Ste.Foy where a small museum of railway equipment has been established in the station. Here is displayed an ex-SNCF 2-8-0 tender engine No. 140C287.

The single track line follows the river closely along the whole route, crossing the river a total of seven times. The valley becomes increasingly narrow as the journey proceeds. The valley sides are steepest and encroach most closely towards the train beyond Giraudière. This section has a succession of short tunnels and viaducts.

The society has brought the experience it gained from operating at Pontcharra to bear on the operation of the Monts du Lyonnais-Brévenne services. Each Sunday during the season, there is a themed operation combining the train journey with excursions and meals. Examples of these tours include farm visits, art exhibitions, a hat museum and organised rambles. This tourist operation appears to have an excellent future. It has a carefully crafted timetable, packaged tourist operations, excellent advertising, steam haulage, beautiful scenery and close proximity to the Lyon conurbation, of approximately one million population.

25. ↑ Refurbished three-car railcar set XABD 2897 stands at Le Puy to form the mid-morning service to St. Georges d'Aurac [59]. *(Photo: A. Oliver)*

26. ↓ The CdF Touristique de la Brevenne [60] is one which utilises a freight-only branch line for Sunday tourist trains. This line crosses the river seven times by handsome viaducts. The loco is ex-Italian Railways 880 157. *(Photo: CFTB)*

27. One of the quarter-scale model trains on the 381mm (15 inch) gauge Chemin de Fer Touristique d'Asne [63]. Railcar X141 passes under the SNCF TGV line as it crosses the river Azergues. *(Photo: AVde38)*

28. The passenger coaches used on the CdF du Haut Rhône [65] are old tramcars from former French and Swiss tramways. At the rear of this train is a 1914 Valenciennes bogie tram. Adjacent are two cars built in 1882 for the Neuchâtel horse tramway. *(Photo: R Haworth)*

29. The 600 metre difference in altitude between upper and lower stations of the St. Hilaire-de-Trouvet funicular [66] can be judged from this view as the car approaches the tunnel. The changes in direction and gradient may be noted. →
(Photo: R. Haworth)

30. ↓ Tram No. 510 on Rue des Docteurs Charcot, near the Bellevue tram depot. This is a PCC car of the 1958 series. The use of a trolley pole for current collection is unusual these days.
(Photo: R Haworth)

31. ↑ One of the original 1933 electric locos of the Chemin de Fer de la Mure [67] climbs high above the Drac Gorge reservoir on a train from St. Georges-de-Commiers. *(Photo: CF de la Mure)*

32. ↓ At La Mure, overlooked by mountains of the Massif de Eerins, the train waits to make the return journey to St. Georges-de-Commiers. *(Photo: R. Haworth)*

61: LE PETIT TRAIN DE LA TÊTE D'OR

✳ At Parc de **La Tête d'Or**, Lyon
✤ Jf/IGN112 B3, ✳ Diesel, ⚒ 600mm, ✱ 1km
☞ SNCF Lyon (La Part-Dieu). Take Metro A then B to Masséna or bus 36 or 41 to park
☛ In N central Lyon. From centre via Rue Garibaldi. Parking beside park
✓ pm. Daily May to Sept inclusive. Also Wed, Sat and Sun rest of year
✉ Office de Tourisme, place Bellecour, BP 2254, Lyon, ✆ 74.42.25.75 or 78.89.53.52

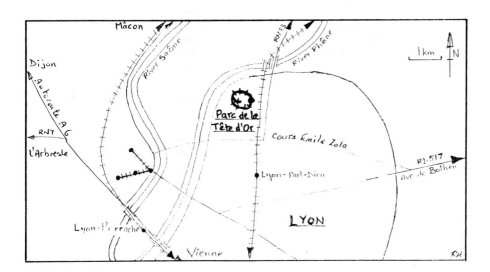

The *Tête d'Or* is a large town park with absolutely magnificent flower displays and many traditional entertainments. It is situated in the north central portion of this large city, close to the Rhône and immediately south of the St. Clair bridge. The TGV line from Paris runs along the eastern edge of the park. It is a popular venue: a lake fills much of the northern part, and has boating, fishing, but also tranquil areas for wildlife. However, each afternoon the raucous sounds of a highly active railway are heard with much whistling and ringing of bells.

In the 1960s M. Didier built the 600mm gauge railway as an added attraction in the park. This has continued to operate each year since it was opened in 1966.

The line is a simple 1km circle of track around the edge of an island, with some short sidings, the longest of which runs to the centre of the island to give access to the railway depot situated beneath the cycle track. The sole station is situated on the eastern side, immediately north of the level crossing. Trains follow a clockwise route; hence seats on the left hand side give the best view of the park across the lake.

The locomotives operating on the line are all four-wheeled ex-industrial diesel locotracteurs suitably repainted in bright colours with various body adaptations in an American "wild west" style. These include a Paris-built Campagne locomotive obtained from quarries in the Isère. It originally pulled trains of gravel for railway ballast for the Est de Lyon railway. There are also two Strasbourg-built engines: a 4 tonne Comessa and a 2.5 tonne Heinz.

Like the trains, the wooden station has an American atmosphere. However, it also contains a number of preserved relics from French standard gauge railways including signalling equipment, lamps and platform trolleys.

62: VOIES FERRÉES DU VELAY

❊ The line runs between SNCF **Dunières** and **Tence** (re-opening to **St.Agrève** is anticipated)
✛ Jf/IGN112 C1 ❊ Diesel (and steam) ⚭ 1000mm ❊ 23 km (38km)
☞ Table 564: SNCF Firminy then SNCF bus (30km) to Dunières
☛ From St.Etienne via RN882 to Bicetre, RD501 to Marlhes then RD1/232.
✓ am & pm. Sun. mid-Jun to end-Sept. Also Wed & Sat in July & Aug.
✉ Office du Tourisme, Place de Chatiague, 43190 Tence, ✆ 71.59.81.99
✉ VFV, 22 rue de la Croix, 43220 Dunières, ✆ 77.39.93.63

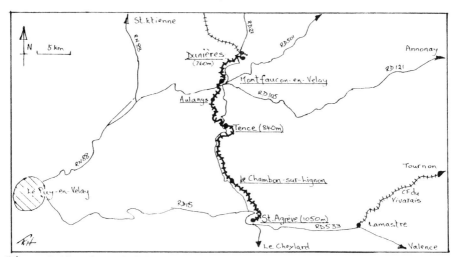

The Réseau du Vivarais was built between 1886 and 1891. This metre gauge network extended to a total length of 200km. It consisted of four lines reaching out from the centre of the Central Massif mountains, to Dunières to the north, La Voulte-sur-Rhône in the south, Tournon to the east and Lavoute-sur-Loire in the west. At its peak, just before WW1, the network transported approaching 750 000 passengers and 200 000 tons of freight per year. The final trains ran in 1968. After closure, two sections were selected as potential tourist lines. The line to the east established itself as the very successful *Vivarais* **(58).** A concession was granted for the professional operation of the northern section from St.Agrève to Dunières. This operated between 1970 and 1986. Despite having a marvellous collection of locomotives and rolling stock and an equally interesting setting, the tourist railway attracted too few passengers and was abandoned following the end of the concession period. However, the desire of local authorities to encourage tourism to the area has given the line a second chance. It is being completely renovated following six years of disuse. The operating programme restarted in the summer of 1993 between Tence and Montfauçon.

The line climbs steadily for much of its 38km length. Starting from Dunières at 765m it reaches a peak about 1km before dropping down to St.Agrève (1050m). It is a noticeably winding route. The railway has much scenic interest and passes through beautiful countryside. The upper section runs through pleasant pasturelands. The general atmosphere is of the alpine foothills of Switzerland. The centre section between Tence and Le Chambon-sur-Lignon runs through the impressive Lignon gorges. Montfauçon-en-Velay, the first station up the line, is a winter sports centre. The scenery changes as the train gains height, from woods and fields in the lower stretches, to forests and pastureland at higher levels.

Remarkably much rolling stock used for the earlier tourist operation remained on site during the period of disuse. These items included an articulated Billard railcar, also conventional Billard, de Dion and Decauville railcars. Steam locomotives included four Mallets: a 1913 Piguet 0-6-6-0T from the Réseau Breton, a 1906 Blanc-Misseron 0-4-4-0T from POC and a Blanc-Misseron/Nord de France 0-4-4-0T of 1906, also an 0-6-0T Henschel and 0-4-0T Borsig from eastern Germany. The steam stock was transferred away during the period of closure. During the initial years of the reinstated services, diesel locomotives have been used. From 1996 the group operating the Vivarais line have been involved in operation of the Velay line, and have transferred to Tence an 0-8-0T Corpet steam locomotive, and De Dion railcar No. 204 is also being prepared for service from 1996. Much of the original freight stock is retained. Although this is now in poor state after years of neglect, its presence adds to the atmosphere of a working, rather than preserved, railway, as do the stations, which retain all the charm of the French rural narrow gauge railway of the first half of the century.

63: CHEMIN DE FER D'ANSE

✳ At **Anse.** The line runs from **Anse-Port (Avenue Jean-Vaucher)** to **Pont St.Bernard**
❖ Jf/IGN112 A2, ✳ Petrol ⚒ 381mm (15 inch) ✳ 2.5km
☞ Table 502: SNCF Anse (1.5km) on line Lyon to Villefranche-sur-Saône
☛ 25 km from Lyon N on RN6 until it crosses the River Azergues at Anse. Parking adjacent
✓ pm. Sun & BH Easter to end-Oct. Also Sat from begin-June to end-Sept
✉ Association de la voie de 38cm, 8 ave de la Libération, 69480 Anse, ℰ 74.60.26.01

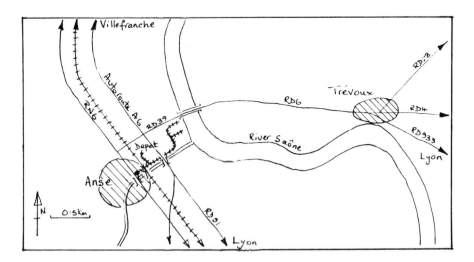

One should not be deceived. A miniature railway on (generally) level track can be thrilling; even exciting! The line built at Anse is the only 15 inch gauge line in France. It has been constructed by a team of enthusiastic model makers who have built all the stock used on the line. The track begins at the southern edge of this small town, which is situated on the River Azergues immediately before it joins the Saône. Autoroutes A6 and A46 and the SNCF line linking Paris with Lyon pass through the town.

This is a truly miniature railway with passengers, two abreast, sitting inside the model carriages and railcars. The sides of the vehicles fold down to permit entry and then, prior to departure, are raised to complete the model profile. Each vehicle is a faithful replica in 1:3.8 scale of present day SNCF stock.

The train leaves from the two-track station and after negotiating the storage loops passes under the SNCF line, which crosses the river, road and miniature railway on a low stone viaduct. The train passes under the autoroute and then without warning swings left straight across the road it has been following since leaving the station. It then runs through farmland to an intermediate terminus at "Stade", the sports ground. Here it immediately reverses (guided, but not driven, by the guard at the back of the train) and makes its way via a brief but sharp gradient and wooded pasture to the municipal camp site, where it terminates at a two-track platform.

The whole trip is undertaken at an apparently breakneck speed (actually limited to 27km/h) which is accentuated by sitting in such a seemingly light vehicle. The crossing of the road is however the most impressive feature to British eyes as the train (long enough to completely block the road) passes without apparent protection, immediately beneath the level of the headlights of the road traffic. This is explained by the fact that the road crossings are regulated by the standards imposed on industrial branch lines, not passenger line requirements.

The depot is situated to the north of the line between the SNCF and A6 bridges. The train has to cross the road (again at an unguarded crossing) to gain access to the depot. The facilities include a modern four track train shed with additional storage tracks, and a preserved full-sized water crane, plus lathe, vertical drill, air compressor etc.

The stock includes 10 unpowered carriages or trailer cars, the original locotracteur of the railway (Y9201), and several power cars numbered after their life-size equivalents (X4901, X131 etc). The building of a substantial 2-6-2 tender steam locomotive was begun in 1983. Visits to the depot are possible on request.

64: TRAIN TOURISTIQUE DE L'ARDÈCHE MÉRIDIONALE

❊ **Montfleury** (Villeneuve-de-Berg) to **Vogüé** (and **St.Jean-le-Centenier**)
✛ Jg/IGN112 D2, ❊ Diesel, ▯ 1435mm, ❊ 6km (11km)
☞ Table 503: SNCF Montélimar then Table 685: SNCF bus (32km to Villeneuve, 45 to Aubenas)
☛ From Montélimar the RN102 crosses the Rhône. It follows the line to St.Jean & Villeneuve
✓ pm Sun & BH: Easter to end-Sept. Also Tues & Weds in July and Aug.
✉ (a) TTAM, gare de Montfleury, 07170 St.Germain
✉ (b) VIADUC-07, BP23, 07200 Aubenas Cedex, ✆ 75.94.76.76 (pm)

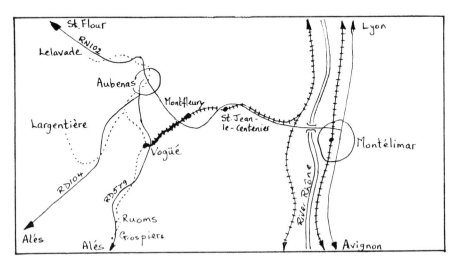

The Ardèche is typified by the various ranges of hills and plateaux to the west of the lower reaches of the River Rhône. These form the south-western part of the Central Massif and a series of cliffs along the west bank of the river. It is an area of soft fruit and wine production but not of intensive agriculture. Rail traffic would not be expected to be heavy and rail access, from the main rail arteries along the Rhône valley, required a penetration through the Vivarais plateau to minimize the requirement for civil engineering.

The primary line ran through this gap from Le Teil to Vogüé. It provided access for a network of lines following the various tributaries of the Ardèche: to the south towards Ruoms and Grospierres and onward to Alés, to the west via St.Sernin to Largentière and to the north via St.Sernin to Aubenas and Lalevade-d'Ardèche. The line south of Grospierres, as far as Robiac, had been closed since the early 1980s, but the rest of the network survived intact until complete closure by SNCF in 1988. Retention until this date was quite remarkable. The Grospierres section, for example, was retained solely for seasonal peach traffic.

In anticipation of the closures, the VIADUC-07 society was formed in 1987 with the aim of preserving at least some of the lines in the southern Ardèche. It is based at Aubenas station where a small museum has been created. The society has acquired a couple of diesel "Picasso" railcars (X3865 and X3989), trailer cars and a couple of ex-industrial diesel locotracteurs. With the support of local authorities a tourist train was operated from Aubenas in 1990 and 1991 under the title of the Train Touristique de l'Ardèche Méridionale (TTAM). However, SNCF had found a buyer for the trackbed to the north and south of Vogüé. The TTAM operation was therefore switched to the easterly route from Vogüé towards Le Teil. The track was lifted from the other lines.

Initial operation began in 1992 between Vogüé and Villeneuve-de-Berg, extending to the main road crossing. A halt, named Montfleury, has been established at Villeneuve. Montfleury has been developed as the base of the TTAM train services. Significant support has been provided by local and regional authorities in the purchasing of track bed. It is anticipated that purchase of the Villeneuve to St.Jean-le-Centenier section will enable services to extend over the 11km between Vogüé and St.Jean with a connection to SNCF.

The present 6km route crosses the Rivers Ardèche and Auzon, both by 200m long bridges. It is situated in beautiful countryside and a primary tourist area. Success of this preservation operation seems assured. In addition to the tourist trains, a collection of 600mm gauge industrial railway items are displayed in the grounds of Montfleury station and the small railway museum is open at Aubenas station.

65: CHEMIN DE FER DU HAUT RHÔNE

✲ From the entrance to holiday camp at **Montalieu-Vallée Bleue** to **Pont-de-Sault Brénaz**
✜ Kf/IGN112 B4, ✲ Diesel & steam, 🚂 600mm, ✲ 4km
☞ SNCF Lyon Part-Dieu (60km), or Table 594: SNCF Ambérieu (20km)
☛ Vallée Bleue is 2km E of Montalieu, 60km E of Lyon: by Autoroute A 42, RN84 & RN75
✓ pm. Sun & BH: Begin-May to end-Sept. Also Wed in Jun, Jul & Aug
✉ CFTM, 2 quai Jean Moulin, 69001 Lyon, ✆ 78.28.83.34

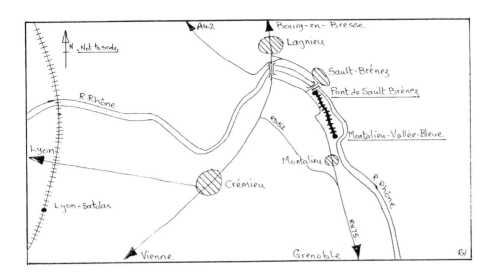

The Chemin de Fer du Haut Rhône is, despite its name, situated in the middle reaches of the Rhône valley to the east of Lyon. It is operated by the well established enthusiast society CFTM (Chemins de Fer Touristiques & de Montagne). CFTM operates two metre gauge lines: the **Vivarais (58)** which connects Tournon and Lamastre, and the **Haut-Velay (62)** from Dunières.

Prior to saving the Vivarais from certain closure in 1969, the CFTM was already operating a 600mm gauge line at Meyzieu to the east of Lyon. It ran from 1960 to 1970 and had a large collection of steam and diesel locomotives. This line was forced to close by the encroaching suburbs of the rapidly expanding city of Lyon. The rolling stock was stored pending access to a suitable site.

The opportunity to build a 600mm line at the present site was taken up in 1988, the tourist train service beginning the following year. The stock restored for this operation includes three steam locomotives: a Decauville 0-6-0T of 1922, a La Meurse 2-6-0T of 1933, and an O&K Mallet 0-4-4-0T of 1905. There are also two diesel locomotives dating from 1935 and 1950. The passenger stock consists exclusively of old tramway carriages which were originally built for the Neuchâtel tramway in 1895, and also two built for the Valenciennes system in 1911 are regularly used.

The line starts at a reconstructed station built in the manner of a small halt on a typical French rural narrow gauge tramway of the early years of the century. Beside the halt is a large, modern three-track depot and workshop. From Montalieu the line runs for the first 2km through a wood in the bottom of the valley to an intermediate halt at Le Source. Here it reaches the River Rhône which it follows for the remaining 2km to Pont-de-Sault-Brénaz.

At the Sault-Brénaz bridge, the Rhône is dammed in connection with the hydroelectric station situated on the island in the centre of the river. The bridge gives access to the island and to the small town of Sault-Brénaz which offers accommodation, post office and shopping facilities. Access to photograph the trains is straightforward along most of the length of the line. The east side of the river is closely bordered by mountains along this stretch which form a beautiful setting at this point.

This is a friendly if unspectacular line. The historic tramway carriages are a delightful feature and a ride should not be missed. The steam operation adds an extra dimension.

66: SAINT HILAIRE-DU-TOUVET FUNICULAR

❋ To **St.Hilaire-du-Touvet** from **Montfort-Crolles**

✢ Kf/IGN112 C6, ✽ Electric funicular, ⚐ 1000mm, ✻ 1.5km

☞ Tables 521/3: SNCF Grenoble (18km) then bus, or SNCF Brignoud (4km)

☛ Immediately beside the Grenoble to Chambéry road RN90; 15km NE of Grenoble

✓ am & pm. Daily begin-Jun to mid-Sept. Also Sat, Sun & BH throughout most of the year

✉ Régie municipale de St.Hilaire, Mairie, 38720 St.Hilaire-du-Touvet, ✆ 76.08.32.31

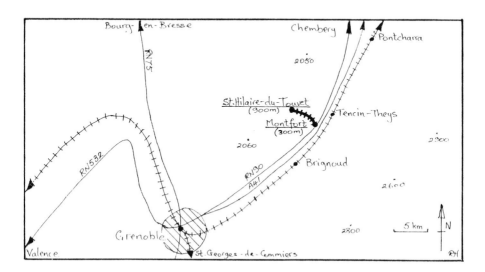

The steepest tunnel in the world is to be found on the funicular linking Montfort with St.Hilaire-du-Touvet. At a gradient of 83% (1 in 1.2) this is also one of the steepest funicular railways in the world. It rises a total of 700m in an absolutely remarkable fashion.

The single track line starts from the rear of a Swiss chalet style station set well back from the RN90. The sloping area in front, which acts as a car park and access road, was the location of a further short funicular connecting the existing line to the road and the tramway which was situated there.

The lower station displays an informative diagram of the route and gradient of the funicular, which was built between 1920 and 1923. The line was constructed to give access to the plateau of St.Hilaire-du-Touvet for the building of curative establishments at an altitude of about 1000m, high up on the west side of the valley of the Isère. It was retained when the construction of the spas was completed in order to act as a transport service due to the inaccessibility of St.Hilaire. The line was taken over by the local authority in 1977 and has been operated essentially as a tourist service since then. A major increase in patronage was gained from the mid-1980s when a hang-glider launching platform was set up close to the upper terminus. Viewing the participants of this sport launching themselves off the precipice and then gliding high over the valley is an added attraction to the mountain walks and restaurants around the upper terminus.

The journey takes 20 minutes in each direction. There is a departure on each hour (half hourly if more than 10 passengers are waiting). Cars leave the upper and lower stations simultaneously, counter-balancing each other. The electric cable winch is situated within the upper station. The mid-line passing place has unusual fixed points. In order for the carriages to pass, there are flanges on both sides of the outer wheels but none on the inner wheels.

The carriages were renewed in 1992 using the chassis of the old ones, which were introduced in 1956. The design of the new carriages is based on traditional format with a combination of open and closed compartments, and balconies at the end to enable the superb view to be appreciated unhindered. The vistas are truly spectacular, stretching 50 miles to the east and south across the heart of the Alps from Mont Blanc to the Vercors Massif. The opportunity to experience this funicular should not be missed.

67: CHEMIN DE FER DE LA MURE

☀ St.Georges de Commiers to La Mure

- ✢ Kg/IGN112 C5, ✿ Electric, ⚒ 1000mm, ✲ 30.1km
- ☞ Table 521: SNCF St.Georges-de-Commiers on the line from Grenoble to Veynes
- ☛ St.Georges is located 15km S of Grenoble via RN75 to Vif and then 3km E to St.Georges
- ✓ am & pm. Sat, Sun & BH: begin-Apr to begin-Oct. Also Daily: May to Sept.
- ✉ Chemin de Fer de La Mure, 38450, St Georges de Commiers, ✆ 76.72.57.11

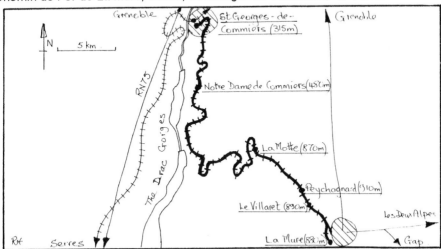

This metre gauge line was opened in 1888 for both passenger and freight traffic. It was built primarily to carry coal from the anthracite mines around La Mure to the standard gauge railway at St.Georges-de-Commiers. La Mure is situated at almost 1000m altitude in the French Alps just south of Grenoble. Regular passenger services were withdrawn in 1955. The coal traffic ceased in 1988. The route selected by the promoters of the line required it to cross a ridge of the Conest mountains and then follow the line of the River Drac in a long and sheer gorge.

At St.Georges is situated the narrow gauge railway depot, carriage and locomotive sheds and the museum collection of rolling stock. The collection being assembled here is concentrating upon narrow gauge mountain railways. A number of items from Swiss and French lines are exhibited. These are mostly of metre gauge. They include bogie carriages and electric railcars from the Swiss Nyon St.Cergue-Morez, Rhätische Bahn and Appenzeller Bahn railways, several old carriages (including a superb saloon) from the St.Gervais to Vallorcine line (71), a rotary snow plough, and freight stock. Items preserved from the La Mure line include the electric railcars of 1927, electric locomotives of 1930, passenger carriages from 1915 to 1935, and freight stock from 1888 to 1932. Original CF de La Mure locomotives built by Sécheron in 1933 and Swiss ex-Rhätische Bahn passenger stock are used to operate the tourist trains.

The line was initially steam operated, but electrified between 1903 and 1911. At 2.5kV dc this was the first high voltage dc line. The quantity of coal carried was large for a metre gauge mountain line. About 250 000 tonnes were transported annually until very recent times.

Soon after leaving St.Georges the train enters a tunnel and emerges right above the town. In the next 20km there are 7 viaducts, 5 large bridges and 18 curved tunnels. The ruling gradient is 1 in 30. Along the first 10km the train clings to the sheer side of the gorge. Twice the train swings away from the gorge to enter long horseshoe tunnels into the mountains to gain height. Over 50% of the line is on curves. At La Motte the train crosses the Loulla torrent on two beautiful viaducts, one above the other. The summit is reached at La Festinière tunnel. Beyond this, the line gently falls to La Mure. Here a short extension was built in 1991 to enable the train to approach the town centre. Greater railway interest, however, lies in the original station where, in the once extensive railway yards, a dozen capstans can be found. These were used in the shunting of wagons by cables connected to a locomotive on an adjacent track and are a rare survival.

The nature of the railway really has to be experienced to be believed. This is one of the most spectacular railway in France and also one of the most enjoyable. An informative and entertaining commentary is provided on the journey. The uphill ride is broken by a couple of photographic stops on top of viaducts. The sensation of climbing out of the carriage on to the parapet of a 35m high viaduct can be imagined. The panorama across the reservoir-filled valley to the various alpine summits is delightful. Take the morning departure from St.Georges and sit on the right for the most spectacular views.

68: CHEMIN DE FER DES HÔPITAUX-NEUFS
CHEMIN DE FER TOURISTIQUE PONTARLIER-VALLORBE

✳ From **Les Hôpitaux-Neufs-Jougne** to **Touillon** and to **Fontaine Ronde**

✧ Le/IGN109 B8, ✳ Steam & diesel, ✇ 1435mm, ✳ 6km.

☞ Table 531: SNCF Pontarlier, SNCF Vallorbe or SNCF bus from SNCF Frasne

☛ The present section is about 15km S of Pontarlier on the RN57 towards Vallorbe (CH)

✓ pm. Also resturant car special on Friday evenings

✉ M. L. Poix, 2 rue de la Seigne, 25370 Les Hôpitaux Vieux

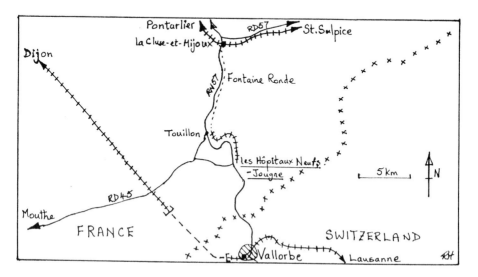

The old single track SNCF railway line between Pontarlier and Vallorbe (Switzerland) was closed in 1969. This line reached a little over 1000m at its middle stretch to the north of Les Hôpitaux-Vieux. The whole line, from the northern junction at La Cluse to just north of Vallorbe, has been lifted.

From a depot at the old station at Les Hopitaux-Neufs, a section of the line is being reconstructed by the CFTPV association. The length available for use by 1995 was 3km. Initial tourist trains ran on 1.5km of track in 1994. The trackbed of much of the rest of the 20km of the old line between Pontarlier and Vallorbe is intact and extension beyond the anticipated 6km operation for 1996 is a strong possibility.

Initial tourist trains used a German (DR) diesel locotracteur, one six-wheeled and two four-wheeled Swiss coaches, and a small 1895-built steam locomotive. This 0-4-0T built by SLM was on loan from the Val de Travers tourist railway in Switzerland. The six-wheeled coach has been converted to a restaurant car. This use of rolling stock of foreign origin is indicative of a shortage of preserved standard gauge French stock, particularly steam locomotives. However, for the 1996 season the steam traction will be an 0-4-0T built by Fives-Lille and hired from the CFT Rhin tourist train operation at Port Rhénan.

The area has a developing skiing and summer tourist industry. There must be significant potential for this thriving tourist railway in this scenic area of the Jura.

69: SNCF SAVOIE LINE: ST.GERVAIS TO VALLORCINE

✵ **St. Gervais** to **Vallorcine** (and to Martigny, Switzerland) via **Chamonix-Mont-Blanc**
✢ Le/IGN112 A9, ✿ Electric (750/800V dc third rail), ⚐ 1000m, ✳ 34km
☞ Tables 513 & 514: SNCF St.Gervais-les-Bains-le-Fayet or CFF/SBB Martigny
☛ Le Fayet is 60km E of Genève and reached directly via RN205
✓ am & pm. Daily: All year. SNCF timetable Table 514
✉ Gare SNCF de St.Gervais, 74190 Le Fayet, ✆ 50.66.50.50

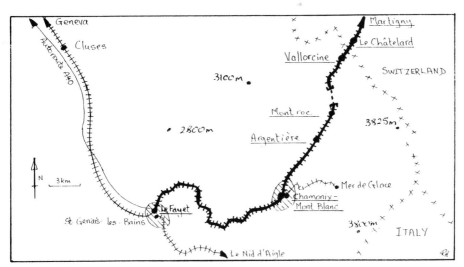

Beginning in 1889, a metre gauge line was created to link the PLM standard gauge railway at St.Gervais-le-Fayet with Chamonix, and to cross the Alps to connect with the Swiss standard gauge network at Martigny. The link was finally completed in 1908. The line is in two sections, meeting at a head-on junction at the French border station of Vallorcine. The French section of the line is adhesion worked throughout; in fact it is one of the steepest adhesion railways in the world, with a gradient of almost 1 in 11. The original rolling stock used the Fell braking system (still used on the Isle of Man) on the steeper sections. By contrast the Swiss section has gradients of 1 in 5 which are rack operated. The line has been electrified with the 750V dc third-rail system from the beginning, but some sections have been replaced by overhead wiring. Through running of trains between the French and Swiss sections was not possible because of the incompatibility of the rack and Fell-fitted stock. Removal of the Fell system in the late 1980s has overcome this and some through trains now operate each day. A change of train is often required at Vallorcine or Châtelard.

The single track line begins from within the pretty SNCF station at St.Gervais-les-Bains- le-Fayet at an altitude of 580m. The initial climb is severe; almost 400m in 9km. Half-way to Chamonix the train crosses the impressively high viaduct of Sainte Marie which has seven stone-built arches. At Chamonix-Mont-Blanc the metre gauge station has all the atmosphere of a major standard gauge junction. This is a result of the importance of the tourist attraction of the town, and of the connection here with the very successful Montenvers rack railway to the Mer de Glace glacier **(71)**. Beyond Chamonix (altitude 1037m), the climb is less steep towards the summit at Montroc (1385m). Here begins a long tunnel, shared in the event of severe snow by road vehicles. Beyond Chamonix the views to the rear are particularly memorable, with Mont Blanc in the background. The whole journey, however, is a constantly changing vista of beautiful alpine scenery. The French-Swiss border is between the stations of Vallorcine and Châtelard. High above the town here is the reservoir of Emosson. At Châtelard-Gietroz station a funicular gives access to a narrow gauge railway (at 1820m) and a further funicular leading to the barrage of the reservoir (at 1930m).

The basic stock used on the French section of the line consists of electric railcars and trailers built by Decauville in 1958, and through railcars from Switzerland. From 1996, modern units, constructed in 1994-95 by Vevey, will operate through services between St. Gervais and Martigny. Two of the original items of rolling stock built in 1901 and 1909 remain on the line. These are modified motor-vans now used as service vehicles and snowploughs.

This line has connections with three other metre-gauge lines: the Swiss Martigny-Châtelard railway at Vallorcine, the Mont Blanc tramway at Le Fayet **(72)** and the Montenvers line at Chamonix **(71)**. The latter two are essentially tourist railways with winter ski traffic and summer rambler and excursion traffic. By contrast, despite some recent modernization, the St.Gervais-Vallorcine-Martigny operation has all the feel of a local line of earlier days.

70: LIGNE DU TONKIN/RIVE BLEUE EXPRESS

※ To **Evian-les-Bains** from **Le Bouveret** (Switzerland) via **St.Gingolf**
✣ Le/IGN109 C9, ❀ Steam and diesel, ⚯ 1435mm, ❀ 20km
☞ Table 513: SNCF Evian-les-Bains or CFF/SBB Le Bouveret
☛ Evian-les-Bains is 42km, and le Bouveret 63km, east of Genève by RN5
✓ am & pm. Sun: End-May to mid-Sept. Also Tues, Thurs, Fri & Sat in Jul & Aug.
✉ M C Pernet, Le Rond-Point, 74500 Neuvecelle, ☎ 50.75.08.47

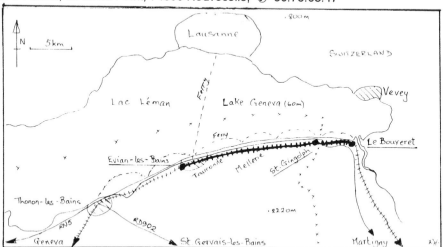

The border between France and Switzerland runs across Lake Geneva (lac Léman): on the southern side of the lake it is at St.Gingolf, 18km east of Evian-les-Bains and 4km west of Le Bouveret. The Chablais Alps rise up immediately along the southern shore of the lake. For at least 100 years this has been an area of genteel spa resorts and residences overlooking the largest lake in central Europe.

The line linking France and Switzerland was built along the south shore of the lake in 1886. It carried international passenger traffic until 1938 and had importance during WW2 when it was the only standard gauge railway linking Switzerland with the unoccupied region of France. Subsequently traffic declined and through traffic was transferred to the international line along the north side of the lake. The final freight trains on this single track line ran at the end of 1987. This left passenger services on the French section west from Evian, with Swiss freight and passenger services east from the border at St.Gingolf to the main line at St.Maurice.

A vigorous campaign was instigated by local authorities on both sides of the border at the time of the withdrawal of services between Evian and St.Gingolf. With financial contributions from Switzerland and France the line has been retained and refurbished for use by tourist trains under a 10 year agreement with SNCF. Since 1986 tourist trains have operated over the 22km section between Evian and le Bouveret. Two separate trains are used: the "Rive Bleue Express" which, despite its name, consists of a small 0-6-0WT steam locomotive built by SLM, Winterthur in 1893, three 1892 carriages with wooden seats and end balconies, and a bar car of 1864 vintage; and "Le Transchablaisien", consisting of an ex-SNCF locotracteur (BB71010) and three 1950-built Swiss carriages. Only one return journey is run on each operational day. This departs from Le Bouveret mid-morning and returns from Evian during the afternoon. A regular boat service operates along the lake and a variety of combinations of train/boat trips is possible. The steam train operates the regular Sunday services and the diesel train the Saturday and weekday ones.

The line runs along the narrow strip of land between the mountains and the lake, terminating at Le Bouveret, where the mountains abruptly give way to the wide valley of the Rhône where it enters the lake. The scenery is quite magnificent. For much of its length, the train journey gives views over the lake. These are interspersed with sections in cutting and tunnel.

The tourist operation has ensured for the present the preservation of the Evian-les-Bains to St.Gingolf line. This is altogether a much rosier picture than a few years ago and a demonstration of how a concerted effort can achieve surprising results. The benefit for all is the opportunity to travel in historic style through a rich and beautiful setting.

At Le Bouveret is situated the Swiss Vapeur Park, with a 1.6km, 184mm (7¼ inch) railway with a large collection of steam locomotives. Trains operate from an extensive station over a 1.5km loop of track. (Le Bouveret Tourist Office, 1892 Le Bouveret, Switzerland. ☎ +25.811101).

71: CHEMIN DE FER CHAMONIX AU MONTENVERS

❄ From **Chamonix-Mont-Blanc** to **Le Montenvers** (La Mer de Glace)
✛ Lf/IGN112 A9, ❋ Electric, ⚒ 1000mm, ❋ 5.4km
☞ Table 514: SNCF Chamonix (direct footbridge connection) **(69)**
☛ From Genève/Annecy. RN205 (E25) is Route Blanche to Chamonix station. Parking at station
✓ am & pm. Daily: mid-May to November
✉ Chemin de Fer Chamonix au Montenvers, BP44, 74401 Chamonix Cedex, ✆ 50.53.12.54

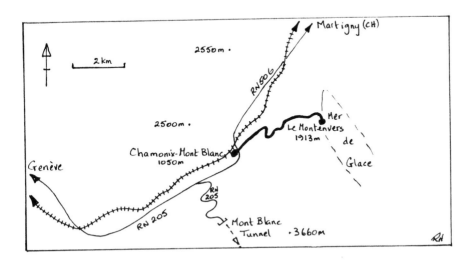

Chamonix-Mont-Blanc is situated in the narrow valley of the River Arve. This together with the valley of the Trient form a natural route through the northern Alps between France and Switzerland. Chamonix is at an altitude of 1037m on the valley floor with mountains close around. Immediately to the north is le Brevent (2520m) and to the south Aiguille du Midi (3840m) and Mont Blanc (4800m). A 7km long glacier, the Mer de Glace, is situated to the east of the town.

In 1909 a metre gauge rack railway was opened to give visitors access to the glacier at Montenvers (1913m). The line, which has a gradient approaching 1 in 4, was operated by steam locomotives until electrified in 1954. Some steam services remained until the early 1980's. Locomotive No. 6 stands on a plinth at Chamonix station where it can be closely approached for inspection. It is understood that No7 and the remains of number 8 are stored at Chamonix. These 0-4-2T locomotives were built in 1923 by SLM, Winterthur (Switzerland) and operated on the Strubb rack system (with horizontally opposed teeth). The chassis of another locomotive has been converted for snow clearance work.

Since 1954 the line has been electrified using overhead supply at 11000v 50Hz. Six single-ended motorized railcars operate the service, with matching trailer cars coupled on the upper end of each train. These motor cars were built, like the steam locomotives, by SLM. The first four entered service in 1954. Two more were supplied in 1965 and 1974.

Three six-wheel diesel locomotives were supplied in 1967 and 1972. These are also fitted with rack/cog equipment. They are primarily for maintenance and support duties but are used to operate relief trains and winter services.

The train starts to climb immediately after it leaves Chamonix. The views are initially restricted by trees covering the nearer slopes. However, on leaving the first long tunnel the views become panoramic across the valley of the Arve to the left and the lower slopes of the mountains to the right. From here on the views are frequently spectacular, especially as the train crosses the curved stone viaduct. The cast iron balustrade adds the final picturesque touch to this setting.

At the upper terminus, impressive views are obtained above the Mer de Glace glacier. This may be approached using the cable car if desired. This was installed in 1961 but completely rebuilt, for greater capacity, in 1974. Food and souvenirs are also available at Montenvers. A combined ticket for train and cable car is available.

Although both the railway and cable car are operated all year, the services are dependent upon the weather, particularly the amount of snow. This can arrive remarkably early. It is recommended that a telephone confirmation regarding the operation of services is made before travel to the line during the winter season, and in October, when maintenance is undertaken..

72: TRAMWAY DU MONT BLANC

✳ From **Le Fayet** to **Bellevue** and **Bionnassay** Glacier towards Mont Blanc summit
✢ Lf/IGN112 B8, ✱ Electric ⚙ 1000mm (rack) ✱ 12.4km
☞ Tables 513 & 514: SNCF St.Gervais-le-Fayet
☛ From Genève (60km) directly via RN205. TMB station faces SNCF station at Le Fayet
✓ am & pm daily. June to September. Restricted Winter service
✉ STMB, 130 avenue de la Gare, 74190 Le Fayet, ☏ 50.47.51.83

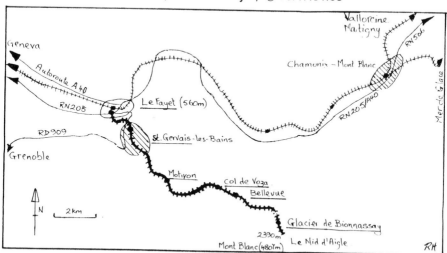

The Tramway du Mont Blanc is more a railway than a tramway and doesn't go to Mont Blanc. However it has much of interest. The plan at the beginning of the century was to build a railway to the summit of Mont Blanc from the valley of the River Arve which forms the main route from France to Switzerland immediately north of the Alps and contains the famous resorts of Chamonix and St.Gervais.

The selected route was well chosen. Starting from an altitude of 560m, it would leave the valley floor at Le Fayet, pass through St.Gervais and then up a long ridge to the secondary summit of Mont Blanc at Dome du Gouter at 4300m. From the beginning finance was a problem which is revealed today by the passing places situated on level sections to avoid the expense of points on the rack rail.

The line opened in sections between 1909 and 1913 until it had reached Le Nid d'Aigle, about half the distance and half the altitude. Progress was halted by WW1 and never resumed. The line was supplied with inadequately-powered 0-4-0T steam rack locos, so that a three hour journey was required to reach a point on the mountain with good views but some 2000m below the summit. This situation was partially improved after WW2 by the introduction of powerful electric railcars. The terminus remained however as the constructors left it before WW1: abruptly stopped in a meadow. This was finally rectified in the late 1980's by a short extension at the Bionnassay Glacier terminus enabling three train sets to be operated when the line is busy.

The line, which is electrified at 11000V ac from overhead wires, begins its route through the streets of Le Fayet. The track is metre gauge with rack on the steeper sections. The first section of rack rail begins as the line begins its first climb amongst the buildings of the town. The depot of the line is at Le Fayet and operations are open to view from the streets. The small station is situated directly outside the SNCF station of St.Gervais-les-Bains-Le Fayet on the international route between Genève and Martigny (both in Switzerland).

Three twin sets of railcars are available on the line. This is just sufficient for the traffic available but provides no reserve stock. Since patronage is good, additional stock might provide increased revenue on peak days and add to the reliability of the service. This is clearly a commercial decision and the railway has continued to survive into the 1990s despite concerns to the contrary ever since the 1960s.

The catenary is removed from the upper section in the winter to avoid damage, hence winter services are cancelled or restricted to the lower section of the line as far as the halt serving the village of Bionassay.

One of the original steam locomotives is preserved by the operating company. It is sometimes exhibited at Le Fayet during summer months. Proposals have been made for the restoration of this locomotive to working order. It is regrettable that neither this nor the development of the railway to its full potential has taken place.

73: STRASBOURG TRAMWAY

✳ Hautepierre to Baggersee and Illkirch via **Strasbourg** SNCF station
✣ Mc/IGN104 C10, ✳ Electric (750V dc o/h), ✇ 1435mm, ✳ 12km (22km)
☞ SNCF Strasbourg. The tramway serves the station on an underground section.
☛ A suggested access point to the tramway is Hautpierre (Junction 4 of Autoroute 351)
✓ am & pm. Daily all year. Tickets (interchangeable with buses) are available in carnet form.
✉ Cie.des transports strasbourgeois, 14 rue de la Garaux Marchandises, 67200 Strasbourg
✉ Tourist Office, Place de la Gare, 67000 Strasbourg ✆ 88.52.28.22

Strasbourg has recently successfully reintroduced trams to the heart of the city. The earlier trams operated from 1878 until 1960. The new tram line runs from Hautepierre in the west of the city to Baggersee in the south. The western section serves the Cronenbourg suburb, and its brewery, close to the tram depot which is situated in an old bus garage. The line passes under the SNCF station (Gare Centrale) in a 1.2km tunnel. It emerges beside the northern arm of the River Ill (Fossé du Faux Rempart) then immediately crosses the river and runs as a traditional tramway alongside and along the centre of cobbled streets through the centre of the town which is pedestrianised and situated on an island in the River Ill. Having crossed the southern arm of the river, it continues southwards along the Rue de la Première Armée and the Route de Colmar which the line follows southwards until it reaches Baggersee, Illkirch and the Canal du Rhône.

Public services began in November 1994 and proved an immediate success with ridership exceeding planning expectations.

The ultra modern trams were designed in Italy and built in UK by ABB, York. and were delivered during 1994 and 1995. Each tramcar has three body sections (plus cab and articulation sections) on a total of four bogies. They have an exceptionally low entry so that only kerb-height platforms are required. The 750V electrical pick-up is by a single pantograph arm.

A southern extension of the line from Illkirch to Cité is possible as is a second line which will in practice be two branches off the existing line towards Hoenheim in the north and Neuhof in the south-eastern suburbs.

74: TRAIN MUSÉE DU MORVAN-BAZOIS

✳ **Tamnay-en-Bazois** to **Château-Chinon**
✣ Id/IGN108 C6, ✳ Diesel, ✇ 1435mm, ✳ 22km
☞ SNCF Nevers (47km)
☛ Tamnay-en-Bazois is on RD978, 47km E of Nevers
✓ Operating dates not known
✉ (a): CFTA Tourisme, 174 rue de la République, 92800 Puteaux, ✆ 46.92.56.56
　 (b): TMMB, La Croisée des Chemins, Tamnay 58110 Chatillon-en-Bazois

The single track, freight only, branch line from Tamnay-en-Bazois to Château-Chinon is operated by CFTA under contract for SNCF. The eastern end of the line enters the 175 000 hectare regional nature park of Morvan. A tourist train has been operated from Tamnay as a joint operation between CFTA and a local association. Initially running southwards along the through route from Tamnay to Cercy-la-Tour, the branch to Château-Chinon has been used since 1988. This line is circuitous, following the contours of the hills. Along the final part of the line, westward views open out across the Morvan. This heavily wooded area rises to 900m. Château-Chinon is an excellent base for exploring the area and the Yonne gorges. Diesel railcars of the 1950s, "Picassos" X3818 and X3876 and also X5800, have operated these occasional services.

75: MUSÉE DE LA MACHINE AGRICOLE ET À VAPEUR

❊ **Ambert**
✧ If/IGN111 F4, ❊ Steam, ⚒ 1435mm
☞ Tables 558 & 565: SNCF Pont de Dore then SNCF bus or via the Train Touristique Livradois-Forez **(54)**
☛ Ambert is E of Clermont-Ferrand. 88km via RN89 and RD906
✓ am & pm. Daily
✉ Musée Agrivap, BP8, rue de l'industrile, 63600 Ambert, ✆ 73.82.43.88

In an old sawmill close to the station in Ambert, a preservation group known as Agrivap have created a museum since 1980. The items displayed include numerous implements and steam operated equipment used on farms in the early years of the twentieth centiury and other industrial and railway relics of the same era. All items are maintained in excellent condition: most are operational. The collection include steam-rollers, stationary and portable steam engines, traction engines and a Cockerill vertical boilered steam locomtive. The Agrivap group also operate freight and passenger services on the rail route running through Ambert **(54)**. The opportunity to combine a visit to a museum with railway exhibits, with travel on this scenic line, is highly recommended.

76: LE PETIT TRAIN DE L'YONNE

❊ From **Massangis** to **Rochefort**
✧ Jd/IGN108 B6, ❊ Diesel, ⚒ 600mm, ❊ 2.5km
☞ Table 570: SNCF Cravant-Bazarnes
☛ Massangis is 45km SE of Auxerre via RN6 then RD11 and RD311
✓ pm. Sun & BH: Begin-May to end-Sept
✉ ATPVM, Angely, 89440 l'Isle-sur-Serein, ✆ 86.33.81.20

This single track 600mm gauge railway runs along the pretty valley of the River Serein. The line is 2.5km in length from Massangis southwards to Rochefort. It has been constructed since 1981 along the trackbed of the old metre gauge Chemin de Fer Départemental de l'Yonne which closed in 1951. The tourist trains have been operating each summer since 1986 from a depot at the southern end of the line. At Massangis, car parking and a picnic site adjoin the departure platform. Half-way along the line there is a passing place, where a refreshment coach is installed on operating days. The rolling stock and railway are immaculately maintained. The motive power consists of ex-industrial 4-wheel diesel locotracteurs built by Compagne, CACL and Deutz in 1910, 1950 and 1953 respectively.

77: ST. ÉTIENNE TRAMWAY

❊ **St.Etienne** (North to south along Rue Charles de Gaulle and Rue Gambetta)
✧ Jf/IGN112 B2, ❊ Electric (600V dc), ⚒ 1000mm, ❊ 10km
☞ SNCF St.Etienne (Gare de Bellevue or Gare de la Terrasse)
☛ St.Etienne is 60km SW of Lyon. Parking in town centre is restricted but easier on Sundays
✓ am & pm. Daily: All year
✉ Office de Tourisme, place Roannelle, 42000 St.Etienne, ✆ 77.25.12.14

St.Étienne has one of the three traditional tramways which survived in France after WW2. Originally opened as a steam tramway in 1881, it was electrified immediately before WW1. The sole remaining line was re-equipped from 1958 with PCC tramcars. A major refurbishment took place from 1981 and the line was extended at both ends. The existing bogie tramcars were renovated, and extra tramcars introduced. The new trams are twin-car articulated units built by Alsthom-ACMV. Additional three-section articulated sets of similar design will be added to the fleet in 1996. The present line connects Hôpital-Nord to Solaure, with intermediate termini at Bellevue and La Terrasse. A second line running east/west is under consideration. A number of trolleybus lines operate in St. Étienne. Historic tram and trolleybuses from the St.Étienne lines are preserved by the operating company. The collection includes trams from the 1907 and 1938 fleets, and trolleybuses of 1947 and 1955 vintage.

78: LYON FUNICULARS

❋ From **St.Jean** to **St.Just** via **Minimes** and to **Fourvière**
✤ Jf/IGN112 B3, ✱ Electric funicular, ⚒ 1300mm and 1000mm, ✻ 0.44km and 0.83km
☞ SNCF Lyon-Part Dieu (TGV) then metro lines B & D or SNCF Lyon-Perrache then A & D
☛ Parking close to Gorge de Loup (metro line D) and SNCF Lyon-Perrache. On street on Sun
✓ am & pm. Daily:All year
✉ Office de Tourisme, place Bellecour, 69002 Lyon, ☎ 78.42.25.75

Two funicular routes survive in the old quarter of Lyon following the renovation programme in 1988 when the third funicular was discontinued. Both lines start from a semi-underground station at St.Jean-Vieux-Lyon, now a combined station with the new metro line D. The more southerly route is the longer and of 1300mm gauge. It climbs to St.Just and has an intermediate (underground) station at Minimes. The 1000mm gauge northerly line terminates behind the enormous church of Notre Dame de Fourvière, for superb views over the city.

79: PETIT TRAIN DU BELVÉDÈRE

❋ Situated close to **Commelle-Vernay**, near Roanne
✤ Jf/IGN111 D4, ✱ Diesel, ⚒ 600mm, ✻ 4km
☞ Tables 561/6/8: SNCF Roanne (8km), SNCF Le Coteau (5km)
☛ Commelle is 95km NE of Lyon via RN7 for 90km then west through Pariqny.
✓ pm. Daily May to October. Also Sundays Nov to Apr.
✉ SCRRV, Mme L Dubanchet, Belvédère de Commelle, 42120 Le Coteau, ☎ 77.68.58.12

At Villerest, 5km south of Roanne, the River Loire is dammed to create a lake about 25km long. The lake fills the narrow valley at this point, les Gorges de la Loire. The narrow gauge railway runs high up on the east side of the steep valley giving excellent views for the passenger. The train is composed of five bogie coaches and a 55hp 0-4-0 diesel hydraulic locotracteur. The locomotive was built by the firm of Soquet in 1989. It is designed to resemble an Austrian steam tank engine, and is hydraulically linked to the carriages so that each axle of the train is driven. This assists the locomotive as the railway is steep in places. The railway was completely rebuilt in 1989 following a fire which destroyed the previous 700mm equipment. It offers an scenic ride, in a lovely setting, on more days than most French tourist lines.

80: TRAIN TOURISTIQUE DES LAVIÈRES

❋ Close to **Is-sur-Tille**
✤ Kd/IGN109 A5, ✱ Petrol & diesel, ⚒ 500mm, ✻ 1.5 km
☞ Table 116: SNCF Is-sur-Tille. The TT site at Combe-Brousselard is 3km west of the station.
☛ Is-sur-Tille is situated 25km N of Dijon via RN74 for 4km then RD3.
✓ pm. Sun & BH: Mid-June to mid-Sept
✉ Association du TTL, 6 rue des Capucins, 21120 Is-sur-Tille, ☎ 80.95.36.36

A 500mm gauge railway has operated here since 1977 adjacent to a growing leisure park in a wooded area just outside the town. This was the site of a quarry from 1900 to 1930. The line has been extended during the winter of 1995/6 to 1.5km. A two-platform station has been added. The stock used for this operation consists of a number of locally constructed or modified vehicles for passenger use from four-wheel four-seat open carriages to an 18-seat bogie baladeuse. These are hauled by one of the two tiny locally-built petrol motors or the Pétolet diesel locotracteur of 1931 vintage.

The original circuit which operated under the name of Chemin de Fer Issois has been further developed since 1992 with an extended track. The revised operation has been renamed as the Train Touristique des Lavières (lava quarry). Services are operated on Sundays and public holiday afternoons. Trains for pre-booked groups are operated on Saturdays from the beginning of May to the end of October. The railway and pleasure park continue to develop. A café and souvenir shop are available at the railway. Additions planned include an 184mm gauge railway, and a model railway in a dedicated building. The park has play areas and various amusement facilities.

81: LES AUTORAILS DE BOURGOGNE FRANCHE-COMTE

✳ Based at **Dijon**. TT trips to locations throughout France and to Switzerland and Belgium
✤ Kd/IGN108 B9, ✸ Diesel, ⚒ 1435mm
☞ SNCF Dijon.Other starting points are occasionally used
☛ Dijon station is to the E of the town. Parking is available. Access possible by TGV
✓ am departure. Dates and locations subject to advertized programme (s.a.e. to address below)
✉ ABFC, 37 rue Lamartine, 21000 Dijon, ✆ 80.35.83.17

Although a railcar based operation with an esoteric title is perhaps not immediately inspiring, the operation of this well established group should not be overlooked. This is a very professional organization offering a varied programme of excellent rail trips throughout France. The association has the aim of using preserved rolling stock to offer tourist train excursions over the SNCF network including lines no longer used by passenger trains. These are to picturesque locations or special events and open days. A programme of about twenty trips is arranged each year. Travel should be pre-booked. Outings have been arranged each year since ABFC's original Picasso railcar (X4039) obtained SNCF authorization in 1987. The stock available to the group now also includes two other Picassos (X4025 and X4051). This is an enterprising operation offering travel on lines not otherwise available.

82: GRENOBLE TRAMWAYS

✳ At **Grenoble**
✤ Kf/IGN1112 C5, ✸ Electric (750V dc o/h), ⚒ 1435mm, ✱ 18.5km
☞ SNCF Grenoble
☛ Parking is available where Tram route A crosses the main E-W road RN90/RN532
✓ am & pm. Daily: All year
✉ SEMITAG, 15 ave Salvador Allende, 38044 Grenoble

Traditional trams were removed from the streets of Grenoble in the 1950s. A completely new system has been installed in stages since 1987. The modern tramway system has been a remarkable success, both in the patronage and also in the way it has been fitted into the city streets. This tramway is a modern version of the traditional tramway with standard gauge tracks laid flush with the roadway constructed of "setts". Line A runs from the SNCF station to the NW of the city and to Echirolle in the S. Line B branches off to the university campus in the E. The network is still being expanded. The modern trams are low-floor articulated three-section sets. Some of the first-generation trams have been preserved and operate on the new network on special occasions.

Trolleybuses, which took over from the earlier trams in the 1950s, continue to operate on several routes.

83: CENTRE D'ANIMATION TECHNOLOGIQUE DE LA MINE ET DES ENERGIES, NOYANT

✳ At **Noyant-d'Allier**
✤ Ie/IGN111 B3, ✸ Various, ⚒ 600mm, ✱ 1.6km
☞ Tables 540 & 567: SNCF Moulins (22km)
☛ Noyant-d'Allier is 100km N of Clermont-Ferrand via RN9 and RD18
✓ am & pm.Sat, Sun & BH begin-May to mid-Sept.
✉ CATME, 6 rue de la Mine, 03210 Noyant-d'Allier, ✆ 70.47.31.51

On the edge of the small village of Noyant situated in an area of rolling hills of agricultural land, are hidden the remains of a coal mine, the Puits Central, closed in 1943. The museum, established here in 1990, has a large collection of mining and quarry railway items. This is housed in the old surface buildings of the mine which has retained part of the pit head winding gear. The rolling stock includes numerous Berry, Deutz, Decauville and Jung diesel locotracteurs, electric trolleys (500V o/h) and an 0-4-0T Orenstein & Koppel steam locomotive. The tourist train carriages are formed of old mine wagons running on a dumbell shaped line. A range of wagons is displayed outside the museum including specialized items: stretcher cars, personnel carrying, and equipment transport vehicles in addition to a range of mineral wagons of various designs.

33. On the dunes beside the Atlantic, the draisines form the Train Touristique Pointe de Grave-Le Verdon [86]. Only the front and rear vehicles seen here retain their diesel engines. →
(Photo: PGVS)

34. ↓ The descent of La Rhune, with St. Jean-de-Luz and the ocean 900 metres below. One of the teak-bodied rack locos uses only the rear arms to contact the 3 kW ac overhead.
(Photo: R. Haworth)

35. ↑ At Guîtres, on the line of the Train Touristique Guîtres-Marcenais [89], the 1924-built 0-4-0T La Meuse loco returns with the weekly train. The semaphore signalling indicates that this is essentially a preservation operation. *(Photo: R. Haworth)*

36. ↓ The regular service of the Guîtres-Marcenais [89] is a single return journey to an isolated halt in the woods near Marcenais. The train halts long enough to allow passengers to stroll through the woods to a water-mill creperie. *(Photo: R. Haworth)*

37. ↑ At Marquèze, loco D4028, a General Electric (USA) BB diesel, brings visitors to the eco-museum on the CdF des Landes de Gascogne. The museum has no public road access.
(Photo: R. Haworth)

38. The CdF du Lac d'Artouste [91] travels through the Pyrenees at almost 2000 metres, with snow around on a June day. In the distance can be seen the barrage of the Artouste reservoir. The Billard locos introduced by SNCF in 1953 continue to display the logo, despite the railway having passed from SNCF control. →
(Photo: R Haworth)

39. ↑ The Quercyrail [92] tourist train follows the valley of the River Lot between Cahors and Capdenac. Railcar 2425 was built by Decauville in 1952, and was withdrawn from SNCF service in the late 1980s. The excellent view forward and to the rear on this scenic trip can be appreciated.   *(Photo: Quercyrail)*

40. ↓ At Latour-de-Carol [97], the 1676mm Spanish gauge, the narrow gauge Cerdagne line, and standard gauge SNCF all meet. Looking north, the RENFE lines are to the left, the SNCF line is on the left of the platform, with two narrow gauge lines to the right.   *(Photo: S. Oliver)*

84: TIGNES FUNICULAR

✳ Tignes (Val Claret) to La Grande Motte
✛ Lf/IGN112 B9, ✽ Electric funicular, ⚒ 1200mm, ✱ 3.5km
☞ Table 512: SNCF Bourg-St.Maurice (30km). Then bus (Autobus Martin, ✆ 79.07.04.49)
☛ Tignes is 110km S of Chamonix via Mont Blanc tunnel, RN90 to Borg-St.M. Then RD902
✓ am & pm. Daily: all year.
✉ Office de Tourisme, le Lac, 73320 Tignes ✆ 79.06.15.55

This modern funicular takes winter and summer visitors to this ski resort from close to the town (at Val Claret, 2110m altitude) to the magnificent alpine panorama on the ridge of La Grande Motte (3032m). The lower funicular station at Val Clareret is immediately at the end of the RD87.

The line which was opened in 1993 is unusual in being in a tunnel for the whole of its length. Also unusual for funiculars is the operation in the form of trains of linked passenger carriages. It is single track for most of its length. The lower section of the line travels in a southerly direction but swings sharply to a south-westerly direction for the final third of the journey. A chair lift links the upper station of the funicular with the summit of La Grande Motte (3656m).

The two stations have platforms on either side of the train for ease of loading. Ridership can be very high in the skiing season and standing is the norm. There are only a few seats at the side of each carriage. There are racks for skis. The funicular close by at Val-d'Isère **[85]** has many similarities with the Tignes system.

85: FUNIVAL FUNICULAR, VAL-D'ISÈRE

✳ Val-d'Isère (La Daille) to Bellevarde
✛ Lf/IGN112 B9, ✽ Electric funicular, ⚒ 1200mm, ✱ 2.3km
☞ Table 512: SNCF Bourg-St.Maurice (30km). Then bus (Autobus Martin, ✆ 79.07.04.49)
☛ Val-d'Isère is 110km S of Chamonix via Mont Blanc tunnel, RN90 to Bourg-St.Maurice, then RD902
✓ am & pm. Daily: all year.
✉ Office de Tourisme, Maison de Val-d'Isère, 73150 Val-d'Isère ✆ 79.06.06.60

The "Funival" funicular at Val-d'Isère has noticeable similarities to the Tignes funicular **[84]** in the adjacent valley in this area of ski resorts. The line was built to increase the capacity of the transport system to the ski slopes above that offered by the existing ski lift. It departs from La Daille to the west of the RD902 road about 2km to the north-west of Val-d'Isère. The lower station is at an altitude of 1785m. The upper is on the flank of the mountain of Bellevarde at 2700m. The peak is at 2826m and is to the west of the town. The funicular began operations in 1987 but full operation did not commence until a year later by which time the speed had been increased. The 2.3km journey is completed in about 5 minutes. The line is supported on a concrete causeway and a viaduct for some of the route but three-quarters of the journey is in a tunnel. The trains are of two cars of modern design: fully enclosed for weather protection but glazed all round so good views are not impeded during the open sections of track. The lighting is bright so that the tunnel section is not oppressive. The skiing season is long (early November to May). The funicular also operates outside these periods.

SOUTH

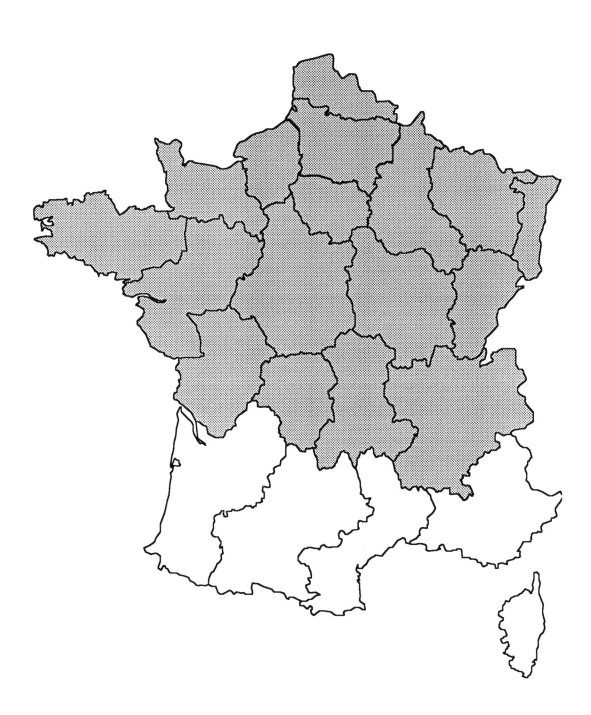

86: TRAIN TOURISTIQUE POINTE DE GRAVE-VERDON-SOULAC (The PGV)

✳ From **La Pointe de Grave-le Verdon** to **Soulac-sur-Mer**
✢ Df/IGN104 A4, ✳ Diesel, ⚒ 1435mm, ✳ 7km
☞ Table 405: SNCF Pointe de Grave or via Table 404: SNCF Royan and ferry
☛ Pointe de Grave is 100km from Bordeaux via RN215. Access also possible by Royan ferry
✓ pm. Sat, Sun & BH from begin-April to end-Sept. Also am & pm Daily in Jul and Aug
✉ Association PGVS, 33123 Le Verdon-sur-Mer ⚒ ✆ 56.09.61.78
✉ Office de Tourisme, rue F. Le Bretton, 33123 Le Verdon-sur-Mer ⚒ ✆ 56.09.61.78

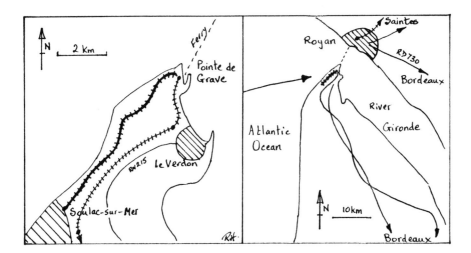

A most unusual tourist train operates north of Bordeaux: a train composed entirely of standard gauge draisines. Each summer since 1986 it has connected La Pointe de Grave with the beaches on the Atlantic coast. Nothing less like a TGV could be imagined than the Pointe de Grave train. However, using the abbreviation of the town name, the initials PGV, have been adopted and the train has humorously been painted in the silver grey livery of the TGV-Alantique.

The draisines were redundant stock from the SNCF depot at Brive. Some of them have been refurbished to act as diesel railcars. The rest have been adapted to become open or closed passenger carriages. All are short, almost square, four-wheel vehicles which are formed into trains of three or four.

The ocean currents have caused sand to accumulate along the shore. This has created a continuous beach along the whole coast and has also caused the River Gironde to travel progressively further north before reaching the sea. At the northern end of the sand spit is le Pointe de Grave with sea on three sides. The developing port town of Le Verdon-sur-Mer is situated immediately to the south. Much of the activity of the area is tourist and recreation-related, with fine beaches, fishing, and boat trips, and off-shore but accessible by boat, a magnificent sixteenth-century lighthouse.

The peninsular has extensive railways largely related to its port activities. Indeed, the single track line used for the tourist train belongs to the Bordeaux port authority. The line has been extended 0.5 km by the association, with the help of a grant from the local département. Trains now operate to Soulac ("Les Arros") where a small station has been built on the northern edge of the town.

Soulac is to the south of La Pointe. However, the train starts its journey by travelling north westwards before swinging in a wide curve to travel south westerly along the remaining 6km of the line. The route runs through the forests of maritime pines which are a feature of the area and then through the sand dunes alongside the beaches of the Atlantic shore of the peninsular.

Access to Le Verdon and La Pointe is possible by ferry from Royan on the west bank of the Gironde, or by road and rail along the peninsular from Bordeaux.

87: TRAMWAYS DU CAP FERRET

❄ Across Cap Ferret from **Belisaire** to **Océan Plage**
✤ Dg/IGN110 C3, ❋ Diesel, ▓ 600 mm, ❋ 2 km
☞ Table 402: SNCF Arcachon then ferry to Bélissaire (Cap Ferret)
☛ From Bordeaux by RD106 or via RN250 and Arcachon ferry
✓ pm daily: mid-June to mid-Sept. Also Sundays in early June
✉ Tramways du Cap Ferret, Mairie du Canon, 33970 Lège-Cap Ferret
✆ 56.03.84.00 or 56.60.52.57. Ferry information: ✆ 56.54.83.01 or 56.54.60.32

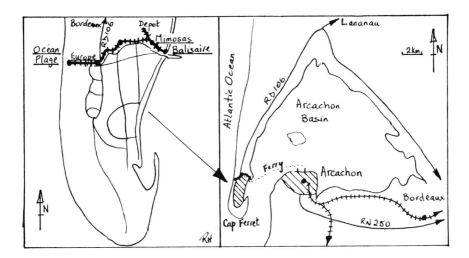

The rebirth of French narrow gauge tourist railways began on Cap Ferret in 1952. The success of this line acted as an example and inspiration for others to develop. Cap Ferret is a long sand spit on the Atlantic coast to the west of Bordeaux, protecting a sea-loch, the Bassin d'Arcachon. It is an area of seaside chalets and hotels set amongst pines.

Although the D106 road gives access direct from Bordeaux, the traditional route for holiday makers to reach the peninsular has been via the ferry from Arcachon, avoiding a 50 km road journey.

Before roads were developed on the peninsular, horse drawn (later petrol tractor) tramways were built south from the ferry terminal to la Pointe and west across the sand dunes to the Atlantic Coast. These 800 mm gauge lines were closed in the 1930's.

The present line re-established the link between the ferry terminal and the beaches. Due to concern of residents, it was necessary for it to deviate from the original route and take a somewhat longer course to the north around the edge of the settlements. Subsequent development has spread beyond the line which, as a consequence, runs between the chalets as a true road-side tramway.

The 600 mm gauge single track starts from a pedestrian area at the ferry terminal at Belisaire, with a halt at Mimosas. At this point the line crosses Avenue de Lauriers, leaving the branch line to the depot to follow the east side of the road. The train runs as a tramway through Avenue des Lilas, then across the Bordeaux road (RD106). The route is wooded along much of its length. After the halt "Europe" the line goes onto the dunes to reach the Atlantic beach at Océan Plage, an enormous expanse of fine sand with good bathing and surfing.

At peak times up to three trains are in use, giving a 15 min service - but usually a single train provides a 40 min service. The carriages used for this service are a mixture of four-wheel and bogie "baladeuses". There are four diesel locotracteurs. Each of the 0-4-0 Schneider ex-industrial locomotives, which were obtained from salt works, has had cabs and chimneys added to give the illusion of a steam locomotive. The other locomotive is a Billard diesel obtained from a forest tramway. It has a body resembling an industrial electric locomotive with a centre cab.

This line continues to do what its promoters intended 40 years ago - offer visitors a practical and enjoyable means of transport across the peninsular.

88: LA RHUNE RACK RAILWAY

⁜ **Col de St.Ignace** to the summit of **La Rhune**
✣ Dh/IGN 113 C3, ✱ Electric ✌ 1000mm (rack) ✱ 4.2km
☞ Table 401: SNCF St.Jean-de-Luz. Then bus from station to Col de St.Ignace
☛ From St.Jean-de-Luz : take D 918 for 6km then D4 via Ascain for 5km to Col de St.Ignace
✓ am & pm. Sat, Sun & B/H: begining May to mid-Nov. Daily: begining Jul to end Sept.
✉ CFTA, gare du col de St.Ignace, Sare, 64310 Ascain, ✆ 59.54.20.26

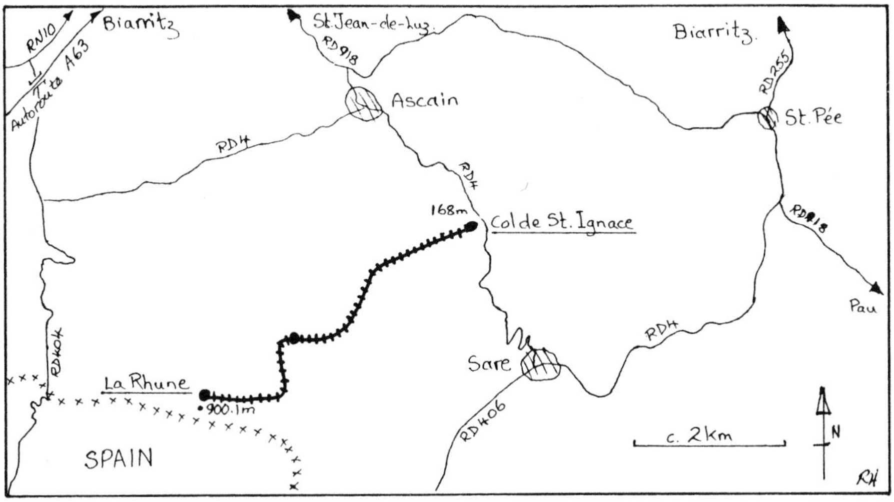

The Pyrénées Mountains rise to over 3000m and form the border between France and Spain. In the Basque country, at the western end, they run down to the Atlantic south of Biarritz and St.Jean-de-Luz. The first significant peak inland from the French coast is La Rhune, 900 m, right on the Spanish border. Due to its situation it affords truly magnificent views over the sea, France and Spain. Building of a rack railway began in 1912 but due to interruption during WW1 was not completed until 1924. It runs to the summit from the Col de St.Ignace which is at 169m altitude. The line length is 4.2 km. It was built as a single track of 1000 mm gauge. The lower section presents a continuous climb, actually beginning in the lower station, but beyond the passing place at Trois-Fontaines (555m altitude) the slope reaches 1 in 4 for the remaining 1.4 km to the summit. Since the outset the line has been operated by overhead electrical supply: initially 3000V 25 Hz three- phase but 50 Hz since 1929. The original operating company used to operate a network of 1000 mm gauge tramways in the region: since 1939, however, the La Rhune line has been the sole survivor. The line operated throughout WW2 for the occupying forces.

The rolling stock consists of four-wheel tractor units and passenger carriages plus some maintenance stock. Trains consist of a tractor unit pushing two carriages from below. The carriages have a bogie at one end and a single rack-connected axle at the other. The 17 tonne 160 hp tractor units were built by Brown-Boveri. They are fitted with cog wheels at front and rear to connect with the Strub rack rail situated centrally between the running rails. They are also unusual in having two overhead electrical contact arms positioned both to the front and to the rear. The first pair operate on the uphill journey and the latter pair on return.

The carriage and tractor units are all wooden bodied, and include the original stock supplied to the line when it opened. However, some transfer of stock between lines took place over the years. In 1938 one set was transferred to the Superbagnères line, then when that line closed in 1966, two tractor units were transferred back to La Rhune.

This single-line railway does not have signalling: control is by telephone. Generally, two trains are in service and depart simultaneously from upper and lower termini. A maximum of three two-car trains operate at peak times: two follow one another, passing the third at Trois-Fontaines. Additional stock was obtained from Switzerland in 1995 to increase capacity. The journey time is 30 minutes. A frequent service operates, dictated in part by demand. Trains run all day from May to November as indicated. Outside this period special trains are available to booked groups, and winter operations are maintained in connection with the transmitter station situated at the summit.

The magnificent views and the vintage stock warrant the effort to visit this line. Trains operate through the seasons, giving the possibility of a Spring or Autumn journey. It should be borne in mind, however, that even in summer, breezes can be chilly at the summit, and warm clothing will be required.

89: LE TRAIN TOURISTIQUE GUÎTRES-MARCENAIS

✳ **Guîtres** to **Marcenais**
✤ Ef/IGN110 B6, ✲ Steam & diesel, ⚒ 1435mm, ✱ 13km
☞ Table 401: SNCF Coutras (6km) or SNCF Libourne (15km)
☛ 40km NE of Bordeaux via RN89 to Libourne then RD910. Station: 1km to W of Guîtres
✓ pm. Sun & BH: Begin-May to end-Oct. Also Tues, Thurs & Sat: in July & Aug
✉ TTGM, ancienne gare SNCF, Guîtres, 33230 Coutras, ✆ 57.69.10.69

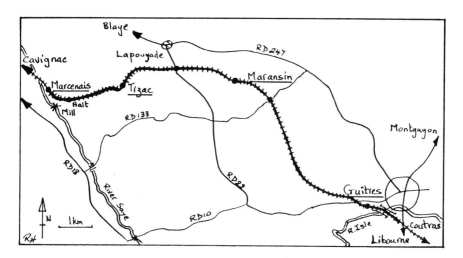

In 1971, SNCF consigned one of its most powerful steam locomotives to the safe keeping of the AATV preservation society. This is the enormous 4-8-2 No 241P9, and remains in the care of the society today, displayed in an external shelter. The society decided to create a museum of local railways, with this enormous locomotive as the main exhibit. A suitable location for the proposed museum was found at Guîtres, a small town with a large 11th to 15th Century abbey, built on a hill overlooking the River Isle.

Guîtres is situated on the old line linking Coutras and Saintes, which was built by the Charantes railway company between 1862 and 1874. The line passed to the control of the "Etat" company in 1878 and formed part of an important north/south route until the Eiffel bridge was opened across the River Dordogne in 1889. From that date the line had only local importance. It lost its passenger services in 1938 and freight in 1965, and was purchased in 1977 by the Gironde *département*. This followed successful tourist train operations by the preservation society: they had purchased three old draisines for this purpose in 1973.

A collection of standard gauge rolling stock has been assembled at Guîtres. In addition to the 4-8-2, there are three small 0-4-0T steam locomotives: a La Meuse of 1924, which operated the first steam trains on the line, and continues to do so; an O & K of 1922, and a SACM built in 1890 which is displayed in unservicable condition outside the station. There are also several draisines of Billard and Smith manufacture, some of which have been de-motorized to act as "baladeuse" style passenger carriages. A Picasso railcar (X 3976, Renault of 1959) and trailer car are used for weekday services during the main season. Historic wagons and carriages and a tricycle track inspection vehicle complete the collection. A set of end-balcony carriages contemporary with the Meuse locomotive are used on the trains.

The 13km section of track used by the TTGM trains is the centre portion of the line from Coutras in the east to Cavignac in the west, which linked the two main lines running north from Bordeaux. The station at Guîtres is a sizeable structure with château characteristics. The line follows a gently twisting route, generally keeping well away from the villages its stations were supposedly built to serve. The countryside is picturesque. This rustic railway is closely encroached upon by hedges and woods in parts, and has all the romance of a Col.Stevens railway. There are two significant structures on the line, a 100m long metal bridge over the River Isle to the east of Guîtres, and a 50m stone bridge across the River Saye at the other end of the route.

This is not a well known line despite having operated for twenty years. The service is generally one return journey from Guîtres on each operating day. An extended break en route gives the opportunity to explore the countryside, visit the picnic site or the mill at Charlot where refreshments are available. The trains runs on to Marcenais to prepare for the return journey.

90: CHEMIN DE FER DES LANDES DE GASCOGNE

❋ **Sabres** to **Marquèze**
✤ Eg/IGN110 D4, ❋ Steam & diesel ⚒ 1435mm ❋ 4km
☞ Table 401: SNCF Labouheyre is 18km from Sabres. Bus service on RN 134
☛ Sabres is on RN134 80km south of Bordeaux
✓ am & pm. Daily: Jun to end-Sept. Also Sat, Sun & BH in May and Oct. Steam: pm Thurs, June to Sept
✉ Ecomusée de la Grande Lande, 40630 Sabres, ✆ 58.07.52.70

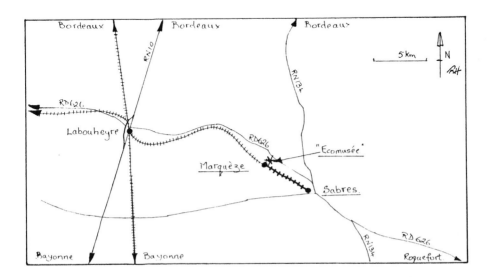

South of Bordeaux is an area of forests covering some 500sq km. This is the Landes de Gascogne Regional Park: the town of Sabres is situated in the centre. The "ecomusée" (a rural life museum) at Marquèze, 4km from Sabres, demonstrates the life which sustained the balance between sheep breeding and forestry until the middle of the nineteenth century.. Marquèze is an early 19th century village which has been completely restored and is operated on traditional lines. There is no road to the village and access is only by train from Sabres. The number of visitors is so great that a 40min interval service is provided.

The railway line used for this service is a section of the 18km branch to Sabres from Labouheyre, one of the many Voies Ferrées des Landes lines which branched off either side of the Midi (now SNCF) main line from Bordeaux to the Spanish border at Hendaye. The Sabres branch was opened in 1890 to carry timber from the forest, cheaply laid on sand ballast and, thanks to the level landscape, with no major engineering works. The line closed in 1969 but was acquired by the regional park administration and reopened over the 4km length from Sabres to Marquèze when the museum opened in 1970. Subsequently services were provided over the 14km stretch from the SNCF station at Labouheyre. This, however, has ceased, and the operating group have moved some of their stock to Labouheyre.

The rolling stock housed at Sabres for this railway is representative of the type of stock previously used on the line. An interesting collection has been built up including a General Electric diesel locomotive, two locotracteurs, a Picasso railcar, draisines and an 0-6-0T steam locomotive: No. 030T1828, a la Meuse of 1903. The railway service is regularly operated by one of the diesel engines. However, on Thursdays in high season the Corpet-Louvet is in operation.

The Sabres-Marquèze railway acts as an integrated part of the living museum. It is a pleasure to experience an occasional steam train offering a genuine public transport service in the 1990's. Because of the sheer extent of the museum it is advisable to take a morning train from Sabres in order to ensure adequate time is available to visit each of the activity sites within the village complex.

91: CHEMIN DE FER DU LAC D'ARTOUSTE

✳ From **La Sagette** (upper station of cable car) to **Lac d' Artouste**
✤ Ei/IGN113 D6, ✿ Diesel, ✦ 500mm, ✱ 8km
☞ Table 410: SNCF Pau then Table 414: SNCF bus (55km) to cable car station at Lac de Fabréges
☛ From Lourdes (60km) or Pau (40km) to Assouste then 15km S on RN134b
✓ am & pm. Daily: end-May to mid/end-Sept
✉ RDSA, 22 ter, rue J-J de Monaix, 64000 Pau, ℭ 59.05.35.69 (Summer)

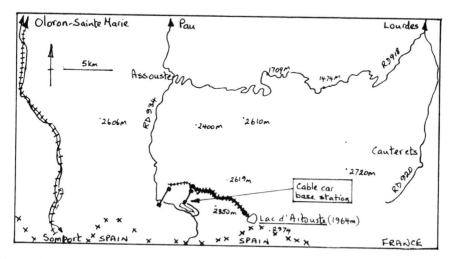

Although the Artouste line was not built as a tourist railway, a more spectacular one would be hard to imagine.

At the beginning of the twentieth century, the Midi railway company decided to electrify its lines wherever hydro-electric power was available. In implementation of this policy, reservoirs were built high in the Pyrennees mountains which form the border between France and Spain. By the end of the 1920's almost 40% of the Midi railway operation was electrified. At this period a power station was constructed at Artouste in the valley of the River Ossau. It was to be supplied by water from Lac d'Artouste, a reservoir built about 1000m above the power station and at about 10km distance, close to the Spanish border. In order to construct the dam, it was necessary to install a cable car from the valley floor to the final altitude of the lake at 2000m and, also, a railway running 8.5km along the side of the valley. The railway was laid on a ledge cut into the rock face mid-way between the mountain peak and the valley floor.

On completion of the construction task in 1932, the Midi company decided not to dismantle the infrastructure but to put it to tourist use. Due to the spectacular nature of the line and the scenery to which it gave access, the project proved an immediate success. In fact, following nationalization of the Midi railways in 1937 SNCF decided to continue to operate the line and renew the track and rolling stock. In 1953 new Billard diesel locomotives were introduced to replace the original Renault machines and in 1957 the very basic original carriages were replaced. The new passenger stock are open bogie carriages with blinds which may be rolled down in the event of inclement weather. The seats are reversed at each end of the line so that passengers face forward on both halves of the journey. Each train has five or six of these twelve-seat carriages. These are usually filled to capacity with up to nine trains in service in high season. The line has been managed by the RDSA company since 1988.

The rolling stock includes thirteen Whitcomb and Billard locotracteurs, fifty-two carriages and a motorized snow plough.

The depot is situated close to the Pic de la Sagette, the upper station of the passenger cable car, and about 1km from the beginning of the line. On the initial section of the line, the view is to the south over the peaks which rise to almost 3000m. Immediately however, a narrow tunnel is entered. On emerging, the train is in the Soussouéou valley. From this point views are to the east with a sheer drop to the left-hand side of the train. For long lengths, the train follows ledges cut in the steep face of the valley with drops of 600m immediately beside the train. Magnificent vistas of the mountains continue throughout the journey.

The journey continues in this fashion for a further 7km. A predetermined break at the terminus permits a walk to the dam or a visit to the buffet. The total time required for the complete trip is three and a half hours. It is advisable to wear warm clothing in appreciation of the altitude (6500 feet). Due to the popularity of this journey, significant waiting may be required at peak times to obtain a place on a train and associated place in a cable car. Early arrival is recommended.

92: TRAIN TOURISTIQUE QUERCYRAIL

❋ From **Cahors** to **Carjac** and **Capdenac**. SNCF bus follows route: Table 445
✛ Gg/IGN110 C11, ❋ Diesel, ⚙ 1435mm, ❋ 71 (46)km
☞ Table 431: SNCF Cahors ☉
☛ 112km N of Toulouse on RN20. Quercyrail trains depart from SNCF Cahors
✓ am & pm.Sun: May to Oct. Also Mon, Thurs & Sats in July & Aug (details below)
✉ Quercyrail, Hôtel de Ville, 46160 Cajac, ✆ 63.40.11.93
✉ Syndicat d'Initiative, place Aristid-Brian, Cahors, ✆ 65.35.09.56

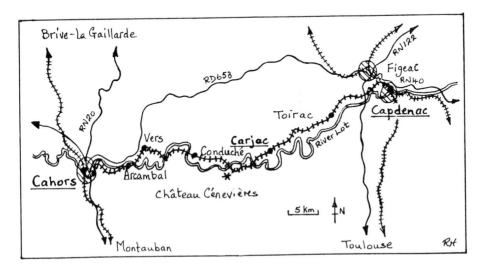

The delightful railway which twists through the meandering valley of the River Lot was finally closed by SNCF in 1989. The line is 71km long and links two through lines running south from Brive to Toulouse. The line has a number of fine civil engineering structures. In all there are fourteen tunnels and six viaducts as the line crosses and re-crosses the river in the narrow valley. The SNCF passenger service has been replaced by a bus service (Table 445) which follows the valley road and is close to the railway throughout its length. From 1984, until SNCF withdrew the final freight service in 1990, an association known as Regiorail operated tourist trains on the line using railcars.

After a lengthy period of negotiations, the *départements* of Aveyron and Lot rented the line in 1993 so that the Regiorail / Train Touristique Quercyrail tourist train service could be re-established. The operation is highly professional with well produced advertising literature. The emphasis is upon preservation of the railway and as a focus for the tourist development of the towns in the valley. This is not a historic train preservation operation. The stock used for the passenger services is beautifully maintained. It comprises 1952 built, Decauville railcar and trailer car (X2425 and XR8232) and railcars X2709/XR7716 which were introduced by SNCF in 1956 for long distance services (Bordeaux-Lyon-Lausanne).

The regular advertised services do not operate along the whole line but over the 46km section from Cahors to Carjac and the 37km section as far as Château Cénevières. Travel along the whole route is possible for pre-arranged groups. It is the longest, and claims with some justification, to be the prettiest preserved railway in France. One train runs on each advertised operating day. Each has a dedicated theme: some with combined rail and boat trips on the River Lot. In 1996 the proposal is for a morning departure from the SNCF station in Cahors on Sundays from May to October and Saturdays in July and August. This makes a three hour journey to Carjac with photographic stops, craft workshop visits and regional food tastings en route. A long lunch time stop at Carjac gives the opportunity for exploration, a leisurely meal or a boat trip. In July and August additional trips depart on Monday and Thursday afternoons from Cahors for a visit to the Château Cénevières.

93: CHEMIN DE FER ET TRAMWAYS DES LACS DE MONCLAR

❈ At **Monclar-de-Quercy**
✧ Gh/IGN114 A2, ✿ Diesel, ⚒ 600mm, ✲ 3km
☞ SNCF Montauban ◉ (20km)
☛ Monclar-de-Quercy is 20k E of Montauban by RD8 via la Salvetat-Belmotot
✓ am & pm. Sat, Sun & BH (Daily for groups): Easter to October
✉ Office de Tourisme, Mairie, 82230 Monclar de Quercy, ✆ 63.30.40.29

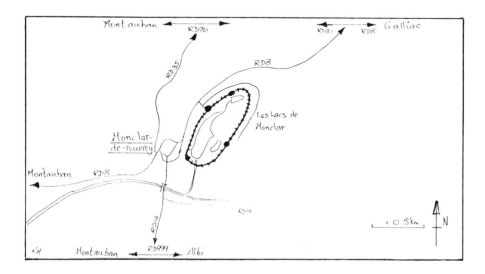

Just to the east of the small town of Monclar-de-Quercy there is a 100 acre leisure park. This is located around some lakes formed by the damming of a tributary of the River Tescounet during the 1970s. The lakes at Monclar are set in a valley amongst the Quercy hills, which rise to about 230m. This is about 100m above the lakes and forms a fine setting for the park.

Since 1987 a narrow gauge railway has gradually been established alongside the lake. However, this is by no means a conventional pleasure park railway. The town council wished to have an unusual attraction. This conformed with the desires of M. Pica & other local railway enthusiasts, who have built some bizarre rolling stock and introduced further unconventional features each year.

The motive power is provided by diesel locomotives: one is an 0-4-0 ex-mine locotracteur operated in its original condition, but another has been disguised as a pseudo steam locomotive. The "steam" locomotive is built in the form of a Garratt articulated engine and is provided with a tender built on the chassis of an old mine wagon. This locomotive is the primary motive power used on the line. Smoke effects are produced by burning material below the chimney.

The passenger stock is perhaps even more unconventional than the fake Garratt. The carriages have been constructed as reduced versions of actual tramcars. Designs from various tramways have been chosen. The pièce-de-résistance is a bogie saloon carriage in the form of a first class Pullman carriage. This beautiful carriage is used as a buffet car. All these vehicles have been built by M. Pica and friends. Each vehicle is of individual design and built upon the chassis of an old mine *berline*.

The track and rolling stock forming the basis of the railway were obtained from a Cévennes coal mine. The line has been built to run along the whole length of the lake from the beach at Baissure Bel Calel through Gare Central past the town to reach the dam at La Glaizo and then run along a local road. The main central station has been built to resemble a period railway structure and incorporates the locomotive and tramcar depot. This, together with its adult sized tramcar carriages, provides the atmosphere of a narrow gauge railway rather than a pleasure park line. All aspects of this railway have been built to an extremely high standard. It is clear that it is operated by true enthusiasts for the entertainment of all members of the family. Well worth a visit.

94: CHEMIN DE FER TOURISTIQUE DU TARN

✳ **St.Lieux-lès-Lavaur** to **Les Martels**
✢ Gh/IGN114 A2, ✽ steam, diesel and diesel/electric, Ⅾ 500mm, ✽ 7km
☞ Tables 444, 450, 451: SNCF St.Sulpice (7km) ◐
☛ From Toulouse 30km by RN88 to St.Sulpice then 8km by RD38 to St.Lieux-les-Lavaur
✓ pm. Sun & BH: Easter to end-October. Also Sat & Mon: mid-Jul to end-Aug
✉ ACOVA, BP 2040, 31018 Toulouse Cedex, ✆ 61.47.44.52

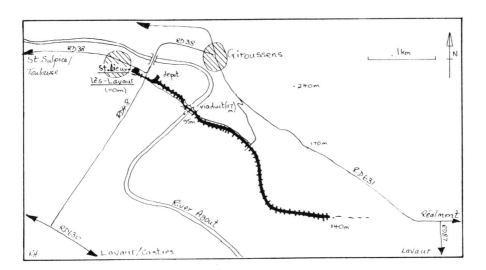

Few reminders of the once extensive network of narrow gauge railways remain in southern France. A notable exception is the CFT du Tarn. In 1975 some enthusiasts in the Toulouse area began the task of building this railway on part of the old trackbed of the Tramways à Vapeur du Tarn. Since then an interesting collection of stock has been assembled, the station facilities at St.Lieux have been developed to present an excellent rural narrow gauge station, and a large depot has been built.

The Tramways à Vapeur du Tarn concern was a small rural network of 600mm gauge railways which reached St.Lieux in 1925. The whole system closed in 1935, but the line through St.Lieux had only a six year existence as its traffic passed to bus operation in 1931. In 1975 the station at St.Lieux-les-Lavaur was threatened with demolition but prompt action by preservationists prevented this. The building and setting have been preserved and retain all the charm and eccentricity of the once common rural narrow gauge railways of France.

The new group have had to reconstruct almost the whole railway infrastructure and obtain stock anew. A gauge of 500mm was chosen. The material preserved includes four steam locomotives: three 0-4-0T Decauvilles (two built in 1931 and one in 1937) and a delightful 0-6-0T Couillet built in Belgium in 1910. At least one steam locomotive is always kept in operational, and immaculate, condition. The line also has three French army WW1 diesel/electric Crochat locomotives and half a dozen ex-industrial diesel and i.c. locomotives together with a locally built draisine. Notwithstanding the immaculate steam engines, the Crochat locomotives are really the delight of this line. Originally built as petrol engines driving six-wheel bogies via an electric generator, during their working life they were converted to diesel-electric operation but the electrical components are original.

The rustic station at St.Lieux incorporates a small loco shed and a ticket office. After leaving the station the train immediately crosses the RD48 Laveur road at an ungated level crossing, and then passes along the centre of the street between houses - a feature typical of the old French rural tramways. Passing the branch into the depot, the line runs in tramway fashion alongside and then along the centre of the single track road including across the bridge over the River Agout. The bridge over the Agout is a notable brick built structure of six arches at 22m above the level of the water, a remarkable structure for an otherwise lightly built tramway.

A museum of narrow gauge railway items has been assembled at St.Lieux.

95: AUTORAIL TOURISTIQUE DU MINERVOIS

✳ **Narbonne** to **Bize-Minervois**
✤ Hh/IGN114 B6, ✳ Diesel ⚓ 1435mm ✳ 20km
☞ Tourist line halt is on rue Paul Vieu, 1km SW of SNCF Narbonne (Tables 432 & 545)
☛ Narbonne is on RN9, RN113 and Autoroute A9(E4) and A61(E49). Halt is to W of town
✓ pm, Sat, Sun & BH: begining July to mid-Sept.
✉ Association des Amis de la 141R1126, 6 rue Cornelle, 11110 Coursan, ✆ 68.27.05.94

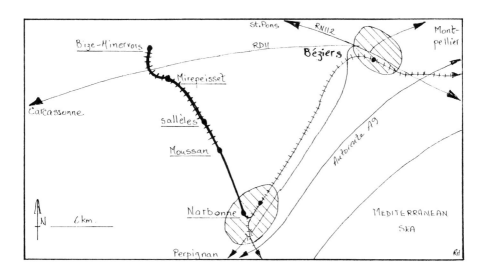

The association which operates these trains was founded in 1980 to preserve the 2-8-2 ex-SNCF locomotive No.141R1126. Then the group turned to the operation of tourist trains with preserved stock on a local line. The idea was, in part, to raise funds for the return of the steam loco to operational condition: this has now been successfully achieved. At that time the 21km line from Narbonne to Bize was used for freight only, on weekdays. Under Government guidance to SNCF, permission was granted for the association to rent the infrastructure to operate a tourist service. The first trains ran in 1983 and have continued every season thereafter.

The railway to Bize was constructed in 1887 to transport wine from the Minervois district. A planned extension to a connection at Labastide on the Castres line was never built. The Bize line lost its passenger service in 1939. Recent freight traffic has consisted of wine, grain and olive products. From Narbonne the branch runs across level countryside, crossing the River Aude on a low 300m long bridge; one of the few major engineering features of this single track line. It runs beside the Robine canal for about 6km and then, after crossing the Canal du Midi, follows a rising route over the final 7km to Bize. The terminal station is on the southern edge of the town. An exhibition of railway equipment and relics is open on tourist train operating days in a preserved railway postal carriage.

The regular Autorail Touristique de Minervois does not start from the SNCF station at Narbonne. The Association have set up a dedicated platform just to the west of the town. "Picasso" railcars (X3846, X3900) and X4028 and trailer car are used to operate the service. These early 1950's railcars are based at Narbonne. The tourist trains are arranged as organized tours with commentary and with scenic stops en-route. Pre-arranged visits are organized to vineyards, an olive oil cooperative or Roman archælogical excavations. Refreshments and souvenirs are available on the train.

In addition to the Narbonne to Bize trains, the operating group also advertise occasional railcar trips on other SNCF lines in the area. These can give opportunities to travel on what are otherwise freight only lines. The whole Narbonne-based set up is a very friendly operation. The number of passengers has remained around 3000 per year, basically restricted by the limited number of trains operated. Additional special trains can be booked in advance by groups at weekends throughout the year. The "Autorail Touristique du Minervois" offers a pleasant way to spend one of the invariable hot and sunny days of a summer weekend in southern France.

96: TRAIN TOURISTIQUE LANGUEDOC ROUSSILLON

✳ **Bédarieux** to **Mons-la-Trivalle** via **Lamalou-les-Bains**
✢ Hh/IGN114 6B, ✳ Diesel, ⚒ 1435mm, ✳ 18km
☞ Table 544: SNCF Bédarieux on line Bézeres to Clermont-Ferrand
☛ Bèdarieux is 70 km W of Montpellier via RN109 and RD908. Station is 2 km S of town
✓ am & pm. Apr to Nov: Sat, Sun & BH: Also Fri in June & Sept. Daily: July & Aug
✉ TTLM, Gare de Lamalou, 34240 Lamalou-les-Bains, ℂ 67.95.77.00

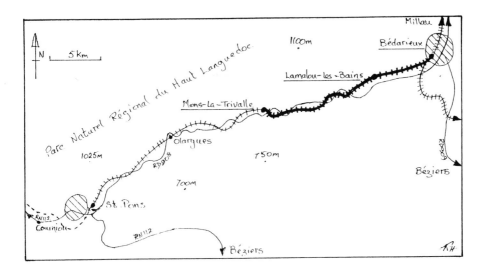

The old SNCF line between Bédarieux and Castres crossed the whole width of what is now the regional nature park of the High Languedoc. This route of almost 100km was opened in stages from 1889. For about 35km from Bédarieux in the east, the route follows the valley of the Rivers Orb and Jaur which flow east towards the Mediterranean. Immediately beyond St.Pons the route tunnels across to the valley of the River Thoré which flows west towards the Atlantic. The eastern half of the route is typified by a series of short tunnels and beautiful light stone viaducts topped with iron balustrades, passing through long stretches of beautiful scenery.

In 1972 SNCF removed the through passenger service, and closed the line to all traffic in 1987. This led to rival schemes to use the route, as a tourist railway or as a cycle track. A partial compromise has been achieved: the track was lifted from the western half of the route as far as St.Pons but remains in place on the 42km from St.Pons to Bédarieux. The 18km section west as far as Mons-la-Trivalle was cleared of encroaching vegetation and opened experimentally for tourist trains in 1992. It is anticipated that an additional 4.5km section, as far as Olargues, could be in use in the near future. The utilization of the whole section to St.Pons remains a possibility.

The initial tourist train operation began with two or three return journeys per day using a diesel locotracteur (Y6424) and two Bruhat carriages all painted in an unconventional pale blue livery. An 0-6-0T steam locomotive (030T8157 *Ilene* was built by SACM in 1952-3) was introduced in the 1993 season. The 1996 season is likely to see services operated by Y6424, and possibly Picasso railcar X3944.

The whole line has a fine and uniform series of structures: stations, bridges and tunnels mouths, with the backdrop of the striking rocky Haut Languedoc mountains. The eastern, lifted, section has many features worthy of attention: most notable perhaps is the 2km long summit tunnel which has a series of air vents on the surface. These unusually each have a rain shelter above. The tunnel is situated just to the west of St.Pons.

The operation is much more accessible to the holiday visitor than many French tourist railways which often operate on Sundays only in high season and in inaccessible locations. The TTLM trains depart from a cross-platform connection at Bédarieux SNCF station and a return service operates, both morning and afternoon, on about 100 days per year. Passengers are taken into some delightful scenery within the wooded and maquis covered mountains. Photographic stops are made en-route. The opportunity is presented to participate in various inclusive excursions from stations along the line including a model railway museum at Bédarieux and caverns and the Héric gorges at Mons. Altogether, this line is a project which deserves to succeed.

97: PETIT TRAIN DE LA CERDAGNE

✳ **Villefranche-de-Conflent** to **Latour-de-Carol** via **Mont-Louis**
✤ Hi/IGN 114 D3, ✹ Electric ⚓ 1115mm ✱ 63km
☞ Tables 436 & 547: SNCF Latour-de-Carol or Villefranche-de-Conflent (via Perpignan)
☛ Latour is on RN20 close to Spanish border. RN116 follows the line.
✓ am & pm, daily. Five return trains per day.
✉ SNCF Gare de Villefranche-Vernet-les-Bains, 66500 Prades ℂ 68.96.09.18

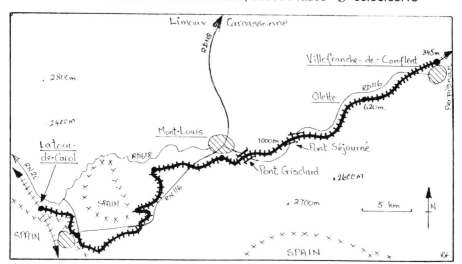

The French national railway, SNCF, continues to operate a narrow gauge line which has survived in the eastern Pyrénées. This mountain range divides France from Spain and rises to over 3000m. The yellow trains still run daily up the 63km line linking Villefranche (on a standard gauge branch from Perpignan) and Latour-de-Carol. Latour is the frontier station on the international trans-Pyrénées line and thus has three gauges of track: the 1115mm of the Cerdagne and also the French and the Spanish standard gauges. Although the Cerdagne train ensures a service for local communities and a useful linking route, it is the leisure market, including the ski resorts along the line, which ensured its survival following the loss of freight traffic after 1974. However, it has been for many years under constant threat of closure. With SNCF under pressure this is still possible. Political pressure from the Catalan nationalists to retain the line is presently effective.

It is a startling line, reaching 1600m along a twisting and turning route punctuated by frequent tunnels and some amazing bridges. From Latour the train passes along the Spanish border and reaches Ur-des-Escaldes via a 350m long curved tunnel. From here to Bourg-Madame the lines passes between two parts of Spain whilst remaining in France. When the timetable allows, a break of journey at Bourg-Madame is recommended: from here a gentle stroll into Puigcerda in Spain is possible. Tight turns and steep gradients lead the train to the summit of the line near Bolquère, which at 1593m is the highest halt on the SNCF network. The downward journey is even more impressive, particularly if a ride is taken in one of the open carriages. Yes - open carriages, just like a fairground ride! The carriages are open topped and open sided. The doors are unlocked. The train rushes through tunnels with walls and roof all within arms reach. The train is running, remember, on third rail electric and at service speed. And all operated by the national rail operator SNCF: not only thrilling, but absolutely amazing.

The line is well known for its civil engineering structures. Two bridges are particularly striking: the 250m long and 80m high Gisclard suspension bridge across the River Têt, and the curved 18 arch and double storey Séjorné Viaduct crossing both river and road. As the line drops towards the well preserved medieval town of Villefranche (415m altitude) the scenery becomes less rugged and the route less tortuous.

The stock is completely original, being built in 1908 for the opening of the line which took place in stages from 1910 to 1924. Electric traction (850V dc) was selected, as hydroelectric power was plentiful and cheap. The line acted as a test-bed at a time when electric traction for French mainline railways was being assessed by the Midi company. Today the modernised power cars act also as passenger stock, usually operating in pairs with a trailer carriage between. They are required to climb gradients of up to 1 in 17. In summer the open carriages with their wooden bench seats are a must - for the sun and for one of the most startling rail journeys in Europe. It is a joy to experience: there is certainly nothing like it in Britain.

98: TRAIN À VAPEUR DES CÉVENNES

✳ From **Anduze** to **St.Jean-du-Gard** via **Bambouseraie**
✢ Ig/IGN114 A9, ✿ Steam and diesel, ⚒ 1435mm, ✱ 13.2km
☞ Table 543: SNCF Alès (18km) then bus (not Sundays)
☛ Anduze is 45km from Nîmes by RD907 or 50km by RD999, RN110, RD907 via Lédignan
✓ am & pm. Sat, Sun & BH: end-Mar to begin-Nov. Also Daily (except some Mons): Apr to end-Aug, and Tues & Weds in Sept.
✉ CITEV, gare du TVC, BP17, 30270 St.Jean-du-Gard, ✆ 66.85.13.17

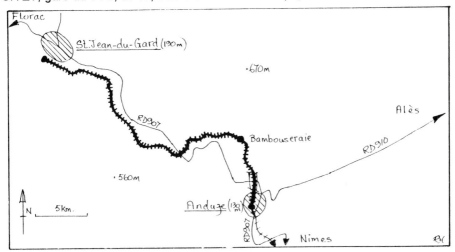

The Cévennes form the southernmost part of the rocky plateau of the Central Massif. It is a region of broad-leaved wooded hillsides and deep valleys. The area has developed the tourist potential of its natural attractions: beautiful scenery, river and country sports, and summer sunshine. Over the past ten years the steam train running along the Gardon valley has developed into one of the major attractions of the region, carrying over 110 000 passengers per year. The success is probably due to the almost daily operation of steam (and diesel) trains over a long season. This is quite exceptional for a French standard gauge tourist railway.

The line from Anduze to St.Jean-du-Gard was operated by the PLM company in 1909 as an extension of its Anduze branch. Passenger services only lasted until 1940: freight service ended in 1977. Just before SNCF commenced lifting the track, its potential for tourist train services was realized, and the local authorities have subsequently purchased the railway. Operation of the train continues to be developed by the CITEV preservation group, based at Conflans-Jarny, where it has preserved a number of steam and diesel locomotives including three 2-8-2s, Nos. 141R73, 141R568, 141R1332, and 2-8-0 No 140C271. This last locomotive was built by North British in 1917. It operated the Anduze to St.Jean tourist trains, almost single-handed, for some years. It was replaced by 0-8-0T No 040TA137. More recently the Train a Vapeur des Cévennes has been operated by a fine ex-colliery 0-6-0T locomotive No 030T8158 built by SACM. Other stock on the line includes two large Schneider diesel locomotives and an unusual Renault single unit railcar No VH24 built in 1934. The first and last trains each day are diesel-operated.

The line from Anduze to St.Jean climbs up the valley almost all the whole way. On leaving Anduze station the train immediately enters an 833m long tunnel. As the locomotive is working hard the atmosphere in the open carriages can be badly affected by smoke. For this reason it is recommended that seats in the closed carriages are selected for the uphill journey. The metal four-wheel carriages have end balconies which enable the atmosphere to be appreciated to best advantage. On emerging from the tunnel, the train passes along the hillside behind the town and then crosses the steel lattice bridge across the wide river valley.

The halt at La Bambouseraie is soon reached. This is the location of a major local attraction: a park of oriental vegetation. A shuttle service of diesel railcars is provided between here and Anduze. The steam train continues to thread its way through the pretty countryside into the mountains, passing disused halts on the way. The line has four stone viaducts, including the beautifully situated Gardon de Malet viaduct which gives lovely views up the rocky valley clothed in chestnut trees.

At St. Jean-du-Gard station a café and picnic site await the traveller. Close by are museums of vintage cars, of telephones, and of the Cévennes countryside.

99: MUSÉE DES TRANSPORTS DE LA BARQUE

✳ Situated at **La Barque-Fuveau**
✣ Kh/IGN115 D5, ✻ Diesel (& steam), ✾ Various gauges, principally 600mm, ✱ 1.8km
☞ Table 522: SNCF Gardanne (8km) or SNCF Aix-en-Provence (12km)
☛ At SNCF freight yard, 12km SE of Aix-en-Provence via RN7 to Le Canet and then RN96
✓ am & pm: Sun & BH all year. Steam operation (pm): third Sunday of each month except Aug
✉ Musée de Transports, gare de La Barque-Fuveau, 13970 La Barque, ✆ 91.98.15.91 (eve.)

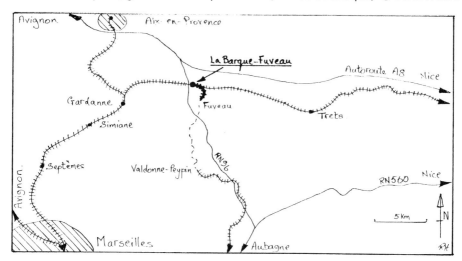

Two SNCF rail lines connect Marseilles and the Rhône valley with the resort towns of the Riviera through to the Italian border. The coastal route via Aubagne is open to all traffic. The inland route remains open only for freight traffic. This line branches from the Marseilles to Aix-en-Provence line at Gardanne. It rejoins the coastal route at Carnoules about 80km to the east. La Barque-Fuveau station is situated at the site of the old junction where a line left the Gardanne-Carnoules route to form a link with the coastal line at Aubagne. This line only survives in its southern section: services over the northern 10km section ceased in 1969. The junction and northern section of line have been removed.

It was also in 1969 that the museum collection of historic transport items was established. The freight yard and goods shed at La Barque are used for this purpose. A maze of railway tracks has been laid in order to display or demonstrate the various items of rolling stock preserved here in excellent condition. The following gauges are accommodated: 400, 500, 525, 600, 640, 750, 800, 1000, and 1435mm. A 1435mm connection to the SNCF line is retained. The majority of these tracks are of minimal length. The 600mm gauge line, however, is about 2km long, having been laid through the museum site and then along part of the trackbed of the old standard gauge line towards Aubagne. It has five halts along its short length.

A large collection of railway equipment has been assembled at La Barque. Much of this has been obtained from industrial sites in the region. The standard gauge items include an 0-4-0T Henschel steam locomotive which was built in 1911, two rail mounted cranes, a Berliet diesel locotracteur of 1926, and an ex-SNCF postal carriage. Over one hundred and fifty 600mm gauge items are on display. These include eight diesel locotracteurs (Pétolat, Decauville, Deutz, LLD, Berry and a Plymouth regauged from 500mm). Subject only to the weather, a passenger train service is provided each Sunday on the 600mm line. A long train of four-wheel baladeuses has been used for this operation for many years. Recently however a train of 6 bogie carriages has been built, which give a more comfortable ride.

Well over a hundred other items of rolling stock are exhibited. These include mining railway items, a stretcher wagon, tank wagons, rail mounted cranes, hopper wagons, flood light wagon, snow plough, two pedal cycle draisines and some tramway equipment. An old trolleybus from the Aix to Marseille line has been set up as a cinema. Vintage transport films are shown on museum opening days. An ex-PLM platform crane from the Aix freight yard has been installed on the platform at La Barque.

This collection of privately owed items is maintained in excellent condition and forms the basis of a very interesting visit. The 600mm gauge line adds active interest. In addition slide presentations are given at certain times, and once a month a local group of model railway engineers operates steam trains on the 127mm (5 inch) track circuit. Special open days are arranged on advertised days each year.

41. The narrow gauge Cerdagne line [97] at the Sejourne viaduct. This structure has 18 arches 200 metres above the river Tet. It consists in fact of two tiers of arches, and is twice as tall as suggested by the photograph!. →
(Photo: French Railways)

42. ↓ On the 600mm gauge La Barque railway [99], a 20hp Berry locotracteur pulls a long train into the "Vieux Chene" halt.
(Photo: J Pollacchi)

43. ↑ Displayed at the Musée Provençal des Transports Urbains et Regionaux at La Barque [99] are five 600mm diesel locotracteurs: a Plymouth, a Berry, two Deutz, and a Petolat. *(Photo: J Pollacchi)*

44. ↓ The Calvi terminus on the Chemin de Fer de la Corse [101]. In 1988 Renault ABH8 railcar 201 and two trailers operated the shuttle service to Île-Rousse. *(Photo: R. Haworth)*

45. The two cars of the Pau funicular [110] are seen at the midway point. The track gauge is one metre. The cars have double-flanged wheels on the outer sides, and rollers on the inner sides, to avoid the need for moveable switches.

→

(Photo: R. Haworth)

46. ↓ At Puget-Théniers on the CdF de Provence [118] is the depot for the steam tourist operation. Seen here are the ex-Reseau Breton 4-6-0T No. E327 built by Fives-Lille, and the Mallet 2-4-6-0T No. E211 built by Henschel.
(Photo: J Banaudo)

47. ↑ The Ecomusée at Breil-sur-Roya [120], between Nice and the Italian border, has a good collection of railway stock, including 2-8-2 No. 141R1108. *(Photo: B. Duchesne)*

48. ↓ A feature of the Train à Vapeur de la Vendée is the link with the Hôtel de France at Mortagne-sur-Sèvre [122]. A high-class restaurant car service is available, using this former Orient Express dining coach. Trains stop on the Barbin Viaduct during the meal. *(Photo: TVV)*

100: CHEMINS DE FER DE PROVENCE

✳ From **Nice** to **Digne-les-Bains** via **La Tinée, Puget-Théniers, Entrevaux** and **Annot.**
✤ Lh/IGN115 C10, ✳ Diesel, ⚐ 1000m ✳ 151km
☞ Nice CP station is 0.5km N of SNCF Nice. Digne is served by coach from SNCF St.Auban.
☛ Parking at Nice. Line follows RN202 and RN 85
✓ CP Diesel service daily, all year: around four trains per day.
✉ CP, 40 rue Clément-Roassal, 06004 Nice Cedex 1, ✆ 93.88.34.72

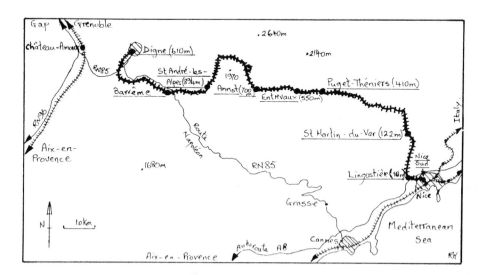

The Alpes-Maritimes in Provence form the SW edge of the Alpine range. They present a range of mountains rising to some 3000m, deeply cut by gorges and narrow valleys formed by rivers flowing to the Mediterranean. Across this mountain range runs the metre gauge Chemins de Fer de Provence (CP). This 151km line is still in genuine public service: it is the last section to remain of the once extensive network of lines of the CF de la Sud de France. It runs from the coast at Nice through the mountains to Digne. The line was constructed in stages between 1890 and 1911.

The line starts from Nice close to sea level and immediately tunnels across to the Var valley which it then follows for the next 70km as far as St.Benoit. Along this section, the line follows the river closely, and crosses it at various points. The width of the valley steadily decreases until it become a narrow gorge. At this point the railway actually runs above the water, the track hanging from the rock walls. Beyond St.Benoit the line cuts through numerous tunnels to gain height. It reaches an altitude of 1022m near Verdon. In all, the line crosses twenty masonry viaducts, a dozen metal bridges, including one of 120m length over the River Bléone, and passes through more than two dozen tunnels. Gradients reach 1 in 30, and curves are as tight as 150m radius, making for an exciting ride. It is a most impressive railway, providing access to the skiing resorts in winter and to the mountains for rambling in summer.

For a metre gauge line to survive as public transport service into the 1990's is remarkable. This survival has not been achieved without considerable difficulty. The future of the line is perpetually precarious. On 5 November 1994 the line was destroyed by a massive storm. Remarkably, it has all been rebuilt. By August 1995 services were restored over all but the 14km section between Entrevaux and Annot. Through services between Nice and Digne are expected to recommence in February 1996.

CP services are operated by a range of diesel railcars and also coaching stock hauled by bogie diesel locomotives. Various elderly Renault (1936-42), Billard (1955-59) and CFD (1971-77) and a modern set built by Soulé in 1984 operate services. Although purchased for the prestige "Alpazar" service linking Nice with the Alpine resorts (via a change to SNCF services at Digne), the Soulé railcars have been employed on the Nice suburban service. The decision to use them only on these short shuttle journeys followed commissioning difficulties. The diesel locomotives are also used for track work and haulage of freight stock. The various locomotives were built by CFD Montmirail works, Brissonneau & Lotz and Henschel. The CP diesel operation is a regular, daily, public service operation. Tourist steam trains operate on the centre section between Puget-Théniers and Annot during the summer - see **118.**

101: CHEMIN DE FER DE LA CORSE

※ Two lines: **Bastia** to **Ajaccio** via **Ponte-Leccia**. **Calvi** to **Ponte-Leccia** via **Ile Rousse**
✤ Ni/IGN116 A4, ✽ Diesel ⅋ 1000mm ✱ 230km
☞ By air from Gatwick (GB), Paris, Nice, or Marseille
☛ Ferry from Nice, Marseille, Toulon, Genoa (I) or Sardinia (I)
✓ am and pm. Daily all year. 6 trains per day.
✉ BP 170, 20294 Bastia, Corsica ✆ 95.31.06.00

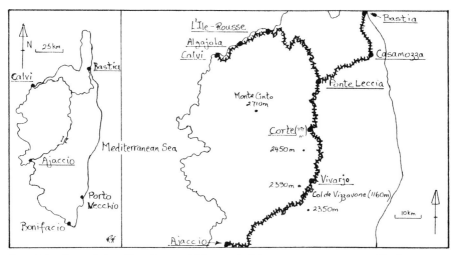

Corsica retains the majority of its railways which were built between 1878 and 1935. The final section of line along the eastern shoreline from Casamozza to Porte Vecchio had a very short existence: it was not reopened after WW2 damage. The rest of the network (Bastia-Ponte Leccia-Corte-Ajaccio and Calvi-Ile Rousse-Ponte Leccia) is in good heart with regular year round passenger services and freight operations. The system has been operated by SNCF since 1983. SNCF timetable 599 gives details of the passenger services.

Corsica is in essence a mountain range rising out of the Mediterranean between France and Italy. The railway runs through and across the mountains. It rises to virtually 1000m, starting from sea level at each of its three terminal points.

The line from Calvi to Ile Rousse follows the northern shore of the island. This is an area of seaside resorts. The railway here is operated as a frequent shuttle service, the "Tramway de la Balagne", which is grafted onto the regular Calvi to Ponte-Leccia services. This section of the route runs right beside the beach in places, close to the hotels but also runs on cliffs high above the sea. After Ile-Rousse the line heads into the hills. It twists and turns between short tunnels reaching 450m altitude at Novella. At Ponte-Leccia, a junction is made with the main route from Bastia to Ajaccio.

The train leaves the northern terminus via the 1422m long Torreta Tunnel. It then runs along the coastal plain to Casamozza. This section of the line is operated as a commuter service into Bastia. Beyond Cassamozza the line heads away from the sea following the valley of the River Golo, crossing the river three times on its way to Ponte Leccia (200m). From the junction here, the line towards Ajaccio begins to climb to 400m at Corte, 475m at Vecchio and 905m at Vizzavona. This section of the route is the most impressive. Between Corte and the Vizzavona summit, the train takes a dozen tunnels, as many viaducts and bridges (including the 140m long, 100m high, Vecchio Viaduct built by Eiffel) and what can only be described as hairpin bends. At this height the line runs along the edge of sheer mountains, cutting through picturesque gorges. The descent to Ajaccio, after the 4km long Vizzavona Tunnel, follows the valley of the River Gravona and is generally less spectacular.

The services have been provided by a varied fleet of diesel railcars for the past forty years. The track and stock have been renewed in recent years. On the main, north-south line, eight modern Soulé twincar sets operate the service. Some of the older railcars survive however, including for the moment four 1950 vintage Renault ABH powercars, CFD railcars, and Billard power and trailer cars built in 1938 and 1949. Freight and works trains are operated by CFD bogies diesel locomotives.

These are a delightful series of lines in magnificent scenery and with guaranteed Mediterranean sun. The railway is clearly destined to survive for many years. This should not be a reason for putting off a visit to the "Scented Isle" but a reason to return again: it is a perfect holiday destination.

102: SNCF LINE BAYONNE TO ST. JEAN-PIED-DE-PORT

✳ **Bayonne** to **St.Jean-Pied-de-Port** (SNCF Table 417)
✤ Dh/IGN113 C3 to C4, ✻ Electric 1500V dc, ⚥ 1435mm, ✻ 50km
☞ Tables 403 & 410: SNCF Bayonne
☛ Bayonne is on RN10 35km N of the Spanish border. St.Jean is to SE via RD932 & RD918
✓ am & pm. Daily: All year
✉ Gare SNCF Bayonne, place Periere, 64100 Bayonne ✆ 59.46.81.63
✉ Gare SNCF, rue du 11 November, 64220 St.Jean-Pied du-Port ✆ 59.55.50.50

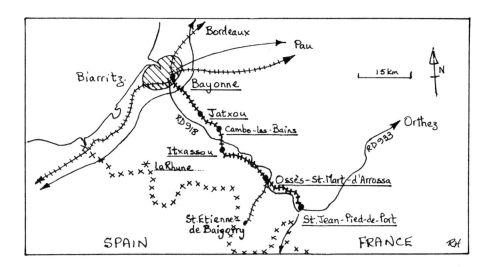

The SNCF train to St.Jean-Pied-de-Port makes a convenient and pleasant means of entering the foothills of the western Pyrenees from the Atlantic coast resorts of south-western France. The route is picturesque rather than outstanding.

As it leaves Bayonne, the main line to Spain swings round behind the town and crosses the River Adour before entering a tunnel. At the end of the tunnel, the lines to Puyoo and to St.Jean-Pied-de-Port turn off the main line. Each of the lines is electrified as a result of an early decision to utilise hydroelectric power for lines close to the Pyrenees. That to St.Jean reaches the valley of the River Nive via a further tunnel. The valley does not narrow until Cambio-les-Bains is reached. This is the heart of the Basque language area of France. Village and station names are distinctive: Itxassou and Jatxou are examples. In this area, the line is passing through the wide valley where the river meanders through reed beds, where marsh harriers can be seen hunting. This is an introduction to the large birds of prey (eagles, vultures etc.) which are commonly seen in the higher Pyrenees.

Between Cambo and St.Martin-d'Arrossa, the river and railway enter a narrow defile through hills which rise to 2000 feet. Here the line passes close to the Spanish border. St.Martin is the junction for the short branch to St.Etienne-de-Baigorry. This has lost its passenger service: an SNCF bus service is available (Table 418).

After 10km of similar scenery, the valley opens out once more as the train approaches the unspoilt terminal station at St.Jean-Pied-de-Port. Both the station and town are worth exploring before the return journey. St.Jean is a small town with a history closely linked with the pilgrim route into Spain. The old town is walled with a citadel. It is only a five minute walk from the station along rue Renaud. The river is crossed by an old stone bridge and flanked by interesting houses.

103: SNCF LINE TOULOUSE TO RODEZ AND RODEZ TO CAPDENAC

✳ **Toulouse** to **Albi** and **Rodez** (SNCF Table 451) and **Rodez** to **Capdenac** (SNCF Table 450)
✢ Gh to Hg/IGN114 B1 to IGN 111 K2, ✳ Diesel, 🚃 1435mm, ✳ 158km
☞ SNCF Toulouse-Matabiau
☛ Rodez is 155km NE of Toulouse via RN88. Albi is 75km from Toulouse via RN88
✓ am & pm. Daily: All year.
✉ Gare SNCF Toulouse-Matabiau, boulevard P. Semard, 31000 Toulouse ✆ 61.62.50.50
✉ GareSNCF Albi-Ville, place Gare, 81000 Albi ✆ 63.54.50.50
✉ Gare SNCF, Avenue de Bordeaux, 12000 Rodez ✆ 65.42.50.50

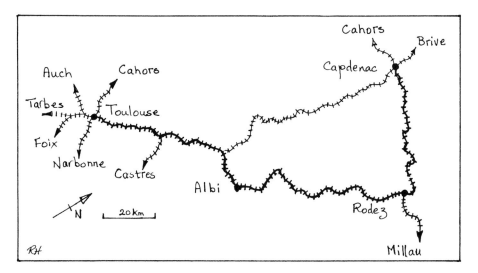

Rodez is a medium sized town with a large sandstone cathedral built on a hill top in the centre of the town. Old town houses crowd below the cathedral. Rodez is the junction of three railway routes: From Toulouse via Albi, from Brive via Capdenac and (now mainly freight) from Sévérac-le-Château on the Clermont-Ferrand to Béziers route.

The town is situated at an altitude of about 2000 feet. Each of the routes involves climbs into the hills. The line from Toulouse follows the wide flat valley of the River Tarn as far as Tessonnières where the direct line to Capdenac heads north. Seventeen km further on the train reaches Albi, another old town with a large cathedral which overshadows the station. Beyond Albi the line crosses the Tarn then strikes north and immediately begins to climb. The route is through an old coal mining area as far as Carmaux.

The line rises some 250m in the next 20km but the X2800 class railcar takes it in its stride. The crossing of the River Viaur is a delight. The train slows and then the country suddenly gives way to a massive trough, with the river far below. This enormous steel lattice arch is the greatest in France at 230m between the support pillars and a track height almost 120m above the river. The train eases its way across. The line then rises to cross the Causse de Limogne and finally swings round the town to enter Rodez. The station has an overall roof and has recently had its facilities improved. There are no trains from Rodez during the extended lunch period.

The route north from Rodez quickly leaves the Toulouse line and crosses the Causse du Comtal. This plateau ends abruptly, and the line makes a lengthy twisting descent hugging the edge of the hillside. There are good views across the country ahead. Before reaching the River Lot the line passes Cransac, another old mining town. It is set in a rural area. The line now follows he south bank of the River Lot and joins the line from Toulouse via Tessonnières just before entering Capdenac station. Capdenac is at the eastern end of the tourist train line from Cahors **[92]**

The highlight of this journey must be the spectacular crossing of the Viaduc de Viaur but the journey has much of interest throughout its varied route. A circular journey is practical in one day: Toulouse, Rodez, Capdenac, Toulouse. A lunch break at Rodez is recommended and probably unavoidable. If this is your intention you should be mindful that the town is situated on the hill high above the station and strenuous walking will be necessary.

104: LE PIC DU JER FUNICULAR

✺ From **Lourdes** to **Le Pic du Jer**
✤ Eh/IGN113 C7, ✲ Funicular, ⚒ 1000mm, ✱ 1.11km
☞ Table 410: SNCF Lourdes (2.5km) Direct bus connection available.
☛ Lourdes is 40km SE of Pau via RD937. Funicular to south of town. Parking adjacent.
✓ am & pm. Daily: Begin-Jan to mid-Nov
✉ Le Funicular du Pic du Jer, 59 ave Francis Lagardère 65100 Lourdes, ✆ 62.94.00.41

The rocky and wooded mountainsides overlooking Lourdes form excellent viewing points over the town and the Pyrénnées. A funicular was opened to the Pic du Jer, a 948m high point to the south of the town, in 1900. The carriages were renewed in 1950. This metre gauge single track system rises a total of 470m with an average incline of 1 in 2 (max. 1 in 1.8). The line is dead straight except at the lower end. Here there is a wide curve just before the line enters an unlined rock tunnel, which is immediately followed by an elegant masonry viaduct. This is broadened in the centre, which is also the centre of the line, to accommodate the passing place for the two carriages. The line is in cuttings for most of the route so, except for the excellent vistas from the viaduct, the views are not generally available until the summit, which is a 10 minute walk from the upper station.

105: LANNEMEZAN HOSPITAL RAILWAY

✺ At **Lannemezan** psychiatric hospital
✤ Fh/IGN113 C9, ✲ Diesel, ⚒ 600mm, ✱ 0.8km
☞ Table 410: SNCF Lannemezan (1.5km)
☛ Lannemezan is 37km E of Tarbes via RN117. The hospital is on this road 2km to the E
✓ pm. Sun & school holidays
✉ Syndicat d'Initiative, place de la République, 65300 Lannemezan, ✆ 62.98.08.31

Since 1958 the train which runs in the grounds of the psychiatric hospital at Lannemezan has given rides to the public each Sunday and throughout the school holidays. The line is of 600mm gauge Decauville portable track and runs for almost a kilometre. It is a single track with a loop at each end to enable the train to reverse. The route through the grounds features a lake, bridge and tunnel, which also acts as the storage for the rolling stock. This consists of a small four-wheel locotracteur, with a body somewhat in the style of a steam locomotive, and a train of four-wheel baladeuses. The site is located at the junction of RN117 and RD929, 2km to the east of the town.

106: LE TRAIN TOURISTIQUE DE LUCHON

✺ From SNCF **Luchon** to the **leisure park** at the aerodrome lake
✤ Fi/IGN113 D9, ✲ Diesel, ⚒ 400mm, ✱ 0.9km
☞ Table 437: SNCF Luchon ☉
☛ Luchon is situated in the central Pyrennées 90km SE of Tarbes via RN117 & RN125
✓ pm. Daily: Begin-Apr to mid-Oct
✉ Hotel de Ville, 31110 Luchon, ✆ 61.79.32.22 or 61.79.20.22

The elegant town of Luchon-Bagnères is situated at an altitude of 640m. Completely surrounded by mountains, it has been a spa for many years and more recently, a resort with an associated winter sports centre at Superbagnères (altitude 2260m) about six kilometres to the south. The development of its tourist attractions has included the construction of a 400mm gauge railway by the local authority. Since 1993 this has offered visitors a pleasant ride from the town along the bank of the rivers Orne and Pique to the town park at the Lac de l'Aérodrome. The park has a lake with beach, boating and fishing. Other amusements include various games and a restaurant. The journey starts from a newly built station on the northern edge of the town. This is situated close to the SNCF station. The single track line has a loop at each end and a passing place half-way along the route. A twin car diesel railcar and baladeuse are used for the operation, with a total capacity of 48 passengers.

107: FUNICULAR DE BARÈGES

❋ From **Barèges** to **Pic d'Ayré**
✥ Fi/IGN113 D8, ❋ Funicular, ⚒ 1000mm, ❋ 1.85km
☞ Table 412: SNCF Barèges (SNCF bus ex-Lourdes)
☛ Barèges is 40km S of Lourdes via RN21, RD921 and RD918
✓ am & pm. Daily: June to September and December to April
✉ Régie Municipale Touristique et Sportive, 65120 Barèges, ✆ 62.97.68.26

Barèges is a spa town and winter sports resort situated in the foothills of the central Pyrennees at an altitude of 1230m. A funicular from the town to a local mountain peak was opened in 1948. This was renovated in 1980 and passengers are now carried in a very modern glass-sided carriage. The metre gauge single track line has been retained with its very narrow support structures. The view from the carriage thus is unimpeded by the bridge structure and gives superb vistas and a great sensation of height from the viaducts. The altitude at the Pic d'Ayré is 2055m, giving a wide panorama over the central Pyrennees, including the Pic du Midi and the Luz Valley. The line has an average inclination of 1 in 2.5, numerous viaducts and a tunnel.

108: CHEMIN DE FER TOURISTIQUE DU MARTEL

❋ **St.Denis-près-Martel** (the SNCF station for St.Denis-lès-Martel) to **Martel**
✥ Gg/IGN110 B11, ❋ Diesel, ⚒ 1435mm, ❋ 6.5km
☞ Table 450: SNCF St.Denis-près-Martel (Lot)
☛ Martel is 33km S of Brive via RN20 & RN140. St.Denis is 6km E of Martel
✓ Time & dates to be announced
✉ CFTHQ, c/o M P Condeville, 27b rue H Cloppet, 78110 Le Vésinet, ✆ 30.53.12.59

The group called the CFT du Haut Quercy are preparing for the operation of tourist trains from St.Denis-près-Martel to Martel on a 6.5km section of the disused SNCF line which used to link the Brive to Capdenac line at St.Denis with the Paris-Brive-Toulouse route at Souillac. The group hope that the operation will be gradually extended westwards beyond Martel. From St.Denis, the line climbs up the scarp rising out of the deep valley of the River Dordogne. There are three short tunnels on the run to Martel. The line is cut through the rocks of the valley side in spectacular fashion. Beyond Martel the route runs across the plateau of the Périgord Noir, at an altitude of about 400m, before the tunnel at Lauméde and the magnificent stone viaduct at Souillac. CFTHQ has three draisines stored in operational condition in readiness for tourist trains, once the track and authority for use of the line are ready. Initial tourist trains are anticipated in 1996. With the line running along a cornice overlooking the Dordogne, this should be a magnificent trip. The purchase of the infrastructure from SNCF by the local authority should guarantee a secure future for this promising operation.

109: GROTTES DE LACAVE

❋ At **Lacave** near **Souillac**
✥ Gg/IGN110 C11, ❋ Battery electric, ⚒ 600 mm, ❋ 0.5 km
☞ Table 431: SNCF Souillac (10km) or SNCF Roc-Amadour-Padirac ⊙ (12km)
☛ Lacave is on RD43, 45km S of Brive-la-Gaillarde via RN20 to Souillac
✓ am & pm. Daily: April to October
✉ Grottes de Lacave, 46200 Souillac, ✆ 65.37.87.03

Tributaries of the river Dordogne flowing south west from the Central Massif have dissolved the lime stone rocks and created natural caverns. Many of these have been opened to the public. The caves at Lacave are particularly renowned for stalactites and underground river formations. Access is from the floor of the gorge. A horizontal narrow gauge railway takes visitors directly into the hillside for about half a kilometre. This is a single track railway totally within a narrow bare rock tunnel. There are no passing places or branches although two trains operate simultaneously. Each consists of two open topped bogie carriages with a small Fenwick battery locomotive situated in the middle. On reaching the end of the train ride, visitors enter a lift. Somewhat suprisingly, this takes them *up* to the caves.

110: PAU FUNICULAR

❊ Between Avenue Jean Biray and Place Royale, **Pau**
✤ Dh/IGN113 C6, ❊ Electric funicular, ⚒ 1000mm, ❊ 0.12km
☞ Tables 410: SNCF Pau. Funicular station is immediately opposite the SNCF station
☛ From Biarritz/Bayonne, Pau is 110km E via RN117
✓ pm. Daily all year. Also am. Mon to Fri
✉ Office de Tourisme, place Royale, 64000 Pau ✆ 50.27.27.08

Pau is an elegant university city which is small enough for its principal sites to be visited on foot. The funicular (no charge) brings one directly from the large SNCF station to the top of the cliff upon which the old town is built. The upper station is on the late 19th century Boulevard des Pyrénnées. This is a long promenade running on a terrace from which there are superb views over the mountains and also over the cliff gardens. Along this boulevard are the principle buildings of the town including the Chateau de Pau.

The funicular is virtually straight. It has two identical closed cars. The track is single at the two stations but almost immediately begins to separate into two tracks to permit the cars to cross at the centre point. As a result, two-thirds of the length of the line is formed of the passing loop. The track is supported on steel trestles giving the whole the appearance of a temporary structure. This is in contrast to the stations, solidly built in classical style in stone. The lower station is situated directly opposite the SNCF station across bridge over the River Ousse.

111: SNCF GORGES DE LA CÈRE LINE

❊ **St. Denis-près-Martel** (the SNCF station for St.Denis-lès-Martel) to **Aurillac**
✤ Hg/IGN111 H1, ❊ Diesel, ⚒ 1435mm, ❊ 76km
☞ Table 450: SNCF St.Denis-près-Martel, SNCF Miécaze or SNCF Aurillac
☛ Aurillac is 160 km SW of Clermont-Ferrand via RN 89 & RD922.
✓ am & pm. Daily (SNCF timetable 556). Fri only through sleeper from Paris
✉ SNCF Gare de St.Denis-près-Martel, 46600 Martel, ✆ 55.23.50.50

The single-track SNCF line running east from St.Denis follows the valleys of the Dordogne, Cère and Authre along the whole route to Aurillac. The line gives access to the group of SNCF operated lines in the mountainous region of Cantal right in the centre of France. It is a particularly picturesque line and the section between Bretenoux-Biars and Miécaze runs through the grand Cère gorges. The nature of this line is indicated by the two dozen tunnels in this 40km stretch, which is well away from encroachment by roads: the railway fighting its own battle with the scenery. SNCF offer up to half a dozen trains per day including a weekend sleeper. A perfect line to ride to experience some the best scenery in France in comfort and gain acccess to the network of lines around the Cantal.

113: CHEMIN DE FER TOURISTIQUE CAUSSE ET ROUGIER

✳ **Tournemire** to **St. Affrique,** and **L'Hospitalet-du-Largac**
✤ Ih/IGN114 A6, ✽ Diesel, 🐇 1435mm, ✳ 16km + 12km
☞ Table 544: SNCF Tournemire on the Clermont-Ferrand to Béziers line
☛ Tournemire is 100km NW of Montpellier via RN109, RN9 to l'Hospitalet, then RD23
✉ Chemin du Fer Causse et Rougier, gare SNCF de Tournemire, 12250 Roquefort
NOTE: Regular operation during 1996 is unlikely.

Tournemire was a railway cross-roads amongst wooded hills at around an altitude of about 500m. Based here, the CFT Causse et Rougier group have been operating a Picasso railcar for a number of years offering weekend railtrips. These have at various times operated over different lines in the area. The railcar used is X3944 repainted in white with a distinctive large butterfly motif. Other stock associated which may be used include a vertical boilered 0-4-0T Cockerill and Picasso X3968. Eastwards a military line runs towards l'Hospitalet-du-Larzac. Plans are centred on establishing regular tourist trains on this line which tunnels across to the valley of the River Cernon, then follows the valley sides via numerous tunnels and viaducts. Authority to utilize this line for regular tourist train operations has yet to be established. The line westward from Tournemire to St. Affrique has delightful viaducts set amongst deciduous forests and could make a superb tourist railway, but the track is in inadequate condition for passenger trains. For the present therefore, regular trains are not operating until the necessary authority and funding have been obtained. During 1995 some trains were operated successfully on the military line: these took place on a few days only. Regular operation may appear by 1997.

114: LA GROTTE DES DEMOISELLES

✳ **Grotte des Demoiselles** at Saint-Bauzille-de-Putois
✤ Ih/IGN114 A8, ✽ Funicular, 🐇 900mm, ✳ 0.16km
☞ Table 545: SNCF Montpellier (40km) then bus
☛ The caves are 40km N of Montpellier via RD986 to St.Bauzille, then 3km E by local road
✓ am & pm. Daily. All year
✉ La Grotte des Fées, 34190 St. Bauzille-de-Putois, ☎ 67.73.70.02

A subterranean twin-track funicular gives access to these marvellous natural caverns. The Demoiselles caves are part of a series of caverns in the limestone hills either side of the River Hérault. They have been opened to the public since the 1920s and are among the premier league of tourist caves in France. They are famous for the stalagmite formations. One of the galleries is claimed to be large enough to fit the Cathedral of Notre Dame within it. The funicular consists of a pair of open topped carriages running through an unlined rock tunnel at an inclination of about 1 in 3. The air temperature in the caverns is about 59 degF.

115: LA GROTTE DE COCALIÈRE

✳ At the **Cocalière** caves
✤ Jg/IGN111 K4, ✽ Diesel, 🐇 712mm, ✳ 1.6km
☞ Tables 543/9: SNCF Alès (25km), SNCF St.Ambroix (7m)
☛ The caves are immediately off RD904, 25km N of Alés. Well sign-posted. Ample parking
✓ am & pm. Daily: Begin-April to end-Oct
✉ Grotte de Cocalière, 30500 Saint-Ambroix, ☎ 66.24.01.57

The natural caverns at Cocalière are essentially linear and not a great depth below the surface. The galleries have been produced by water action flowing down into the subterranean river running below the public viewing caverns. The temperature within the cave is a steady 56 degF. The tour takes the form of a walk along the length of the caverns, emerging about a mile from the entrance. The journey back is provided by a narrow gauge railway running on the surface. A train of baladeuses is hauled by a tractor unit which carries fake steam engine-outline bodywork. The tractor, somewhat unusually, has rear wheels with rubber tyres which run on tarmac laid on the outside of the railway track. The front bogie of the tractor and all wheels of the train carriages run on the rails.

116: PETIT TRAIN DE DOMAINE DE MÉJANES

※ At **Méjanes** beside the Étang de Vaccarès
✣ Jh/IGN114 B10, ❋ Diesel or petrol, ⚇ 600mm, ❋ 3km
☞ Table 503: SNCF Arles (25km). Bus available all year
☛ The Méjanes site is 23km SW of Arles via RD570 to Albaron then RD37
✓ am & pm. All season
✉ Office de Tourisme, 5 avenue Van Gogh, 13732 Les Saintes-Maries-de-la-Mer Cedex,
✆ 90.97.82.55 or Méjanes: 90.49.60.34

In the middle of the delta of the River Rhône is a long-established holiday centre based on a traditional ranch of the Camargue. A narrow gauge railway runs around the site and along the marshy shore of the large lake, the Étang de Vaccarès. The station is laid out to standard gauge practice with platforms and parallel tracks. The main route is in the form of an almost square loop of about 3km length. The trains are composed of steam-outline locotracteurs and closed coaches in traditional railway style. The marshes and temperature make this a haven for mosquitoes: suitable clothing or cream are a must.

117: GALERIE DES TRANSPORTS, MARSEILLES

※ At **Noailles** tram-metro interchange, **Marseilles**
✣ Kh/IGN115 D5, ❋ Electric, ⚇ 1435mm, ❋ 0km
☞ SNCF Marseilles: Gare de la Blancarde and tram 68 or Gare de St.Charles and metro M2
☛ Parking is available at St.Pierre, then tram 68: or at Palais de Congrès, then metro M2
✓ am & pm. Wed to Sat: All year
✉ Galerie des transports, place du Marchédes Capuchins, 13001 Marseilles, ✆ 91.54.15.15

The construction of the interchange station between the new metro (line M2) and the one remaining Marseilles tram (line 68) immediately beside the previous terminal station for the trams, freed it for use as a exhibition hall for the collection of urban tram etc stock of the city. The collection contains old tramcars and models, and is available for inspection each afternoon.. Historic tramcars are also exhibited in the station itself where the double-track tramway broadens to three lines in the terminal station. This is at the lower end of the steep tunnel running under the Noailles area of the town, emerging as a traditional street tramway with reserved track in the centre of Boulevard Chave as far as St.Pierre. The Marseilles urban network includes trolleybuses. The new metro lines are 1435mm gauge but with additional wheels with rubber tyres running on concrete strips outside the rail lines. The metro is electrified by third rail. The tramway has overhead (pantograph) electrical collection.

At St. Giniez to the south of the city centre is the old tramway electric sub-station, which houses a collection of old Marseilles trolleybuses and other items of urban transport. These may be viewed on advertised dates.

118: TRAINS DES PIGNES: STEAM ON THE CF DE PROVENCE

※ From **Puget-Théniers** to **Annot** (and occasionally to **Nice** and **Digne**)
❖ Lh/IGN115 C9, ❋ Steam, ⚙ 1000mm, ✳ 20km (151km)
☞ Table 519: Puget-Théniers is on the Chemin de Fer de Provence line from Nice **(100)**
☛ Puget-Théniers is 65km NW of Nice via RN202
✓ Suns: Begin-May to mid-Oct
✉ GECP, Dépôt des locomotives, 06260 Puget-Théniers ✆ 93.82.10.17

The Chemin de Fer Provence **(100)** is a metre gauge public service line running for 151km from the coast at Nice through the Alpes-maritimes to Digne. About half way along the line is Puget-Théniers. A society of railway preservation enthusiasts known by the abbreviation "GECP", is based here. From May to October the GECP group operates steam trains on one of the most beautiful sections, between Puget-Théniers and Annot. Occasional trains are also run to Digne and to Nice. An ex-Reseau Breton 4-6-0T No. E327 hauls the tourist trains, and an ex-Portuguese Railway 2-4-6-0T No. E211 will re-enter service after overhaul. Also maintained at Puget-Théniers is a wooden carriage and a six-wheeled crane (both built in 1891 and previously used by the CF de la Sud de France); nine freight vehicles and two vintage locotracteurs. The steam train operate on specific days throughout the summer but the programme is not regular. Services are however well advertised. Pre-booking is recommended.

These are magnificent locomotives running through magnificent scenery, on a public-service metre-gauge railway. This is an experience it is worth planning a holiday around.

119: SNCF/FS TENDE LINE

※ **Nice** to **Cuneo** (Italy) via **Breil-sur-Roya** and **Tende**
❖ Mh/IGN115 C11, ❋ Diesel, ⚙ 1435mm, ✳ 80km
☞ Table 506: SNCF Nice-Ville, SNCF Breil-sur-Roya or FS Cuneo (Coni)
☛ Nice-Ville station is in the centre of the city on Avenue Thiers and Avenue Durante
✓ am & pm. Daily: All year (SNCF timetable 506)
✉ Gare SNCF de Nice-Ville, 06049 Nice Cédex ✆ 93.87.50.50

The international route from Nice to Turin via Tende has been described as "one of the most beautiful alpine routes" and "one of the most beautiful lines in Europe". It opened in stages from 1887, the final link being made in 1928. It was comprehensively destroyed by military action in 1945. The extremities in France, in the south, and in Italy, in the north, were rapidly re-opened after WW2. However, due to the damage to the civil engineering structures, the high section was not reopened until 1979. This follows the valley of the River Roya, twisting and turning as it climbs towards the 6km long border tunnel. The innumerable tunnels include three complete spiral tunnels on the French side and another on the Italian side. The Italian FS line from Ventimiglia to Cuneo joins at Breil-sur-Roya, and its trains form the main through service..

120: ECOMUSÉE DU HAUT-PAYS

※ **Breil-sur-Roya**
❖ Mh/IGN115 C11, ❋ Steam, diesel & elec, ⚙ 1435mm, ✳ 0km
☞ Table 506: SNCF Breil-sur-Roya
☛ Breil is 25km N of Ventimiglia (Italy) via RN204
✓ am & pm. Sat & Sun: June to Sept. Also Mon, Wed to Fri in Jul & Aug
✉ L'Ecomusée du Haut-Pays, gare SNCF, 06540 Breil-sur-Roya, ✆ 93.04.99.76

The Ecomusée du Haut Pays at Breil has a significant railway collection including a large 2-8-2 steam locomotive (141R1108), an ex-Marseille tramcar (1267) and diesel railcars (X2719, XR7708) and a locotracteur (Y2423). The museum is housed in the old locomotive depot and has a turntable and extensive track available for use in the yard. The museum contains an excellent model railway depicting the complex lines meeting at Breil where the lines to Nice and Ventimiglia twice cross over one another within the mountain. Breil is a pleasant town set in the narrow valley below the station: bar, buffet, and left luggage facilities are available here.

WEST

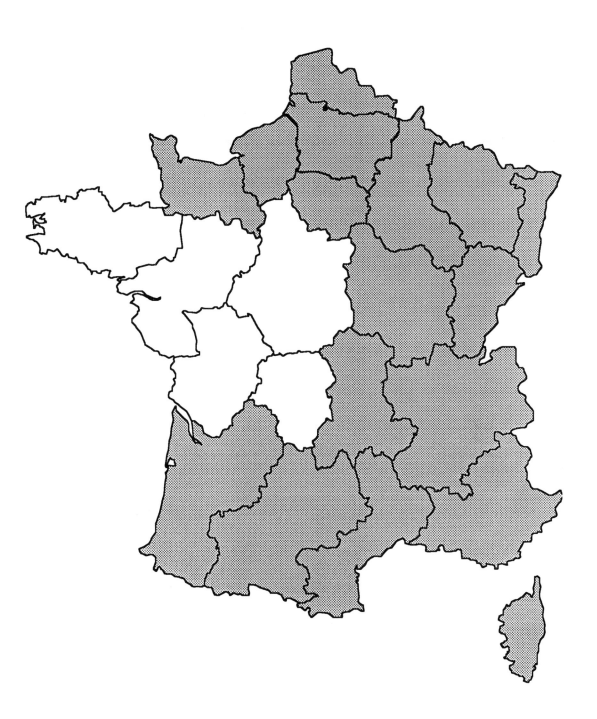

121: LA MINE BLEUE AT NOYANT-LA-GRAVOYÈRE

⁂ The Blue Mine is situated at **Noyant-la-Gravoyère** near Segré
✣ Ed/IGN106 A3, ❃ Battery electric, ✌ 600mm, ❃ 1km
☞ Table 372/4: SNCF Châteaubriant (35km), SNCF Angers (42km)
☛ Segré is 42km NW of Angers. La Mine Bleue is just N of RD775 5km to E
✓ am & pm. Daily: Begin-Mar to mid-Nov. Not Tues in Mar, Apr, Oct & Nov
✉ La Mine Bleue, BP10, 49780 Noyant-la-Gravoyère, ✆ 41.61.55.60

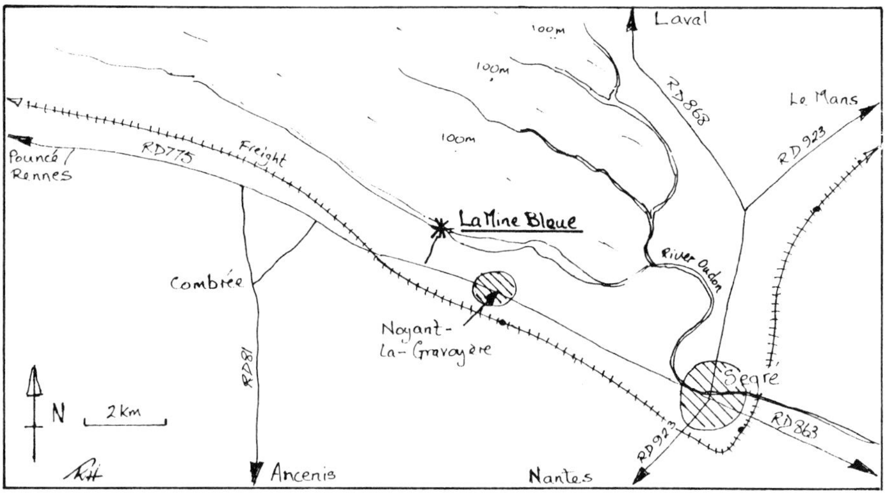

Slate mining was a major activity at the "Blue Mine" at Noyant-la-Gravoyère between 1900 and 1936. The remaining activities have been refurbished and preserved over the past few years and opened as a museum of the slate industry. The surface installations are stone-built sheds illustrating the various aspects of slate cutting and preparation. Each is connected by a narrow gauge railway. This system was operated manually and is nominally of 600mm gauge.

The museum is in a newly-constructed purpose-designed building of stone matching the working facilities. A rope-worked incline is preserved and demonstrates how the wagons were transferred from the underground to surface lines. A lift transports visitors to the underground workings 15m below the surface. The lift replaces an earlier funicular access which was originally operated by a steam driven winch.

Visitors are carried from the foot of the lift to the beginning of the tour of the mine galleries by a 600mm railway. The two trains consist of two bogie open carriages and a battery electric locotracteur. These ex-colliery locomotives run round the train at each end of the journey.

The mine tour visits five caverns created by the extraction of the slate. The various dioramas and lectures vividly demonstrate the difficulties and dangers of slate extraction undertaken using crawling boards hung from the roof of the galleries. This is an interesting and memorable tour. It is strongly recommended that visitors take a pullover as the temperature in the galleries is a constant 13 deg C (55deg F). It is necessary to wear safety helmets.

Locomotives displayed at the surface are Decauville and Hillard diesel locotracteurs from various mines and quarries.

If the visit to the preserved mine at Noyant-la-Gravoyère has raised interest in the slate industry and its railways, this can be indulged further in the area. At Renazé, 15km west, is a museum of the slate industry **(135).** At Trélazé, in the eastern suburbs of Angers, about 45km to the east of the "Blue Mine", the extraction of slate and its fashioning are still important industries.

122: TRAIN À VAPEUR DE VENDÉE

❋ **Mortagne-sur-Sèvre** to **Les Herbiers** via **St.Laurent-sur-Sèvre** and **Les Épesses**
✛ Ee/IGN107 B4, ❋ Steam ⚒ 1435mm ❋ 22km
☞ Table 386/7: SNCF Cholet is 11km from Mortagne.
☛ Mortagne-sur-Sèvre station is on RN160 10km SSE of Cholet (49)
✓ am & pm. Fri, Sat & Sun from begin-Jun to end-Sept. Also Weds & Thurs in July & Aug.
✉ (a) Office du Tourisme, 4 Grand Rue, 85500 Les Herbieres, ✆ 51.92.92.92
   (b) Diner trains: Hôtel de France, place du docteur Pichat, 85290 Mortagne-sur-Sèvre,
   ✆ 51.65.03.37

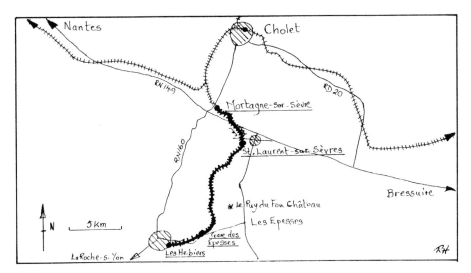

When the standard gauge line from Cholet to Fontenay-le-Comte was being built, the religious authorities persuaded the promoters of the line to bring it close to St.Laurent-sur-Sèvre for the convenience of pilgrimages to the Montfort tomb there. The town continues to nestle around the abbey church in the valley. To reach it the train crosses the River Sèvre on the eleven arch Barbin Viaduct. Like other features of the line, this 300m long 38m high structure is built in white limestone. It strides majestically above the trees of the wooded valley and forms a perfect setting for photography on this delightful line.

Regular passenger services ceased in 1939. The viaducts were blown up in 1944. But thankfully, the structures were rebuilt after the war using the same stone. Freight services continued as far as Les Herbiers throughout the 1980s. As a result, when the steam train services began in 1985 the line was intact and the structures (bridges, viaducts, stations) remained in matching material and style. The line has three significant viaducts and runs for 22 km through pretty, undulating, wooded pastureland: in many ways the perfect setting for a tourist railway. The track is single throughout. This adds to the impression of height of the viaducts along the line.

The immaculately maintained stock is operated as a tourist train, not as a preservation operation. As a result there are none of the rusting hulks of stock at stations along the track, so often found on preservation lines.

The operation forms part of a co-ordinated tourist development of the region and is supported by the local authority. The train contains a bar carriage and is wired to enable a commentary to be presented during the journey. The line is known for "wine and dine" special services which utilize the magnificently restored, ex-Orient Express, dining car. A *son et lumière* light and sound spectacle, involving many hundreds of actors, is a major event in summer evenings at the Puy-du-Fou Château which is situated close to the southern part of the line. Special trains have run in connection with these events.

The tourist train depot is at St.Laurent-sur-Sèvre. At Les Épesses station there is a small museum of railway relics. The return leg of the journey is broken here to allow passengers to visit the museum. Recently the steam locomotive has been a Fives-Lille 0-6-0T No 030T6 on hire from the Richelieu depot of the Trains à Vapeur de Touraine **(127)**. Steam engine driving courses are available at St. Laurent-sur-Sèvre.

123: CHEMIN DE FER TOURISTIQUE DE LA SEUDRE

※ **Saujon** to **La Tremblade** via **Mornac**
✛ Ef/IGN107 D4, ✳ Steam and diesel, ⚒ 1435mm, ✺ 21km
☞ Direct connection at SNCF Saujon (on Royan to Saintes line), Table 404
☛ From La Rochelle: 50km S on RN137. From Saintes: 25km SSW on RN150
✓ am & pm. Sun: June to Sept. Also Wed & BH in Jul & Aug
✉ CFTS, BP12, 17600 Saujou, ℗ 46.36.64.59

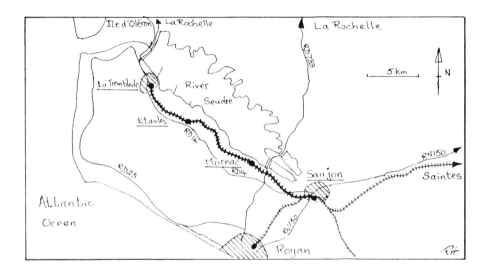

The effect of the sea on the mid-west coast of France has caused the River Seudre to reach the Atlantic Ocean via a long estuary encircled by two arms of the mainland and the Ile d'Oléron. Saujon is situated where the river initially enters the estuary. La Tremblade is about 20 km downstream immediately before the river enters the ocean. The estuary has proved to be an ideal site for the farming of oysters and as a consequence they formed an important part of the goods traffic each December right up to final closure of the line.

The railway was opened in 1877. It was built by local enterprise as the final stage in a project to link the coastal area to the main network at Saujon. Financial problems arose immediately. Despite this, the passenger service survived until just after WW2 (although some seasonal and mixed trains continued) and freight until 1980.

Although some dismantling took place the infrastructure remained essentially intact and agreement was obtained for a tourist passenger service to be operated. Stock was obtained, and after much track work etc, initial services were begun in 1984. The operation has now stabilized and morning and afternoon trains are run, as indicated, from June to September (special trains for groups may be booked outside these times). The steam service operates as follows: Chaillevette-La Tremblade-Saujon-Chaillevette. A diesel service supplies a connection from La Tremblade for the initial steam train trip Saujon to La Tremblade in the morning and a final connection at the end of the day. There are also one steam and one diesel return journeys. This operation gives, in effect, two out and return runs per day from both ends of the line each with steam for at least half of each trip.

An historic 0-6-0T Schneider locomotive, "Progress", of 1891 is used on the line. This engine has a distinctly antiquated appearance and is possibly the oldest loco in use on any French standard gauge tourist railway. In addition a 1945 built SACM 0-6-0T, "Delphine", is available for services together with two large diesel locomotives, BB71017 and CC65004, and a "Picasso" railcar of 1955. The railcar, number X3926, was one of the few of this design built as combined first/second class units. It has a trailer car available. A rich collection of old coaching and freight stock is preserved. The steam depot is at Mornac and is open for viewing on certain journeys.

The line has a high proportion of British visitors due to its proximity to the popular camping area along this coast. It is perhaps the most accessible of the three tourist lines in the area (Seudre (**123**), Oléron (**133**), and Pointe-de-Grave (**86**)). The line has continued to operate successfully each season for the ten years since it was created. The location in the heart of a tourist area and its SNCF connection will have played no small part. However, the use of steam traction as its primary motive power and its astutely planned timetable are probably the heart of its success.

124: CHEMIN DE FER TOURISTIQUE DE LA SARTHE

✳ **Connerré-Beillé** to **Bonnétable** via **Tuffé** and **Prévelles**
✥ Fc/IGN102 D8, ✲ Steam and diesel, ⛟ 1438mm ✲ 17.8km
☞ Table 350: SNCF Connerré-Beillé
☛ Connerré is on RN23, 25km east of Le Mans. The station and depot is 1.5km N of Connerré.
    Access is alongside the grain silo.
✓ am & pm, Sundays in July and Aug (Operation for pre-arranged groups Apr to Oct)
✉ TRANSVAP, 3 chemin de la herse, 72160 Connerré, ☏ 43.85.05.03

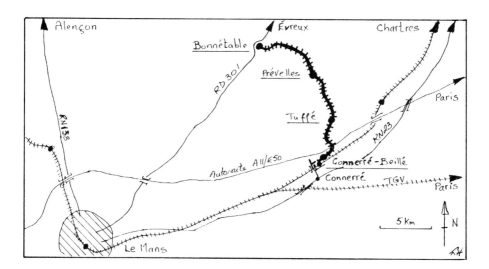

Where the TGV Atlantique joins the conventional Paris to Le Mans line is the extensive station and rail yards of Connerré-Beillé. These are situated some distance from the town and about 25 km east of Le Mans. At this point the 45 km long *départemental* standard gauge line linking Mamers and St.Calais (MStC) connected with the SNCF system until it was closed in 1977. Passenger services had ceased in 1965. An 0-6-0T steam locomotive built by SACM operated some freight services and occasional passenger specials until 1967.

The preservation society TRANSVAP have a large collection of stock preserved at the old Connerré depot of the MStC Département railway, which was built in 1870. By agreement with the *département*, which still owns the facilities, the Transports Vapeur Association (TRANSVAP) has operated tourist trains along the remaining 18 km of track to Bonnétable. The first trains ran on part of the line in 1979. Regular steam and diesel services now operate on Sundays in season. The single track route runs along the valley of the River Huisne through pleasantly rural and undeveloped countryside. This is largely meadows and woods.

The rail-cars include Renault, Verny and Billard examples and an ex-SNCF "Picasso" which operates some services. Other motive power includes a British built 0-4-0T Bagnall saddle tank built in 1917, an ex-MStC diesel locotracteur, and an 0-6-0T Corpet-Louvet of 1923 which operates the afternoon trains. The preserved stock includes some historic freight wagons dating from the 1870s and two cranes of 1869 and 1871 vintage. Many of these and some of the collection of petrol and diesel rail-cars are from the old MStC line.

The layout of the interesting depot at Bonnétable has changed little since pre-preservation days. It includes three wagon turntables and a wagon transverser. The depot is in effect a living museum. The equipment in the workshop appears unchanged since the last century. The TRANSVAP are essentially a preservation group. The stock is excellently maintained and visitors are made very welcome. A visit to the depot with the preserved atmosphere of the 1870s is particularly worthwhile. Of all the preservation sites in France, the depot at Connerré gives the most complete picture of what a typical *départemental* branch line operation involved.

Also recently established at this site is an association which has a collection of operating 600 mm gauge stock and museum. Information is available from APEMVE, 1 rue de AGN, 72360 Mayet.

125: PAPEA. PARC D'ATTRACTIONS

✷ **Papea** at Le Mans
✧ Fc/IGN106 6A, ✺ Diesel, ⌇ 600mm & 400mm, ✻ 2.5 km & 0.3 km respectively
☞ SNCF Le Mans then suburban bus.
☛ Papea is in the suburbs of Le Mans; 3 km to the East. Access is via RN 23
✓ am and pm daily. From beginning April to end of Oct.
✉ Parc d'Attractions, Papea 72530 Yvré-l'Évèque, ✆ 43.89.61.05

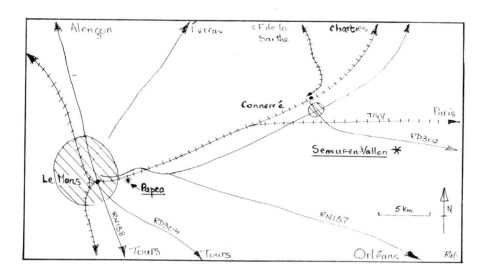

In the eastern suburbs of Le Mans between the Le Mans to Paris main (TGV Atlantique) line and the River Huisne, a large pleasure park was laid out in 1971. This is recorded as having involved a great deal of earth work and management of the river. The results are still obvious today from the water features and the routeing of the park railway. The park offers a wide range of attractions for all ages. These attractions include two narrow gauge railways both operated by steam outline diesel locomotives and open carriage stock.

The smaller of the two systems has one Lombardini locomotive of unusual 0-4-6 wheel arrangement. The first passenger carriage has two seats only. It acts as the tender as part of the illusion of a "wild west" locomotive. The brightly coloured train follows a basically circular 400m long track which has a single siding. There is also a short piece of double track, one half of which has a false tunnel. This acts as the train shed. The only passengers permitted on this line are children.

The other railway is an altogether larger affair which, although showings sign of age, remains impressive. The track is conventionally laid out as two loops with a long single track connection. The total length runs to 2.5 km. The terminal loop is situated in a wood, reasonably close to the park entrance and to the 400 mm gauge railway. The station is situated on the south side of this loop. This has sheltered seating and two covered platforms long enough to accommodate trains of six bogie carriages. From the station the train follows a lengthy route through the woods and across the river. It then runs right round the edge of the large lake before re-crossing the river and returning by the previous route through the woods to the station.

The stock of this line consist of two sets of six, bogie "baladeuse" coaches. Unusually these have old cinema seats, which ensure a very comfortable ride. Two diesel mechanical locomotives are maintained to operate the trains. Two others are displayed out of use.

The primary motive power is a 1938 built Campagne industrial locomotive which has been cladded to resemble a steam locomotive. The adaptations include a bell, headlight and cow-catcher, in 'wild west' style. It has also received a painted face in recent years as has the Lombardini on the smaller railway. The reserve locomotive is an unmodified Arn-Fung industrial engine which retains its drab industrial paintwork.

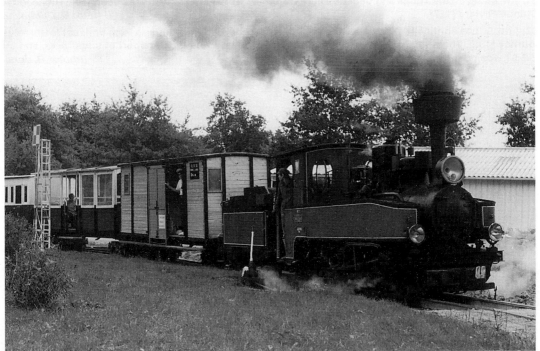

49, 50. Two views of the Train Historique du Lac de Rillé, which runs for 2.5 km through a wooded park [126]. The principal loco is "Polska", an 0-8-0 tender engine built by Henschel in 1918.

(Photos: AECFM (above), J. David (below))

51. ↑ Working on the Trains à Vapeur de Touraine, 0-8-0T No. 040TA137 waits to depart from Richelieu for Chinon-Rivière [127]. *(Photo: B. Duchesne)*

52. ↓ No. 9 "Les Fontinelles" of the Musée des Transports de Pithiviers departs from Bellébat for its return journey [132]. The primary function of the Pithiviers Tramway was the transport of sugar beet, and this 2-6-0T was built for use in a sugar refinery. *(Photo: R. Jones*

53. ↑ At the Pithiviers depot, the immaculate Decauville 0-6-2T "La Matroy" prepares to take a passenger train to Bellébat [132]. *(Photo: R. Jones)*

54. ↓ Pithiviers No. 4, a Henschel 0-8-0T built in 1917, brings an afternoon train into Pithiviers [132]. *(Photo: R. Jones)*

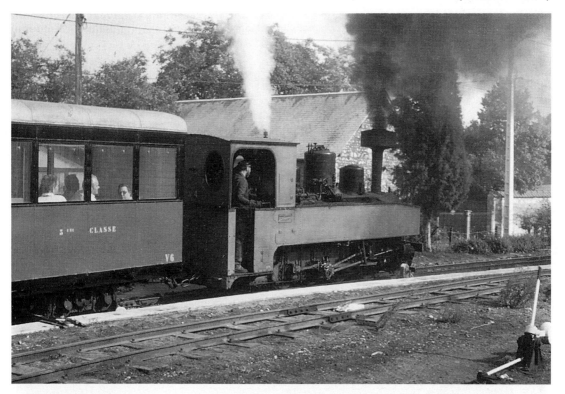

55. ↑ Adults and children ride on what appears to be a toy train, but in practice is a powerful 4-2-4 loco with a petrol engine and "Wild West" outline. The Omlande Parc d'Attraction [136].*(Photo: R. Haworth)*

56. ↓ The former PLM 4-6-2 express loco 231K8 of the FACS Society is seen here at Bercy station preparing for a special train. This loco is one used on main line steam excusrsions.   *(Photo: T. Duchesne)*

126: TRAIN HISTORIQUE DU LAC DE RILLÉ

❉ Located at the **Lac de Rillé** leisure park
✤ Fd/IGN106 B6, ❋ Steam & diesel, ⚒ 600mm, ❋ 2.5km
☞ SNCF Tours ◉ (35km)
☛ From Tours, the park is approached from the east via RN152, to Langeais, then RD57
✓ pm. Sun & BH: begin-May to end-Sept. Also (diesel) Wed & Sat: mid-July to mid-Aug
✉ ACEFM, Marcilly-sur-Maulne, 37330 Château-la-Vallière, ✆ 47.24.80.19

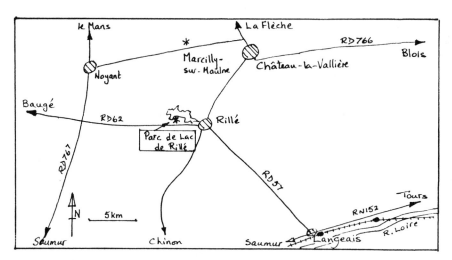

Since 1977 ACEFM, a small group of enthusiasts, has assembled an interesting collection of narrow gauge locomotives and various items of rolling stock at Marcilly-sur-Maulne. The large five-track locomotive shed, with its complex track layout and turntable, was until 1990 the base of a 1.5km tourist line situated here. This lightly laid line ran alongside several farm fields and linked the depot and station to the car park.

The rolling stock preserved by the ACEFM group includes two DFB steam locomotives obtained from Poland: "Polska" an 0-8-0T+T Henschel and an 0-4-0T Orenstein & Koppel and also a number of diesel locotracteurs: built by Ruston, Billard, CACL, Comessa, Berry, Paviers and a number by Decauville. The coaching stock contains two particularly interesting items: "Petit Anjou" a four compartment closed bogie coach from the old "Anjou" line and a wooded luggage van built in 1890. A number of the items were originally of metre gauge and have been regauged to 600mm.

Despite the very friendly and welcoming nature of this set up at Marcilly, it did not attract a large number of visitors, due to being situated away from traditional tourist areas. As a result it was decided in 1989 to create a purely tourist operation at a major leisure complex being developed about 15km from Marcilly and to use the Marcilly site as a maintenance depot and support base. The stock used to operate the railway is taken from the pool maintained at Marcilly. This decision has resulted in a very successful railway at the Château de Rillé park which has been created beside a large lake formed by damming the River Lathan to produce a reservoir.

The line was built in 1990. It was extended in 1992/3 to reach the lake. It now has a length of 2.5km and a further extension is planned. The site is a very pleasant, partially wooded, country park. The railway, which is in the form of an irregular circle, runs through the woods in the area of the lake. A three-track depot building has been constructed: this shelters the operational stock and that undergoing maintenance. The Marcilly facilities are used for long term and major work on locomotives.

Services on Sunday are generally steam operated by "Polska". The summer midweek services are exclusively diesel hauled. A number of the small four-wheel Decauville diesel locotracteurs have been moved from Marcilly and are based at Rillé. It should be appreciated that movement of locomotives and carriage stock between sites will continue so that the rolling stock operating the railway can be expected to vary from time to time.

The collection of stock maintained by the ACEFM group is excellent and well worth a visit in its own right. This combined with the pleasures of steam train operations means that a visit to the newly established railway is strongly recommended. A genuine welcome awaits visitors. Steam locomotive driving lessons are offered. English visitors are made very welcome: an English guide can be made available for visiting groups.

127: TRAINS À VAPEUR DE TOURAINE

✳ **Richelieu** to **Ligré Rivière**
✣ Fd/IGN106 C6, ✿ Steam & diesel ⚒ 1435mm ✱ 12km
☞ Table 422: SNCF Chinon
☛ At Richelieu via RN147 to Loudin then RD61.
✓ pm. Sat & Sun: mid-May to begin-Oct. Also additional in Jun & Jul.
✉ TVT, Gare de Richelieu, 37120 Richelieu, ✆ 47.58.12.97 or 47.58.10.13

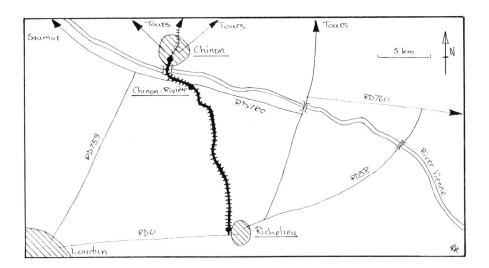

Richelieu and Chinon are two historic towns situated in the Loire Valley. Richelieu remains as built by Cardinal Richelieu and is a unique and delightful survival. The station is situated beside the town walls. Chinon has one of the most renowned châteaux in the Loire Valley. The standard gauge railway used by the tourist train links these two tourist sites. It runs across the valley bottom, a pleasant area of wooded pasture land, passing close to a small château on the way.

Following acquisition of the section of line to Ligré-Rivière by the local authority, a tourist train service was established by AJECTA, a nationwide French railway preservation society. The operation is now operated by Trains à Vapeur de Touraine (TVT).

This line has had mixed fortunes since the start of its tourist operation. The freight services were initially very successful, including services on other lines in the region. They were however adversely affected by the transfer of freight to road services, and ceased in 1992. The tourist train operations have at various times run through to Chinon (by agreement with SNCF in respect of the Ligré to Chinon section) but at other times have been cut back to Ligré-Rivière with, on occasion, a linking railcar service to Chinon. At the time of writing, the TVT operates a diesel service between Richelieu and Ligré. Use of the Ligré to Chinon section will require much work to bring the track up to adequate standard. The stock is subject to change, with loans and hirings. As on many tourist lines in France, the number of trains per day is low (one or two return journeys only). For a line in a major tourist area, having extensive motive power and the support of the local authorities, the annual passenger loadings, of around 9,000 in recent years is hardly compatible with its potential. However, this train is well worth riding. A friendly welcome from members of the operating association awaits.

The motive power based at Richelieu includes steam tank and large tender locomotives, diesel electric freight locomotives, diesel locotracteurs and diesel railcars. The steam stock includes a 1910-built 0-6-0T, an 1883 built 2-6-0, and two 2-8-2s, a 4-6-0 and an 0-8-0T. Diesel locomotives are available for commercial freight service.

128: CHEMIN DE FER DU BLANC À ARGENT

❋ **Romorantin** to **Salbris** and **Luçay-le-Mâle** (Table 426)
✛ Gd/IGN106 B10, ❋ Diesel, ⚒ 1000mm, ❋ 67km
☞ Tables 430, 473: SNCF Salbris or SNCF Gièvres
☛ Situated 60km S of Orléans via RN20 to Salbris then RD724 to Romorantin
✓ am & pm. Daily all year
✉ (a) Chemin de Fer du Blanc à Argent, gare de CFBA, 41200 Romorantin ✆ 54.76.06.71
   (b) Office du Tourisme, Boulevard de la République, 41300 Salbris ✆ 54.96.15.52
   (c) SABA, La Mairie, 36180 Heugnes

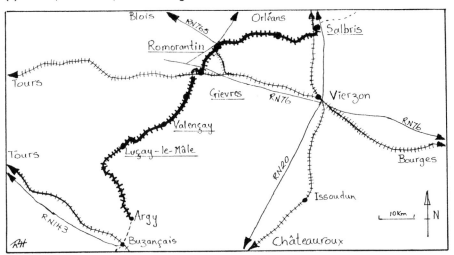

Originally linking the towns of Argent and Le Blanc, a distance of 195 km, the CFBA railway has gradually retreated at each end of the line. The present passenger service, which is operated by SNCF, now links Salbris with Luçay-le-Mâle over the central 67 km section. Until 1989 the CFBA carried significant quantities of freight, but this required man-handling at the change of gauge. The freight trains operated from Salbris to Buzançais. The exchange yards remain largely intact at Romorantin, with metre and standard gauge tracks. The CFBA now offers only a passenger service. Romorantin, which still forms the heart of operations, is situated at the end of a short standard gauge branch from Villefranche-sur-Cher, close to the centre of the narrow gauge line.

All services are operated by diesel railcars. The complex timetable has up to half a dozen trains per day from Romorantin north-eastwards to Salbris and south to Gièvres. At these points connections are made with SNCF services on the lines from Paris to Vierzon and Vierzon to Tours respectively.

Following closure of the freight services, two locotracteurs remain on the CFBA. These were constructed locally in 1951 on the chassis of 1901 steam locomotives. The stock of passenger railcars also retains interest, with many historic items. Two power units were built in 1983 by CFD Montmirail. These modern cars are named after towns on the line and carry appropriate coats of arms. Five motor cars built by Verney in 1951 are still in service. Four of these have been modernised and rebodied to match the CFD units. The fifth Verney unit and the sole remaining de Dion-Bouton railcar remain in original condition. They are held in reserve and used for occasional special operations.

The Salbris terminus is situated immediately in front of the standard gauge station. The CBA line initially runs south parallel to the main line before crossing it to run, for the following 25km, through a patchwork area of wild forest, lakes, marsh and occasional fields. The pretty market town of Romorantin is entered via a picturesque four-arch stone bridge over the River Sauldre. As the line leaves the town it passes the Prévostiere air base which has its own halt. The line runs through open woodland to reach Gièvres, where it shares the SNCF station. It then swings sharply south under the standard gauge line and enters the most picturesque section: an area of rich agricultural country. The train crosses the undulating countryside perpendicular to the valleys of the Rivers Cher and Fouzon and the disused Berry Canal. This requires a series of metal viaducts which, apart from the bridge at Romorantin, are the only significant engineering structures on the line. The train reaches the elegant château style station at Valençay and finally the minimal platforms at Luçay-le-Mâle. A newly-formed preservation group have saved the disused Luçay to Argy section. Details are available from Salbris tourist office. The SABA preservation group has accumulated a collection of rolling stock including diesel locotracteur from the Boulogne port railway, and balcony-end coaches from Switzerland.

129: PARC FLORAL, ORLÉANS

❋ A circuit from Terminus Station at the **Parc Floral** at **Orléans**

✛ Gd/IGN106 A10, ❋ Diesel, ⚒ 600mm, ❋ 2.5km

☞ Tables 400, 430: SNCF Orléans

☛ From Orléans take RN20 south for 6km (or via the centre of Olivet) then follow D14 (Avenue du Parc Floral) towards St.Cyr-en-Val for 2km. Park entry on left.

✓ pm. Daily except Fri: Begin-May to mid-Sept. Also a limited service in April

✉ Parc Floral, 45100 Orléans-la-Source ℂ 38.63.33.17

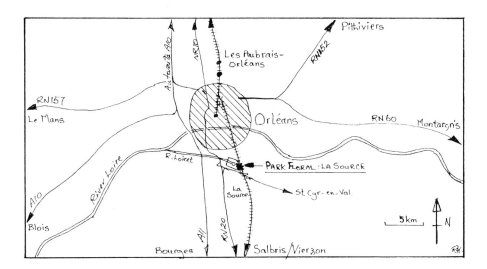

The River Loiret which is a tributary of the River Loire has its source in a lake to the south east of Orléans. Here it emerges as a full sized river. A floral park was created around the location in 1967 for a garden festival of the type held more recently in Britain. A very extensive 600mm gauge railway was built for this event. The system was operated by 0-4-0 Henschel and Gmeinder diesel locomotives. A 1944 Gmeinder locomotive continues to operate a seasonal service around the remaining 2.5 km circuit of track. The locomotive is dressed to resemble a steam tram locomotive with cow-catcher, spark arresting chimney and side skirts. Brightly painted in red and yellow, it has a train of matching open sided bogie carriages. After 2.30pm, the train offers a half hourly service from three stations (Terminus, La Rocaille and Pont Blanc) giving an alternative means of viewing this immaculately maintained park. The terminal station is situated on the loop at the end of the single line track.

The attractions of the park are not limited to the railway. There are refreshment facilities, children entertainments, exotic birds etc. and the gardens are truly magnificent, being maintained to a very high standard.

130: CHEMIN DE FER TOURISTIQUE LIMOUSIN - PÉRIGORD
VIENNE VÉZÈRE VAPEUR

※ **Limoges** to **Ussel** line (see also SNCF Table 465)
✧ Gf to Hf/IGN110 A10 to IGN 111 E1/F1/F2, ✸ Steam & diesel, ὖ 1435mm, ✳ 117km
☞ SNCF Limoges
☛ The tourist trains operate from the SNCF station at Limoges
✓ am & pm. Various Sun, Mon, Wed & Sat: May to August. Various destinations (see below)
✉ Vienne Vézère Vapeur, le Mairie, 87120 Eymoutiers ☏ 55.69.10.21
✉ CFTLP, 11-13 ave Berthelot, 87100 Limoges ☏ 55.77.26.65
✉ Office de Tourisme, boulevard Fleurus, 87000 Limoges ☏ 55.34.46.87

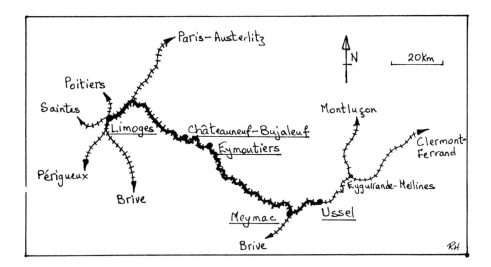

A large ex-SNCF 2-8-2T steam locomotive, No. 141TD740, hauls rail excursions on the SNCF line between Limoges and Ussel. This excellently maintained locomotive was built in 1932 by the Compagnie des Chemins de Fer de l'Est (one of the railways which subsequently formed part of SNCF). The locomotive operated passenger trains in the Paris suburbs. It was withdrawn from SNCF service in 1968. It was destined for the National Railway Museum at Mulhouse but was sold by SNCF to the Chemin de Fer Limousin-Périgord (CFTLP) association in 1981.

Since 1982 steam train excursions have been operated using the CFTLP locomotive and a train of four bogie coaches of 1931 to 1935 vintage. The Vienne Vézère Vapeur operation is based at Limoges and operates to Chateauneuf-Bujaleuf (40km), Eymoutiers (49km), Meymac (99km) and Ussel (112km). This route was built by the CF de l'Etat around 1880 and has a large number of tunnels and magnificent viaducts including some curved examples, for instance those at Farges and St.Léonard-de-Noblet. The tourist train operation is supported by the state and by the local authorities situated along the route and its future seems assured.

The various steam train trips include entrance to various activities in the price. For example, the Limoges to Eymoutiers trip combines visits to the towns and museums at St.Léonard, and Eymoutiers and coach travel from the stations to the various sites. Amongst other points of interest at the stopping off places: Eymoutiers has a model train museum, with over 1000 items, and at St.Léonard-de-Noblet there is a railway history museum. The other trips have similar arrangements. At Ussel a turntable is used to turn the locomotive. The four hour break of journey at Ussel gives ample time to observe this and enjoy lunch.

The CFTLP is one of the longest steam train journeys available in France on a regular basis. The train and scenery are wonderful, and passengers are given a real "day out". The train has a limited capacity and pre-booking is strongly recommended. Tickets may be purchased from the addresses indicated above, and also from the Offices de Tourisme/ Syndicat de Tourisme at each of the settlements along the route.

131: CHEMIN DE FER TOURISTIQUE DE PUISAYE

✳ From **Charny** to **St. Sauveur-en-Puisaye** via **Toucy**
✢ Hd/IGN108 B4, ✤ Diesel, ⚒ 1435mm, ✳ 44km
☞ Table 540: SNCF Montargis
☛ Montargis is 80km E of Orléans by RN60. Toucy is 24km W of Auxerre by RD965.
✓ Service temporarily suspended
✉ AATY, avenue de la gare, 89130 Toucy, ✆ 86.44.05.58

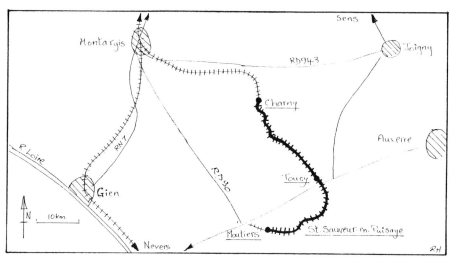

SNCF have recently withdrawn most services from the lines situated in the rural area of the border between the départements of Loiret and Yonne, to the south-east of Montargis which is some 120km south of Paris. From 1987 to 1992, the AATY enthusiast group operated a tourist train each year on parts of the old line between Montargis and Auxerre. The line was opened in two stages. In 1874 a line was built to link Montargis and Sens. This takes a basically easterly route following the valley of the River Ouanne as far as Triguères at which point it turns north-easterly to Sens. In 1884 a link was opened southwards from Triguères to Clamency and Toucy where the line extended on to St.Fargeau. The furthest extent of the track has not been used for some years but remains in situ. Passenger services ceased in 1938 but freight operations have continued on parts of the network until recent years. This enabled the line to be rented from SNCF between 1987 and 1992, so that tourist trains could be operated on days with no freight services.

After the initial operations in 1987, the tourist train services operated between the SNCF station at Montargis and the lake and park at Etang de Moutiers; a total distance of 82km, making this the longest volunteer operated tourist line in France. However, since the end of 1991 SNCF have withdrawn freight services from the southern section of the line beyond Charny. As a result operations in 1992 and 1993 were limited to the 40km northern section from Montargis to Charny using Châteaurenard as a base.

The southern section of the line is now being purchased by the local authorities through which the route passes: therefore the train will return to the Charny to St.Sauveur section.

The society has available the following ex-SNCF diesel railcars; two "Picasso" units (Nos X3871 and X3814), a trailer car (XR7920), and an ex-SNCF luxury twin railcar set (X2716/XR7762). The twin car set has been fitted out with dining and buffet facilities. AATY also have three draisines from the 1930s and a small diesel locotracteur.

The route followed by the northern section of the line is essentially rural with numerous stations each serving a charming village in the gentle valley of the River Ouanne. The countryside has the appearance and atmosphere of the English New Forest with frequent copses of broadleaf trees. The southern section gradually becomes more wooded. The line continues to follow the River Ouanne as far as Toucy and the River Loing at Moutiers. Beyond Toucy the line twists and turns through the woods. Each of the pretty stations is a suitable base for country walks.

As an additional attraction for the railway-minded visitor, a small museum has been established at Toucy station presenting small railway items, documents and plans etc. The Toucy station exhibits can be visited on Saturdays, Sundays and public holidays during the season.

132: TRAIN À VAPEUR DE PITHIVIERS

☀ From **Pithiviers** to **Bellébat**
✢ He/IGN103 D5, ✿ Steam, ♒ 600mm, ✽ 4km
☞ Table 400: SNCF Étampes (from Paris Austerlitz), 30 km, then bus
☛ Situated 80km S of Paris via RN20 to Étampes, then RD921 to Pithiviers
✓ pm. Sun & BH: begin-May to mid-Oct
✉ TVP, Office de Tourisme, rue Carnot, 45300 Pithiviers, ☏ 38.30.50.02

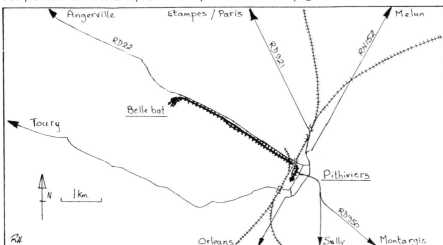

Pithiviers is situated on a plateau of open farmland and isolated trees which forms the Beauce region to the south of Paris. This area of heavy rich soils is an ideal location for maize, wheat and, particularly, sugar beet production. Sugar refineries were built at Toury, Sermaises and Pithiviers. Decauville, the major French builder of light railway equipment, was the main driving force behind the establishment of the 600 mm gauge system in France. The Company built and operated a line between Pithiviers and Toury to demonstrate the commercial potential of their rail system. This was opened in 1892 and grew rapidly to satisfy the traffic available. Management of the network was taken over by the Loiret *Département*. The Tramway de Pithiviers à Toury (TPT) survived WW1 intact and continued to expand, linking the sugar factories with the innumerable branches and railheads of individual farms and fields. The lines ran along the side of the roads and lanes, in true tramway fashion. At its peak the TPT was operated by 24 steam locomotives. Naturally these were initially Decauville designs but, following WW1, war surplus, reparations and new stock was introduced. This explains the variety of stock now preserved at Pithiviers. Following WW2, road transport severely encroached on the traffic. Rail passenger services were withdrawn in 1952 and the final sugar beet was transported in 1964. At closure, ten steam locomotives remained on the system which had survived into the preservation era. A group of enthusiasts were encouraged by the success of narrow gauge preservation in Great Britain. They resolved to use the old TPT depot at Pithiviers to form a base and museum of narrow gauge railways.

The line starts from a station of typical Decauville design and runs beside the depot before swinging sharply left to pass under the SNCF line. It then runs as a tramway beside the road all the way to the terminus called "Bellébat". In a copse here a small station has been built to a design based on a typical halt of a rural tramway. Just after the SNCF bridge, the 600mm gauge track crosses, on the level, a 1435 mm standard gauge siding. This is the only such crossing remaining in France. In the region originally served by the TPT it is still possible to find indications of the old system. These relics include typical Decauville wooden station buildings now used as barns, at least one rail weighbridge at a farm entrance and the remains of rail-served stock pits.

The stock preserved at Pithiviers is one of the most extensive collection of narrow gauge steam locomotives in France. The majority are in operational state and used on the line from time to time. All are maintained in immaculate condition. The delightful little 0-4-0T Schneider of 1870 is claimed to be the oldest operational locomotive in France. Other item include two 0-4-0T Decauville (1905 & 1919), two 0-6-0Ts: Blanc-Misseron (1902) and Decauville (1928), a unique 0-6-2T Decauville (1902), a number of 0-8-0Ts including Henschels (1916 & 1917), Hartmann (1918), and "Pithiviers", a Franco-Belge of 1944; a 2-6-0T La Meuse of 1905 and a 2-6-2T Alco-Cooke of 1916. In addition there are diesel locotracteurs built by Gmeinder and Plymouth and the sole remaining petrol-electric railcar built by Crochat in 1922 for passenger services on the original TPT system. The Crochat, Blanc-Misseron, Franco-Belge and 0-6-0T Decauville have all survived from the original Pithiviers-Toury network. This is truly a collection not to be missed.

133: ST. TROJAN TRAMWAY

✽ **St.Trojan-les-Bains** to **Maumusson** via **Gatseau** (Ile d'Oléron)
✢ Md/IGN104 D9, ✽ Diesel, ⚲ 600mm, ✱ 6km
☞ Table 394: SNCF Rochefort then bus (40km) to St.Trojan (Boulevard du Préventerium)
☛ Causeway on RD728 to island. Then D26 and D126 to St.Trojan
✓ pm, daily: Easter to begin-Oct. Also am, in July & Aug.
✉ STTST, Boulevard du Corps-Franc-Marin, 17370 St.Trojan-les-Bains
✆ 46.76.01.26 (46.74.35.34 in closed season)

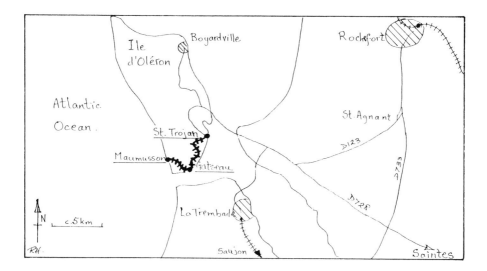

This is not a tramway in the English use of the word. Just lots of little four wheeled diesel locomotives with steam outline bodies and carriages like fairground rides, gaudily painted like the locos, operating a public transport service - so delightful and typically French!

The Ile d'Oléron is reached by a causeway from the mainland on the Atlantic coast. The southern area of the island is extensively wooded with maritime pines and encircled with fine beaches and sand dunes. It is a popular holiday resort. In the 1960's the idea of a transport system to link the resorts and beaches was developed and a single-track of 600 mm gauge line was opened between St.Trojan and the southern beach at Gatseau in 1963. The success of the operation led to the extension to the Atlantic beach at Maumusson in 1965. Passing places and signalling were introduced, to enable a service frequency of 20 minutes to be operated. This requires 4 trains in service at once.

The small station at St.Trojan is situated to the west of the town. About 250 m after leaving the station, the train enters the forest, which is the major feature of the journey. It then runs beside the beaches to Gatseau. On this section of the line there is a depot situated in a clearing and various passing loops where trains can pass. The route onward to Maumusson also runs through the forest until crossing the dunes onto the beach at the terminus. Here a triangle is provided, as at St.Trojan, to enable the locomotive to reverse. In summer a buffet wagon is placed at the end of the line.

The winds on the west coast can be severe. Winter damage was so bad in 1990, for example, that it caused the line to be completely relaid at Maumusson and at Gatseau. Despite these problems, more than 60 000 passengers are carried each year. During the peak months of July and August three trains give a 20 minute service interval, and night trains are run. These carry searchlights to illuminate the forest on each side for the delight of the pasengers.

The stock consists of nine diesel locomotives since the risk of fire has prevented use of steam traction. The locomotives are ex-industrial items of Deutz-Ruston and Billard manufacture. Some are rebodied to resemble (after a fashion) steam engines. However, the Billards continue to exhibit their industrial pedigree. The carriages are bogie baladeuses built on DFB chassis.

134: CHEMIN DE FER DU CENTRE BRETAGNE

✳ **Loudéac** to **Pontivy** and **St. Nicholas des Eaux**
✤ Cc/IGN105 B7, ✿ Diesel, 𝄥 1435mm, ✿ 35km
☞ Tables 351, 353: SNCF St.Brieuc (40km), then train or bus, Table 371
☛ Loudéac is 40km to the S of St.Brieuc via RN168
✓ Time & dates of operation to be announced
✉ CFCB, rue Pierre Loti, BP 341, 22600 Loudéac, ✆ 96.72.58.65
✉ Syndicat d'Initiative, place General de Gaulle, 22600 Loudéac (Summer only) ✆ 96.28.25.17

The association Chemin de Fer du Centre Bretagne was formed to promote the railway network in the middle of Brittany. It is appropriately based at Loudéac, half way along the St.Brieuc to Auray route which crosses central Brittany from north to south. The northern half of the line from St.Brieuc to Loudéac has a few passenger trains per day. South of Loudéac the line was closed in 1968.

The association has based its "Picasso" railcar X3890 at Loudéac. It has been thoroughly overhauled and modernised by the association and is expected in 1996 to operate tourist trains along the line south of Loudéac as far as St.Nicholas des Eaux. This is a rural line and very picturesque, especially after Pontivy where it follows the Blavet valley.

135: MUSEÉS DE L'ARDOISE AT TRÉLAZÉ AND AT RENAZÉ

✳ At **Trélazé** and **Renazé**
✤ Renazé: Ec/IGN106 A2, ✿ Diesel, 𝄥 600mm, ✿ 0.5km. Trélazé: Ed/IGN106 B4
☞ Trélazé: Tables 375 & 390: SNCF Angers (6km)
☞ Renazé: Tables 370/2/4: SNCF Châteaubriant (26km)
☛ Trélazé is immediately to the east of Angers.
☛ Renazé is 115km WSW of Le Mans. RN157 to Laval then RN171
✓ pm. Daily: July to Sept. Also Sat & BH most of year.
✉ Musée de l'Ardoise, 32 Chemin de la Maraîchère, 49800 Trélazé ✆ 41.69.04.71

Trélazé is the centre of a still-active slate industry. Here a delightful museum of the industry has been created in a sixteenth century slate workers dwelling. There is a large collection of mine wagons at the museum and in the car park. Also in the back streets of Trélazé it is possible to observe part of the once extensive narrow gauge railways which are part of the slate operation. The slate mine (les Fresnors Mines de Trélazé) has a 600mm gauge railway with Gmeinder and Comessa diesel locotracteurs. This railway is likely to be replaced by road transport in the near future. The slate quarries (Les Grands Carreaux) have a 1000mm system with 400V dc overhead pick-up and five steeple-cab locomotives which ceased commercial operation in 1995. Renazé has a small museum dedicated to the slate industry of this rural area. The museum has a short 600mm gauge railway for the demonstration of the preserved stock displayed there. Amongst the railway equipment is a number of small diesel locomotives obtained from various slate mines of the region.

136: OMLANDE PARC D'ATTRACTION

❋ **Omlande** Near Brion
✤ Ed/IGN107 A7, ❋ lc, ⚒ 600mm, ❋ 1.5km
☞ Tables 376, 390: SNCF Saumur
☛ Omlande is 34km E of Angers via RN147, to Beaufort-en-Vallée, then RD7 to level crossing
✓ am & pm Daily: Mid-Apr to mid-Sept
✉ Omlande Parc d'Attraction, Le Bois Thomas, 49250 Brion, ☎ 41.57.43.19 or 41.45.64.07

The Omlande pleasure park is one of many such sites in France containing a collection of simple family entertainments in a wooded setting. Omlande covers an area almost twenty-five acres of heathland to the north of the River Loire. Amongst the numerous attractions is a narrow gauge railway to take visitors between the various points of interest in the park and to act as a pleasure ride in its own right. The main station is situated immediately inside the entrance gate beyond the car park. The entrance fee covers all attractions including the train ride.

The train consists of two bogie open topped carriages and a locomotive built to resemble a "wild west" locomotive and tender; the whole having a 4-2-4 wheel arrangement. The tender is used as additional space for seating.

137: LE PETIT TRAIN DE L'HÔTEL DE PIERRE-BRUNE

❋ At **Pierre-Brune** near Mervent
✤ Ee/IGN107 C5, ❋ Diesel, ⚒ 600mm, ❋ 2.5km
☞ Tables 388 & 394: SNCF Bus Fontenay-le-Comte (6km)
☛ Situated 35km NW of Niort via RN148 to Fontenay then RD65
✓ am & pm. Easter to begin-Nov.
✉ Hôtel de Pierre-Brune, Mervent, 85200 Fontenay-le-Comte, ☎ 51.00.20.18/51.00.25.53

The forest of Mervent , which covers 13 square kilometres of Vendée, is located around artificial lakes created by damming the River Vendée and tributaries. This is in effect an area of parkland used for outdoor pursuits and relaxation. Pierre-Brune is in the centre of this area. A pleasure park has been created beside the large hotel situated here in the midst of the forest: amusements are offered including a narrow gauge railway. This runs for 2.5km through the forest crossing streams and passing through a tunnel. The stock consists of a number of brightly painted diesel 0-4-0 locotracteurs and baladeuse carriages.

138: CHEMIN DE FER DE SEMUR-EN-VALLON

❋ **Semur-en-Vallon**
✤ Fc/IGN106 A7, ❋ Diesel, ⚒ 600mm, ❋ 3km
☞ Table 350: SNCF Connerré-Beillé (15km)
☛ Semur-en-Vallon is 40km E of Le Mans via RN23 (Connerré), RD302 (Dollon) & RD84
✓ pm. Sundays & BH: May to Sept. Also Sats in July & Aug.
✉ Comité des Fêtes,La Mairie, Semur-en-Vallon, 72160 Connerré, ☎ 43.71.30.36

Semur-en-Vallon is a quiet village situated in a peaceful valley well off the regular tourist route. Just to the west of the village is an extensive area of woodland and a lake. Originally running beside the lake, the 600mm gauge railway has been completely revised and relaid within the woods. Close to the car park, the station has an extremely complex set of railway lines which cross over each other before running in various directions into the woods. A variety of rides is possible along the valley floor and into the woods which spread up the sides of the gentle valley. Ex-industrial diesel locotracteurs are used for the passenger trains. This is an interesting railway operated by an enthusiastic team. It is situated close to the tourist train based at Connerré-Beillé which also operates on Sundays in the summer season.

At Semur-en-Vallon, a museum of railway and agricultural equipment has been established. In the collection are both standard and narrow gauge items including original equipment and a Paris Metro trailer.

139: MAMERS TO CHÉRANCÉ CYCLE RAILWAY

✳ **Mamers** to **Chérancé**
✣ Fc/IGN102 D7, ✲ Pedal power, 🜊 1435mm, ✲ 17km
☞ Table 335 SNCF Alençon (25km Mamers)
☛ Mamers is 40km N of Le Mans via RD301 to St.Cosme-en-Vairais then RD2
✓ am & pm. July & Aug.
✉ Office du Tourisme, Place de la République, 72600 Mamers ℭ 43.97.60.63
✉ Points of departure: Mamers (ℭ 43.33.91.56) and Chérancé (ℭ 43.33.12.90)

The freight line branching to the east from the SNCF Le Mans to Alençon line at La Hutte- Coulombiers has been closed by SNCF and Mamers has lost its last railway services. The line is now being used for a tourist operation. Like a number of other lines (e.g. Magnières, Bussière-Gallant and la Roche-sur-Yon) a rail-cycle hire service has been set up. The cycles are built for two pedalers and two riders The line is the longest in France used for this purpose. Hire of the four-wheel four-seat cycles is available at two points, Mamers (level crossing) and Chérancé, which are some 17km apart. This is a long journey on such a machine so presumably most riders explore one end of the line at a time. In fine weather these cycle railways can be a delightful way to spend a day, with a picnic and a drink along the way in the quiet of the countryside. Don't forget to remove your vehicle from the track to allow others to pass: it is, remember, a single track used in both directions!

140: TRAIN TOURISTIQUE DE LA VALLÉE DU LOIR

✳ **Thoré-la-Rochette** and **Vendôme** to **Trôo** via **Varennes** and **Montoire-sur-le-Loir**
✣ Fd/IGN106 A8, ✲ Diesel, 🜊 1435mm, ✲ 18km
☞ Table 420: SNCF Vendôme (9km), Table 399: SNCF Vendôme-Villiers TGV (6km)
☛ Thoré-la-Rochette is about 40km NW of Blois via RD957 to Vendôme the RD917
✓ pm. Sat, Sun & BH: Begin-July to end-Aug Also am Suns, mid-July to mid-Aug.
✉ TTVL, Marie de Thoré-la-Rochette, 41100 Thoré-la-Rochette, ℭ 54.72.80.82

The River Loir is a tributary on the right bank of the River Loire. In its middle reaches, north of Tour, its valley cuts through a plateau of about 150m altitude. This is a pleasant area of woods and fields and a reasonable setting for a tourist train. Such a train has been introduced in the past few years on part of the SNCF branch from Vendôme to Trôo. The base of this operation is at Thoré-la-Rochette. The regular operation uses a preserved railcar (X2419) at weekends in the summer season from Thoré to the western terminus of the line at Trôo. Occasional trips are operated along the whole line. At Varennes, to the east of Thoré, the line crosses the line of the TGV Atlantique immediately before meeting the Tours to Chartres line at Borde-Beurre. Combined rail excursions are arranged. The ticket price includes entry to Trôo museum, the wine museum at Trôo, and regional product tasting at Thoré station.

141: LE TRAIN D'UNION

✳ **Château du Loir** and occasional TT runs to Bessé-sur-Braye
✣ Fd/IGN106 A6, ✲ Diesel, 🜊 1435mm, ✲ 35km
☞ Table 335: SNCF Château-du-Loir ⊙
☛ Château-du-Loir is 40km S of Le Mans via RN138(E502). The station is 2km to S
✓ The TT operates on advertised days only. The Château-du-Loir centre is open weekends
✉ Syndicate d'Initiative, 72500 Château-du-Loir, ℭ 43.44.56.60

Château-du-Loir is a rural railway cross roads where the PO railway met the Etat system. It still retains a passenger service between Le Mans and Tours and some freight services. The ten-track roundhouse and turntable from the old locomotive depot remain in the modernised freight yard to the west of the station. Built by the Etat railway, it has been disued by SNCF since 1954. A group of local enthusiasts (AAFVDL) have, since 1989, arranged occasional tourist trains along a section of the freight only line along the valley of the Rivers Loir and Braye as far as Bessé-sur-Braye. By hiring stock for this operation, AAFVDL have been able to offer a variety of rolling stock including a 2-8-2 steam locomotive as well as the ubiquitous "Picasso" railcar. At weekends, a display of local railway memorabilia and models AAFVDL is presented in the old buffet of the station. The model of the roundhouse in 1920 is particularly impressive.

142: CHEMIN DE FER D'ÉTIVAL

❆ At **Étival** near Le Mans
✣ Fd/IGN106 A5, ✽ Diesel (steam), ⚒ 600mm, ✽ 0.3km
☞ SNCF Le Mans (10km), SNCF Voivres-lès-le Mans (3km)
☛ Étival is 12km SW of Le Mans via RD309
✓ pm. Sundays and BH: Begin-May to end-Sept
✉ M.B.Bommert, ℂ 43.47.12.14

A 600mm gauge line has been laid out at Étival, close to Le Mans by the Association du Train à Vapeur de l'Herpiniere. A short train of baladeuse stock offers rides here each Sunday and public holiday from May to September. The present service is operated by an Orenstein & Koppel diesel locotracteur. A locally built steam locomotive will operate in future. This is a vertical boilered tank engine based on the design of the old Tramways de la Sarthe Blanc-Misseron locomotives. Two full-size examples of these magnificent metre gauge engines can be seen at the Vallée du Sausseron transport museum at Valmondois, Butry.

143: LE PETIT TRAIN DE WICHITA

❆ **Parc Pasteur**, rue Eugène Vignat, Orléans
✣ Gd/IGN106 A10, ✽ Steam, ⚒ 320mm, ✽ 0.1km
☞ Table 490: SNCF Orléans-Ville (0.5km)
☛ Parc Pasteur is close to the centre of Orléans beside Rue Eugene Vignat N of the ring road
✓ pm. Sun in May to Nov. Also Tues from May to mid Oct and Thurs & Sat in Jul & Aug
✉ Office de Tourisme, Bd Aristide-Briand, Carré St.Vincent, 45000, ℂ 38.53.05.95

There is a small and immaculately maintained town park in the centre of Orléans. A circuit of 320mm track is laid on the ground running across the lawns and between the flower beds. The cause of this luxurious setting dates back to 1952 when Orléans was presented with the complete railway by its twin town of Wichita, USA. The 4-4-0 outside cylinder locomotive was built at Houston in 1949. It is of a "Wild West" style. It pulls three carriages each capable of carrying 4 children (adults not permitted to ride). The line is a single circuit with the stock stored when not in use in an artificial well-camouflaged tunnel.

144: BUSSIÈRE-GALLANT CYCLE RAILWAY

❆ **Bussière-Gallant** to **Châlus**
✣ Gf/IGN107 D10, ✽ Pedal power, ⚒ 1435mm, ✽ 5km
☞ Table 440 & 458 SNCF Bussiére-Gallant
☛ Bussiére-Gallant is 42 km SSW of Limoges via RN21 then 6km E to Bussiére station.
✓ am & pm. July & Aug.
✉ Plan d'eau "les Ribières", 87230 Bussière-Gallant ℂ 55.78.86.47
✉ Le Mairie, 87230 Bussière-Gallant, ℂ 55.78.80.26

As at Magnières, Mamers and la Roche-sur-Yon, the line between Bussière-Gallant and Châlus offers the experience of propelling your own "engine" on a rural railway. The line from Bussière-Gallant to Saillat-Chaussenon had for some years only a freight service as far as Oradour-sur-Varyes. Once this ceased operation in 1987 the local authority began negotiations to save the line. Now a 5km section is rented from SNCF and since 1994 has been made available for the exclusive use of four wheel rail-cycles. The line runs through the delightful valley of the River Dronne and on a fine day a relaxing, if tiring, time can be spent enjoying the quiet countryside. As this is a single track railway it is necessary for one cycle to be removed from the line when two meet. This is a shorter line than the others of this type in France. This should not deter you: A ten-km cycle ride on one of these vehicles can require quite some effort, unless all members of the party participate in the pedaling.

145: NANTES TRAMWAY

✳ **Nantes**
✢ Dd/IGN107 A3, ✱ Electric 750V dc o/h, ⚊ 1435mm, ✱ 26km
☞ SNCF Nantes
☛ Parking at Place de la Bourse, close to "Gare SNCF" on tramway line No.1
✓ am & pm. Daily: All year
✉ SEMITAN, 3 rue Bellier, 44046 Nantes

Nantes is the city where the era of modern French tramways was established in 1985. The previous tramway in Nantes was closed in 1958 after almost 80 years service. The modern system has expanded since 1985 and now has two lines with a third planned.

Line No.1 links Bellvue in the west of the city with Beaujoire in the east via the SNCF station. Other than the extension to the Beaujoire stadium, the eastern section of the line is laid beside the SNCF tracks to Châteaubriant. The line here is elevated above the streets, but after Malakoff the line runs at street level as a traditional tramway. It follows the a series of wide boulevards, and the infrastructure has been adapted to incorporate the tram with connecting bus services and pedestrianised central area. The tramway depot is at Dalby. Line No.2 links La Nöe to the NE with Trocardière to the south of the city. It crosses line No.1 in the commercial centre about 1km from the SNCF station. The depot is at the Trocardière terminus.

The Alsthom built tramcar sets can operate in pairs. Each has three sections. The centre section is unpowered and has a low entrance for ease of access.

Associations arranging Tourist Trains on SNCF main lines

The following organisations operate, or arrange trips on, steam or other preserved stock on SNCF main lines. These are not usually on a regular basis. Trips are frequently advertised in the railway press, and/or advertised locally. This list is not comprehensive. When writing for information, please enclose an addressed envelope and an International Reply Coupon. A number of the UK agents specialising in overseas rail enthusiast trips often offer package visits to France which incorporate main line operations with preserved stock.

Pacific Vapeur Club, BP115, 76303 Sotteville-les-Rouen Cedex ✆ 35.72.30.55

AJECTA, BP1, 77650 Longueville ✆ 64.08.60.62, (1)64.60.26.26 or (1)43.86.94.49 **[See 19]**

Autorails Bourgogne-Franche-Comté, 37 rue Lamartine, 21000 Dijon **[See 81]**

CFTV, BP152, 02124 St.Quentin Cedex ✆ 23.07.88.02 **[See 18]**

CFTR, 16 rue des Cordiers,68600 Andolsheim ✆ 89.71.51.42 or 89.72.55.97 **[See 26]**

AAMCS, Office du Tourisme, 91 Grand place, 59230 St.Amand ✆ 27.48.13.13 **[See15]**

Agrivap, BP8, rue de l'industrile, 63600 Ambert ✆ 73.82.43.88 **[See 54/75]**

Association des Amis de la 141R1126, 6 rue Cornelle, 11110 Coursan ✆ 68.27.05.94 **[See 95]**

International Ferroviaire Club, 46 ave. de Savigny, 93600 Aulnay sous Bois ✆ (1)43.84.78.17

Association 141R420, BP7, 63830 Durtol

FACS, SNCF Gare de l'Est, place de 11 Novembre, 75475 Paris Cedex 10 ✆ (1) 44.41.10.57

CITEV, gare du TVC, BP17, 30270 St.Jean du Gard ✆ 66.85.13.17 **[See 98]**

MFPN, 64 rue de Coucelles, 77290 Mitry-Mory ✆ 64.27.33.84 or (1)34.12.00.60

VVV, le Marie,87100 Limo ges ✆ 55.69.10.21

CFTLP, 11-13 ave Berthelot, 87100 Limoges ✆ 55.77.26.65 **[See 130]**

BIBLIOGRAPHY

General and specific information

Institut Géographique National maps: Green series (1cm:1km) or Red series (2cm:2.5km)

Various books on individual tourist railways. Les Editions du Cabri, 06540 Breil-sur-Roya.

SNCF timetables (set of four). Available from French Railways Ltd, 179 Piccadilly, London W1V 0BA

France. Michelin Guide

The Traveller in France: Reference Guide. French Government Tourist Office, 179 Piccadilly, London W1V 0BA

French Railways: Locomotives and Railcars. **B Gavin, D Haydock & P Fox.** Platform 5 Publishing.

High Speed in Europe. **D Haydock.** Platform 5 Publishing.

European Railway Atlas: France etc. **M G Ball.** Ian Allan Publishing.

La Voie de 60 et les CF Militaires. AMTP, 7 rue Lacuée, 75012 Paris

Today's Railways - The European Railway Magazine. Platform 5 Publishing.

Railway Societies in Britain

The Narrow Gauge Railway Society, Membership Sec.: P Slater, Wayside, Stibb, Bude, EX23 9RG

The SNCF Society, Membership Sec.: J Rowcroft, 13 Highlands Road, Seaford, BN25 1SL

Continental Railway Circle. Subscriptions: E G Pearson, 1 Midhurst Ct., Haslemere Rd, London N8 9QR

Industrial Railway Society. 47 Waverley Gardens, London NW10 7EE

French Railway Journals

Calendar-year subscriptions to some of the following magazines are available through **Rapid Transit Publications,** 37 Wellesley Road, Ilford, IG1 4JX. French books on railway and tramway subjects can also be ordered via this service.

La Vie du Rail. 11 rue de Milan, 75440 Paris Cédex 09

Voie Étroite. APPEVA, BP106, 80001 Amiens

Connaissance du Rail. Editions de l'Ormet, BP 12, 03330 Bellenaves

Voies Ferrées. Presses et Éditions Ferroviaires, 31 rue Colonel Bougault, 38100 Grenoble

CdF Regionaux & Urbains. FACS-UNECTO, Gare de l'Est, 75475 Paris Cedex 10

Rail Passion. 11 rue de Milan, 75440 Paris Cédex 09

INDEX

Light face shows Page Numbers. **Bold** type shows Railway Numbers